GOOD STUFF

GOOD STUFF

Courage, Resilience, Gratitude, Generosity, Forgiveness, and Sacrifice

SALMAN AKHTAR

ROWMAN & LITTLEFIELD
Lanham • Boulder • New York • London

Published by Jason Aronson
A wholly owned subsidiary of The Rowman & Littlefield Publishing Group, Inc.
4501 Forbes Boulevard, Suite 200, Lanham, Maryland 20706
www.rowman.com

10 Thornbury Road, Plymouth PL6 7PP, United Kingdom

First Rowman & Littlefield paperback edition 2014

British Library Cataloguing in Publication Information Available

Library of Congress Cataloging-in-Publication Data

The hardback edition of this book was previously cataloged by the Library of Congress as follows:

Akhtar, Salman, 1946 July 31–
Good stuff : courage, resilience, gratitude, generosity, forgiveness, and sacrifice / Salman Akhtar.
pages cm
Includes bibliographical references and index.
1. Character. 2. Virtue. 3. Resilience (Personality trait) I. Title.
BF818.A36 2013
179'.9—dc23
2012045065

ISBN: 978-0-7657-0976-9 (cloth : alk. paper)
ISBN: 978-1-4422-3816-9 (pbk. : alk. paper)
ISBN: 978-0-7657-0977-6 (electronic)

∞™ The paper used in this publication meets the minimum requirements of American National Standard for Information Sciences—Permanence of Paper for Printed Library Materials, ANSI/NISO Z39.48-1992.

Printed in the United States of America

To

JENNIFER BONOVITZ

naturally

CONTENTS

ACKNOWLEDGMENTS

A number of psychoanalytic colleagues have helped sharpen my thinking about the themes contained in this book. Some have reviewed earlier drafts of these chapters. Others have offered valuable comments in an informal way. Still others have brought important reading material to my attention. Prominent among these individuals are my wife Dr. Monisha Akhtar, and Drs. Ira Brenner, Jennifer Bonovitz, Ralph and Lana Fishkin, Axel Hoffer, Susan Levine, Afaf Mahfouz, Frank Maleson, Henri Parens, Nadia Ramzy, Shahrzad Siassi, Melvin Singer, Stuart Twemlow, and Vamik Volkan. Dr. Michael Vergare, Chairman of the Department of Psychiatry and Senior Vice President of Academic Affairs at Jefferson Medical College (my academic base for over thirty years) has offered unwavering support for my intellectual pursuits. Drs. Rajnish Mago and Stephen Schwartz have been critically sound readers of my scribblings. And, within the Jefferson "family," Drs. Solange Margery Bertoglia, Jonathan Beatty, Karl Doghramji, and Deanna Nobleza have provided useful "holding" functions and, in this indirect fashion, supported my creativity. My good friend, Dr. J. Anderson Thomson, Jr., introduced me to the ethological and evolution-related literature and thus greatly enriched my understanding of phenomena addressed in this book. Ms. Smita Kamble put me in touch with Mr. Stephen Crawford, who was kind enough to share his unpublished work on generosity with me. Dr. Glenda Wrenn and Ms. Archana Varma have graciously permitted me to include some co-authored material (for chapters 1 and 6, respectively) in this book. My assistant, Jan Wright, prepared the manuscript with her usual skill, diligence, and good humor. To all these individuals, I offer my deepest gratitude.

PREFACE

The founder of psychoanalysis, Sigmund Freud, held a rather dismal view of human nature. He declared that belief in human goodness was an "evil illusion" (1933, p. 104) and regarded vast swathes of humanity to be "good for nothing in life" (1905, p. 263), "antisocial and anticultural" (1927, p. 7) at their core, and fundamentally "lazy and unintelligent (1927, p. 7). Freud's followers upheld this skeptical, if not cynical, view of man and looked at any positive traits with suspicion. They strenuously looked for the repudiated anguish or warded-off anxiety that, they believed, invariably lurked underneath sunny and enjoyable attributes of personality.

Over time, however, a shift occurred. British analysts (e.g., W. R. D. Fairbairn, Donald Winnicott, Michael Balint) who were not affiliated with either Anna Freud or Melanie Klein, challenged the notion of "primary narcissism" and replaced it with "primary love." They accorded greater importance to object relations than to instinctual discharge. They regarded psychopathology to result not from the inherent battle between life and death instincts (and, between these instincts and the superego) but from impingement, abuse, overstimulation, or neglect by the child's early caretakers. The essentially romantic ethic of this perspective made it possible to discern goodness in human beings, which was intrinsic and natural, not merely defensive or sublimatory. Across the Atlantic, the work of Erik Erikson rendered it possible to see human development as providing, at each step of the way, personally gratifying outcomes of age-specific tasks and challenges. Ground was thus set for psychoanalytic psychology of mental health.

Sporadic papers now began to appear on specific healthy character traits as well. Prominent among these were Ralph Greenson's (1962) paper on enthusiasm, Leo Rangell's (1963) paper on friendship, Martin Bergman's (1971) paper on love, Warren Poland's (1971) paper on tact, Chasseguet-Smirgel's (1988) paper on humor, to name a few. I myself contributed to this trend by writing the first psychoanalytic essay fully devoted to the issue of forgiveness (Akhtar, 2002). A major step in the beginning consolidation of psychoanalytic interest in healthy, adaptive, and genuinely pleasurable aspects of human experience was taken in 2009 when the IPA (International Psychoanalytical Association) commissioned a comprehensive edited volume on these emotions and ego capacities (Akhtar, 2009a). There, I brought together the scattered psychoanalytic literature and invited updates and critiques from distinguished psychoanalysts around the world. I thought my work was done and I could put the issue to rest.

That did not turn out to be the case. Emotions and behaviors not included in that volume (e.g., generosity, gratitude, sacrifice) kept tugging at the sleeve of my psychoanalytic attention. Other topics (e.g., resilience, forgiveness, and courage), though addressed in the IPA volume, demanded further explication. As a result, I decided to write this book. I have divided the book's contents in two parts: Part I addresses Positive Attributes and Part II, Positive Actions. The former contains chapters on Courage, Resilience, and Gratitude. The latter contains chapters on Generosity, Forgiveness, and Sacrifice. Together, the six chapters constitute a harmonious gestalt of the relational scenarios that assure enrichment of human experience. Allow me, at this point, to offer thumbnail sketches of each of these chapters.

I begin the first chapter of the book by considering the etymology and definition of the word "courage" and by elucidating the relationship of courage to power, wisdom, faith, joy, and self-affirmation. I make a brief foray into the phenomena of counterphobia and cowardice and then proceed to the developmental origins of courage as a character trait. I then devote a somewhat larger section to the technical implications of the aforementioned ideas and conclude by making some synthesizing remarks and by touching upon areas that might still have remained unaddressed.

The next chapter is devoted to resilience. In it, I tackle the following questions:

- What determines whether positive or negative consequences will predominate in the aftermath of trauma?
- What regulates their proportion?
- Is the outcome of trauma a once-and-for-all occurrence or subject to psychic elaboration, layering, and modification?
- Do pretraumatic ego assets matter more in governing the outcome of trauma than the ameliorative influences that follow it?
- What is the role of intelligence, inborn talents, imagination, and fantasy here?
- How and to what extent do societal institutions and cultural containers help transform the impact of individual or group trauma?

The third chapter is devoted to the experience of gratitude. I begin my discourse by delineating its phenomenological scope and its developmental origins. Following this, I describe the psychopathology that exists in this realm, including: (i) anxious deflection of gratitude, (ii) guilty intensification of gratitude, (iii) narcissistic denial of gratitude, and (iv) sociopathic absence of gratitude. Then I demonstrate the clinical significance of gratitude and underscore the value of (i) feeling and expressing gratitude in response to the patient's gestures of kindness, (ii) appreciating and accepting the patient's healthy gratitude, (iii) diagnosing and interpreting the patient's conflicts around gratitude, (iv) making developmentally oriented interventions with the gradual enhancement of the capacity for gratitude as a result of analytic work, and, (v) avoiding countertransference pitfalls in this realm. I conclude by making some synthesizing remarks and noting areas that might warrant further attention. This brings the Part I of the book to an end.

Part II of the book opens with a chapter on generosity. I start it by defining the concept of generosity and tracing its developmental origins. I then delineate its various pathological forms, including (i) unrelenting generosity, (ii) begrudging generosity, (iii) fluctuating generosity, (iv) controlling generosity, and (v) beguiling generosity. Following this, I highlight the impact of knowing the nature and significance of generosity upon the clinical situation. This is evident in six different ways, namely, (i) having and maintaining an attitude of generosity toward the patient, (ii) listening and intervening with an attitude of generosity,(iii) recognizing and accepting the patient's healthy generosity, (iv) diagnosing and interpreting the patient's pathological generosity, (v) unmasking and interpreting defenses against generosity, and (vi) remaining vigilant toward countertransference pitfalls in such work. I conclude by making some synthesizing remarks and noting the impact of age, gender, and culture upon the capacity and differential patterns of generosity.

Like generosity, the phenomenon of forgiveness remains dynamically, technically, and socially important enough to warrant serious attention from the discipline. The next chapter of my book is aimed to fill this lacuna. I begin by highlighting the psychodynamics of giving and seeking forgiveness. I then attempt to elucidate the evolutionary and developmental correlates of these phenomena. Following this, I discuss the various psychopathological syndromes involving forgiveness. These include (i) inability to forgive, (ii) premature forgiveness, (iii) excessive forgiveness, (iv) pseudo-forgiveness, (v) relentless forgiveness-seeking, (vi) inability to accept forgiveness, (vii) inability to seek forgiveness, and (viii) imbalance between capacities for self-forgiveness and forgiveness toward others. While this chapter has also appeared in an earlier book of mine (Akhtar, 2003), it seemed imperative to include it in this collection of essays on positive character traits as well. To compensate for this repetition, I have appended a freshly-written postscript which covers the psychoanalytic literature on forgiveness that has appeared since the original 2002 publication of my paper.

The last chapter of my book offers an elucidation of the concept of sacrifice and, in particular, its phenomenological (e.g., etymology, definition, and forms), dynamic (e.g., instinctual, self-based, and moral), sociocultural; and clinical aspects. The aim of this discourse is to enhance knowledge in this in optimally studied area, and to enlarge the mental space in which clinical and cultural meanings of sacrifice can be explored and beneficially utilized.

To come back, full circle, to the opening paragraph of this Preface, my purpose in writing this book and offering these socio-clinical meditations is to temper Freud's view that human beings are essentially "bad" and whatever goodness they can muster is largely defensive. This should not be taken to mean that I am siding with Winnicott's perspective which suggests that human beings are fundamentally "good." My attempt is to synthesize these "classic" and "romantic" visions of psychoanalysis (Strenger, 1989). It is my conviction that both "bad" and "good" attributes exist as hard-wired potentials that can be evoked, accentuated, or diminished by experiences during the formative years of childhood. Nonetheless, by elucidating the origins, dynamics, social pleasures, and clinical benefits of courage, resilience, gratitude, generosity, forgiveness, and sacrifice, I have shed light on a corner of human experience that has remained inadequately understood by psychoanalysts and other mental health professionals. It is my hope that familiarity with these matters will enhance the empathic capacity and technical proficiency of all clinicians. More importantly, it might soften their view of their patients' struggles, of their own private quandaries, and of mankind's dilemmas at large. This, I would like to believe, is *Good Stuff*!

Part I

POSITIVE ATTRIBUTES

1

COURAGE

Despite Freud's referring to himself as a "conquistador" (cited in Gay, 1988), and despite psychoanalysts's daily bravery in exposing themselves to an onslaught of projections, psychoanalysis has paid little attention to the phenomenon of courage. Scattered references do exist in the analytic literature but a comprehensive survey of them which would result in a harmonious gestalt of observations is lacking. Unanswered questions continue to abound in this realm. What, for instance, is the relationship of courage to fearlessness? How are courage and self-affirmation tied to each other? Are there subtypes of courage? Does courage grow out of wisdom or is it the other way around? What childhood experiences contribute to the origin of courage? What makes some people act boldly and others cowardly? And, of course, what are the implications of such questions for the conduct of psychoanalysis and psychotherapy?

In this chapter, I will attempt to answer some of these questions. I will begin by considering the etymology and definition of the word "courage" and by elucidating the relationship of courage to power, wisdom, faith, joy, and self-affirmation. I will make a brief foray into the phenomena of counterphobia and cowardice and then proceed to the developmental origins of courage as a character trait. I will devote a somewhat larger section to the technical implications of the aforementioned ideas and conclude by making some synthesizing remarks and by touching upon areas that might still have remained unaddressed.

ETYMOLOGY, DEFINITION, AND SUBTYPES

> Courage is not simply one of the virtues, but the form of every virtue at the testing point, which means at the point of highest reality. . . . A chastity or honesty or mercy which yields to danger will be chaste or honest or merciful only on conditions. Pilate was merciful till it became risky. (Lewis, 1942, p. 21)

> Almost all heroic individuals face grave crises while they are still on the road to reaching the ultimate decision that they will remain faithful to their selves, whatever the cost. (Kohut, 1985, pp. 15–16)

The English word "courage" is derived from the French *coeur,* which literally means "heart." And since "heart" has traditionally (and metaphorically) been regarded as the seat of emotion, spirit, and strength of character, the implication of such etymology is clear: courage involves the capacity to bear difficulties without wincing, to dare and be innovative, and to do what is needed regardless of its frightening consequences. The equivalents of "courage" in Latin (*fortitude*) and Greek (*andreia'*) stand for strength and manliness, respectively. Hindi, national language of the populous India, has two corresponding words, *saahas*, which denotes the capacity to bear hardship and *veerta,* which implies bravery and is closely related to *veer*, i.e., "semen." The phallocentric foundations of courage in Greek and Hindi have most likely evolved from its early restriction to military personnel; the soldier with his willingness to tolerate hardship and injury and even sacrifice his life was upheld in ancient times (and, to a considerable extent, still is) the epitome of courage.

This brings up the important point that courage is not synonymous with fearlessness. A fearless person is either foolhardy—the "danger denying type" of Glover (1940)—or is operating under the protection of someone vigilant and powerful. A courageous person, in contrast, knows that his stance and his actions can have adverse consequences: financial loss, social isolation, personal ridicule, physical punishment, and so on. And yet, he braces himself to encounter their impending onslaught. Only then can he face destruction and death and not betray the meaningful core of his existence. John Wayne, the movie actor who personified boldness in his roles, quipped that "courage is being scared to death and saddling up anyway" (downloaded from *www. Thinkexist. com*). General William T. Sherman (after whom the Sherman Tank is named) declared courage to be "a perfect sensibility of the measure of danger and a mental willingness to endure it" (cited in Kidder, 2006, p. 9).

The courageous man accords great weight to his own thoughts and perceptions. He needs no consensus and does not depend upon others' approval. He can stand on his own even when others do not agree with him or oppose him. Courage becomes for him "an exceptional state of mind allowing and producing an extraordinary form of behavior" (Coles, 1965, p. 85). Such behavior can occur in three realms: (i) physical, (ii) intellectual, and (iii) moral. A brief consideration of each follows.

- *Physical courage* involves knowingly taking risks of bodily harm for purposes that often include altruism. Military personnel, firefighters, life guards, and those in charge of various security and rescue operations embody such courage. However, physical courage can appear in non-altruistic contexts as well. Risky sports like rock-climbing and white water rafting, thrills like bungee jumping and roller-coaster riding, and working with lions and tigers in a circus or zoo also demand physical courage. Altruism and thrill-seeking are not the only motivators of physical courage, however. At times, self-interest and the need to survive can lead to daring acts as well. Such was the case with Aron Ralston, the rock-climber who had to amputate his own arm, since he was trapped in crevice and would have died otherwise (nationalgeographic. com/news).
- *Intellectual courage* refers to the capacity for "out-of-the-box" thinking and for looking at problems in fresh and unexpected ways. Copernicus, Galileo, Darwin, Newton, and Freud showed this sort of courage in evolving new paradigms of thought. Intellectual courage propels imagination and buttresses authenticity. It contributes to the capacity to create literary metaphors such as "what is sadder than a train stopped in rain" (à la Pablo Neruda), envision juxtaposed visual perspectives (à la Pablo Picasso), take leaps of faith in scientific creativity (à la Albert Einstein), and come up with inventions (à la Thomas Edison). W. H. Auden's quip that "there is no creativity without audacity" refers to this very type of courage.

- *Moral courage* involves being truthful to one's convictions under circumstances that do not support or even punish such honesty.[1]

The phrase "moral courage" itself is a relatively recent arrival in English, having been used for the first time less than two centuries ago (Colton, 1822). It denotes willingness to expose oneself to suffering that involves not the body but the mind and the "heart." The morally courageous person is rock-solid in his beliefs. It might have taken him time, trial and error, much soul searching and personal anguish to arrive at his ideological stance but once he has come to that point, he holds on tightly to it. He refuses to be bought, bribed, or silenced by intimidation. The lives of Mahatmas Gandhi (Erikson, 1969; Gandhi, 1929), Martin Luther King, Jr. (Frady, 2006; Akhtar and Blue, 2012), and Nelson Mandela (1994) provide shining illustrations of moral courage.[2] What is even more striking than their brave non-violent revolts against colonialism and racist oppression is that they had the spiritual fortitude to not hate their oppressors *per se*; their refusal to accept *status quo* was directed at grave social injustices around them and not at individuals who perpetuated such violations of human dignity.

Compartmentalization of courage into physical, intellectual, and moral categories is, however, not water-tight. There is much overlap between them. Physical courage often emanates from moral courage; Levine (2006) makes this point by stating that courage refers to "a conscious decision to tolerate risk or pain for the purpose of achieving a higher goal" (p. 36). Moral courage itself grows out of insights consequent upon intellectual courage. And, acts of physical courage might receive guidance from perspectives arising out of intellectual courage. Matters are not clean-cut, it seems. Moreover, there exist forms of courage that do not fit neatly in any of these categories. The heroism of lovers in great epics of the East and West is a case in point here. Testimony to romantic valor is sprinkled throughout the pages of the West's *Romeo and Juliet* (circa 1562), Iraqi *Majnun-Laila* (circa 650), the Persian *Shirin-Farhad* (circa 1000), and the Indian *Heer Ranjha* (circa 1700). Illustrated in real life by King Edward VIII (1894–1972), such an attribute can be best termed 'romantic courage.' Ruling over the powerful British Empire, he abdicated the throne for Wallis Simpson (1896–1986), a woman with whom he had fallen in love. To give up immense wealth and great authority in order to marry a twice-divorced, foreign-born "commoner" must have required nerves of steel and a heart full of courage.[3]

It should be acknowledged, however, that acts of courage (or, at least, seeming courage) are not always based upon the "noble" emotions of love and altruism. Avoidance of shame, too, can lead to seeming bravery; this happens, for instance, when frightened parents join their children on a rollercoaster ride to elude being mocked. Rage can accentuate the desire for combat and the resulting foolhardy assertiveness can come across as courage. Impulsivity can propel one to circumvent fear. Most of the phenomena mentioned here are better designated as "pseudo-courage." They involve either a perfunctory tip of the hat to the dangers involved or, worse, they are associated with libidinization of fear, risk, and suffering. In this context, it is pertinent to note Levine's (2009) comment upon the similarities and differences between courage and masochism.

> Courage does not necessarily feel very good in the moment of the act and the risk; conversely, masochistic acts may not always engender conscious displeasure (although they often do). Perhaps this is not curious, for masochism and courage may share an affective tone of suspenseful anxiety. There is a similarity in the conscious affect produced, for it is the presence of risk that characterizes both a courageous and a masochistic act. How is one to distinguish "worthwhile risk" (Maleson, 1984, p. 336) from masochistic strivings? One answer to this question is that in masochism, the painful state itself represents the aim, while in courage, it represents the means to an end." (pp. 38–39)

At the same time, Levine recommends that "we increase our cynicism and seek the underlying masochism in courage" (p. 40), arguing that "it is as much masochism as courage that influences the willingness of some clinicians to endure the rigors of clinical work" (p. 41). O'Neil (2009) disagrees with this view. I will return to this tension while elucidating the technical implications of the concept of courage. At this point, I want to move on to two other reactions to fear; one resembles courage but in actuality is different and the other is the opposite of courage.

COUNTERPHOBIA AND COWADICE

> Counterphobia refers to the unconscious effort to deny or overcome a phobic tendency by seeking contact with the dreaded object or situation. For example, a person might take up mountain climbing in order to deal with an underlying fear of heights. Realistically regulated counterphobic mechanisms may be quite adaptive, as when the choice to become a physician originates in an effort to master a fear of disease. (More and Fine, 1990, p. 145)

> What good is a conviction about honesty or fairness without a willingness to put those values into action in the face of adversity? Of what use is a code of ethics that hangs on the wall, unimplemented? Without the courage to act, virtuous conviction is pointless and paralytic. (Kidder, 2006, p. 71)

The phenomenon of courage has two psychopathological counterparts. One is marked by a peculiarly exaggerated absence of fear. The other is characterized by a weak-kneed response to life's challenges. The former leads to behaviors that are at best called "foolhardy" while the latter results in gutless avoidance of risks. The two syndromes are those of counterphobia and cowardice.

Counterphobia

This refers to an unconscious attitude of the ego which propels the individual to undertake, and even enjoy, the very activities that arouse fear and anxiety in him. However, there is a rigid and exaggerated quality to such behavior. According to Fenichel (1945),

> The obsessive manner of the search for the once-feared situations shows that the anxiety has not been completely overcome. The patients continuously try to repeat the way in which in childhood other anxieties gradually had been mastered by active repetitions of exciting situations. The counterphobic pleasure is a repetition of the child's "functional" pleasure of "I do not need to be afraid anymore" (Silberer, 1909). And, as in the child, the type of pleasure achieved proves that the person is by no means really convinced of his mastery, and that before engaging in any such activity, he passes

> through an anxious tension of expectation, the overcoming of which is enjoyed. (p. 480)

A common example of counterphobic attitude is the social and motoric dare-devilry of adolescents (e.g., driving at high speeds, experimenting with drugs, defying social etiquette, confronting the high school principal). Another illustration is the strikingly rapid assimilation into the host culture on the part of some immigrants (Akhtar, 1999a). They adopt the new local customs in a magical way in order to deflect the social anxiety of being "different." More examples can be given. An individual who accepts the recommendation of a major surgery in the blink of an eye is most likely showing a counterphobic attitude. The grotesque youthfulness of some aging narcissists (Kernberg, 1980) and the 'gallows humor' of some terminally ill individuals also belies a defensive avoidance of approaching threats. In all these situations, there is a suspicious absence of expectable fear. The fact is that fear exists but is kept in abeyance by forceful self-assurances to the contrary. Gleefully proclaiming "look, ma, no hands!" the inner child is unaware that mother's visual attention has itself become a variety of "hands," so to speak. Seepage of fear and of the subterranean need for reassurance both accompany counterphobia.

Less recognized is the frequent overlap between counterphobia and repetition-compulsion. While many character traits (e.g., outrageousness, cockiness) betray such dynamic, it is most convincingly evident in the symptoms of the so-called post-traumatic disorder. Weiss (1965) emphatically makes this point by saying,

> If one survives the initial onslaught of outrageous fortune, one then returns to meet it again compulsively, to prove to oneself that the thing one feared might happen did not in actuality happen, while all the while the original and unresolved anxiety forbids final proof. In effect, one strives to ritualize, to enclose within a rigid framework of intention, what had originally been a unique and unforeseen accident. (p. 136)

Such linkage between counterphobia and repetition-compulsion also open up the possibility of seeing the former containing the unconscious hope of redress.[4]

Cowardice

Beginning with Freud's (1909) widely known study of Little Hans to numerous subsequent contributions to the psychoanalytic understanding of phobia (e.g., Rangell, 1952; Wangh, 1959; Tyson, 1978; Sandler, 1989; Kulish, 1996; Campbell and Pile, 2011), psychoanalysts are familiar with a focal reign of terror upon the ego. They are knowledgeable about the intricate mechanisms that lead to a phobia. What they know less about is the personality trait of cowardice. Even the concept of "phobic character" does not provide us any insights on cowardice. Introduced by Fenichel (1945), the designation is reserved for individuals "whose reactive behavior limits itself to the avoidance of situations originally wished-for" (p. 527). Elaborating on Fenichel's proposal, Mackinnon and Michels (1971) emphasized that more common than ego-dystonic, monosymptomatic phobia is the use of fearful avoidance as a character defense, adding that such an individual is "constantly imaging himself in situations of danger while pursuing the course of greatest safety" (p. 49). Of note here is the implication that the fears felt by such a person are imaginary. Cowardice, in contrast, involves a recoil from plausible, if not actual, threats.

A habitual reaction to threat and danger, cowardice is a response to fear of actual harm. In this way, cowardice is akin to courage and counterphobia. Of course, the three lead to entirely different sort of behavior. In courage, one perseveres despite fear. In counterphobia, one refuses to acknowledge fear and acts in a foolhardy manner. In cowardice, there is a "crippling of the will" (Menaker, 1979, p. 93); one succumbs to fear and withdraws from the "combat."[5]

Like courage, cowardice can be evident in physical, intellectual, and moral realms. The coward reacts to confrontation with distress. In part, this is due to "automatic anxiety" (Freud, 1926), i.e., the spontaneous reaction of helpless dread in the face of a massively traumatic situation. And, in part, this is due to projection of the coward's own anger. Unable to express his resentment directly, the coward attributes vicious intent to his opponent and gets terrified. Consequently, he postpones the "debate," falsely concurs with his adversary, or, worse, flees the situation in reality. Recognition of his timidity fills him up with shame and self-disgust; these are often drowned in drink or covered over by the narcissistic fantasy of having deliberately engineered his defeat. The spineless combatant of yesterday thus transforms himself into the lofty bestower of victory to others.

But there is more to cowardice than its narcissistic dynamic. The base of cowardice is formed by a "thin-skinned" (Rosenfeld, 1971) psyche which is the consequence of weak maternal containment of early infantile anxieties (Bick, 1968). The cowardly individual tends to get affectively overwhelmed while facing a narcissistic threat; withdrawal from a full encounter with it follows. Deficient identification with the same-sex parent also contributes to such psychic vulnerability. The most important etiological factor in cowardice, however, is a condensation of body mutilation anxieties (including, of course, castration anxiety) and a dread of separation and aloneness. An "ocnophile" (Balint, 1968) par-excellence, the coward clings to his objects and is willing to sacrifice dignity at the altar of relatedness. All cowardice, at the bottom, is the fear of being disliked and being alone. Meltzer (1973) notes:

> Where dependence on good internal objects is rendered infeasible by damaging masturbatory attacks and where dependence on a good external object in unavailable or not acknowledged, an addictive relationship to a bad part of the self—the submission to tyranny takes place. An illusion of safety is promulgated by the omniscience of the destructive part. . . . Where a dread of loss of an addictive relation to a tyrant is found in psychic structure, the problem of terror will be found at its core, as the force behind the dread and the submission. (p. 78)

Meltzer's proposal has implications for the technical handling of individuals trapped in relationships with narcissistic-sadistic partners (see "Technical Implications" section below). However, before discussing them, it is pertinent to consider the relationship of courage to other phenomena, both positive and negative ones.

RELATIONSHIP TO JOY, FAITH, AND WISDOM

> Joy is fed by two sources: (i) the child's inner awareness of significant forward move into a psychological realm of new and exciting experiences, and—of even greater importance—(ii) his participation in the glow of pride and joy that emanates from the parental self objects. (Kohut, 1977, p. 236)

> Courage allows a person to better manage the threatening passions of life: love, hate, and anger are prime motivators; fear in the face of danger and anxiety in the face of risk must be overcome. Courage involves conviction, determination, risk, and uncertainty. Courage expresses, often, the realization of ideals central to a person's sense of self. (O'Neil, 2009, p. 55)

Courage has close structural and dynamic ties with certain other psychological phenomena including joy, faith, and wisdom. The relationship is at times linear and at other times dialectical; in either case, the overlap is nuanced and complex.

Courage and Joy

Elsewhere, while delineating various kinds of happiness, I designated joy as an "assertion-based happiness" (Akhtar, 2010).[6] Here, I quote from that paper of mine:

> Joy refers to the happiness that accompanies the experience of confidence and self-assertion. Pleasurable exercise of ego functions and finding efficacy in one's actions also gives rise to joy. . . . A similar kind of happiness results from the robust use of object related ego functions (G. Klein, 1976). The delight one feels in pleasing people one loves, and the "ego pleasure" in synthesis and effectiveness belong in this realm. (pp. 229, 230)

Like joy, courage has close ties with efficacy and authenticity. Self-affirmation ("I know and accept who I am"), self-expression ("I act in accordance with my convictions"), and self-actualization ("I strive to become what I aspire to be") are three facets of courageous contact with one's true self. For them to work in unison requires courage and, when they do operate harmoniously, the resulting emotion is joy. Courage gives rise to psychic truthfulness and joy follows it. Traffic can move in the opposite direction as well. However, the joy produced by courage is real while the courage produced by joy is often counterphobic in nature (since the capacity to estimate risks is compromised during a joyous state).

Courage and Faith

Since courage involves perseverance and honest self-expression while facing challenge and adversity, it needs to draw upon whatever psychic strength one can muster. Freud's (1917) declaration that having received unconditional love from mother during childhood gives one life-long confidence speaks to an important—perhaps, the most important—source of such strength. Abraham's (1924) comment about the salutary impact of early oral gratification echoes Freud's sentiment. And, later concepts of "object constancy" (Spitz, 1946; Hartmann, 1952; A. Freud, 1965; Mahler et al., 1975) give a developmentally-anchored, nuanced glimpse of what keeps us going despite frustrations, hardships, and challenges in our life's course.

Such internal sources of fortitude are not the only source of faith in ourselves. Cultural and societal structures also offer support in times of doubt and distress. Religious belief, ethnic belonging, patriotism, and genuine commitment to a philosophical system or creative pathway (e.g., writing, painting, music) can also sustain faith and add to courage. Feeling 'protected' by the majesty of such civic and cultural institutions, the individual can become able to bear more, do more, and express more. In other words, he can be more courageous. The lives of great artists and writers, social activists and freedom-fighters, founders of nations, and originators of fresh thought systems, give ample testimony to the relationship between faith and courage.[7]

Courage and Wisdom

Tillich (1952) traces the relationship of courage to wisdom to the beginning of the modern world in Stoicism and Neo-Stoicism. Directed at conquering the anxieties of life and death, these philosophies centered upon the tension between individual righteousness and a sense of cosmic resignation (as opposed to cosmic salvation, offered by Christianity). Tillich notes:

> One event especially gave the Stoics' courage lasting power—the death of Socrates. That became for the whole ancient world both a fact and a symbol. It showed the human situation in the face of fate and death. It showed a courage which could affirm life because it could affirm death. And it brought a profound change in the traditional meaning of courage. In Socrates the heroic courage of the past was made rational and universal. A democratic idea of courage was created as against the aristocratic idea of it. Soldierly fortitude was transcended by the courage of wisdom. (p. 11)

A philosophical consolation and a strong-willed acceptance of the inevitable calamities of life and nature thus implied a higher form of courage than gallantry on the war-front. Stoic courage is based upon the dominance of reason in man and leads to a life of acceptance and fortitude. And, if logic dictates, the same courage can result in suicide.[8] However, a caveat needs to be entered here.

> The Stoic recommendation of suicide is not directed to those who are conquered by life by to those who have conquered life, are able both to live and to die, and can choose freely between them. Suicide as an escape, dictated by fear, contradicts the Stoic courage to be. (Tillich, 1952, p. 12)

Such Western notions have recently been compared by Jeste and Vahia (2008) with the conceptualization of wisdom in ancient Indian scriptures, especially the highly-revered and widely influential *Bhagavad Gita* (circa fifth century BCE). Employing meticulous lexicographic methods, these authors found both similarities and differences in the East-West views of wisdom. The Eastern perspective subsumed renunciation of acquisitiveness and a complete faith in God under wisdom while the Western perspective included personal well-being and clarity about life goals as well. More importantly, the definition of wisdom from both Eastern and Western perspectives included the domains of knowledge, emotional restraint, pro-social attitudes, and the capacity for appropriate action in the face of uncertainty. Jeste and Vahia noted:

> Living in the face of uncertainty and understanding real and potential conflicts between personal and societal goals is essential; however, such moral or practical dilemmas should lead, not to inaction, but to well-chosen and decisive action. (p. 204)

Such capacity for acting rationally and in accordance with one's ethical principles when faced with uncertainty is the crux of "moral decision-making" (Jeste and Meeks, 2008) and testifies to the inherent link between courage and wisdom. Courage arises from the wisdom of trusting one's powers of reason. In this way, courage seems to be the product of wisdom. On the other hand, courage may be needed to trust one's logical self in the first place. The relationship between courage and wisdom might therefore be dialectical, with one capacity-lending strength to the other. And, both capacities are vulnerable to deterioration in the face of instinctual desires and defensive inhibitions.

DEVELOPMENTAL ORIGINS

> If a man has been his mother's undisputed darling, he retains throughout life the triumphant feeling, the confidence in success, which not seldom brings actual success along with it. (Freud, 1917, p. 156)

> We need to fight for ourselves and stand up for who we are and what we want to become. We need to be warriors instead of victims, fighters instead of followers. Why a warrior? Because a warrior lives and acts with great strength, integrity, and commitment. A warrior has ignited the courage within. (Ford, 2012, p. 3)

It is not easy to figure out how and when courage develops in the course of life. Few psychoanalytic texts trace the origins of courage. Instead they offer observations on "confidence in success" (Freud, 1917), "imperturbable optimism" (Abraham, 1924), "optimism that is not lacerated by reality" (Glover, 1941), "confident expectation" (Benedek, 1938), and "basic trust" (Erikson, 1950). These concepts might have a bearing on the understanding of courage but are not related to courage in a linear fashion. The work of the four most prominent child analysts—Melanie Klein, Margaret Mahler, Donald Winnicott, and Anna Freud—is a little more explicit in this regard but, in all honesty, it too fails to draw a composite and convincing ontogenetic profile of courage's development.

Klein (1932) placed the consolidation in the phase of adolescence. She noted the powerful reaction formations against sexuality that emerge around this time and shift the ego-id struggles in the realm of morality and ethics. The resulting new principles and freshly idealized father-imagos are used by the child for disengagement from his early objects.

> By doing so he is able to call up his original positive attachment to his father and increase it with less risk of coming into collision with him. This event corresponds to a splitting of his father imago. The exalted and admired father can now be loved and adored while the 'bad father—often represented by his real father or by a substitute such as a schoolmaster—summons very strange feelings of hatred

> which are common at this period of development. And in the aggressive relationship to the hated father the boy reassures himself that he is his father's match and will not be castrated by him. In his relation to the admired father-imago he can satisfy himself that he possesses a powerful and helpful father, and can also identity himself with him; out of all this he draws a greater belief in his own constructive capacities and sexual potency. . . . It is here that his activities and achievements come in. By means of those achievements, whether physical or intellectual, which call for courage, strength and enterprise, among other things, he proves to himself that the castration he dreads so much has not happened to him, and that he is not impotent. (p. 189)

Mahler (1942) similarly emphasized the period of adolescence and reported the case of a teenager who shed his inhibitions and became "quite courageous in sports" (p. 157) by identifying with an athletic instructor at his school. Anna Freud (1956) viewed courage in the context of anxiety and declared that courage "is no more than the individual's ability to deal with the external threats on their own ground and prevent the bulk of them from joining forces with the manifold dangers lurking in the Id (p. 431). But what leads to the capacity to prevent the external-internal conflation was not made clear by her. Winnicott said little about courage and Jan Abram (2007), who has combed through his language, found no mention of this topic. Winnicott's notions of the capacity for tolerating aloneness and of the object's "survival" (1958, 1969) do, however, contribute to the understanding of courage in an indirect fashion.

These meager offerings on courage in the classic literature on early development are hardly improved upon by later child analysts of renown (Greenacre, 1971; Sarnoff, 1976; Greenspan, 1989; Lichtenberg, 1989; Stern, 1985). While these contributors talk about exploratory and assertive activities of the growing child and about the impact of maternal enthusiasm upon their consolidation, they do not refer to courage specifically. In contrast is the clarity of the following passage.

> It is an attribute that develops gradually and its precursors can be observed quite early. It is related both to temperament and to the affective messages given by caregivers. Take for example the visual cliff experiments conducted by Sorce et al. (1985). Infants 9 to 12 months old will not cross over the visual cliff if the parent on the

> other side makes a fearful face. When the infant reaches the edge of the "cliff" he/she looks for a signal from the parent. If the parent smiles and nods the baby will cross over. This is an example of the child's use of social referencing to overcome fear of a perceived danger. Parents who are not overly fearful themselves and who can inspire confidence in their children are facilitating exploration and providing their children with opportunities to practice overcoming avoidance of fear producing situations. So, you could say that courage is closely related to encouragement from significant others. (Jennifer Bonovitz, personal communication, September 24, 2012)

Putting her observations together with the literature cited above and my own speculations regarding the ontogenesis of courage, leads me to conclude that courage evolves around the following six developmental steps.

- *Constitutional factors*: The literature on temperament or the genetically-received, hard-wired affect-motor propensities (Kagan, 1984; Chess and Thomas, 1986) has demonstrated that children differ in their inherent assertiveness, novelty-seeking, and tolerance of frustration. Children with high levels of these three attributes display "proto-courage" and are likely to evolve into courageous adults, provided, of course, that the care-taking environment affirms and upholds these attributes in a sustained and loving manner.
- *Establishment of the "protective shield"*: The notion of a "protective shield" was inherent in Freud's (1895) earliest speculations regarding mental trauma but was not properly elucidated until his much later work, *Beyond the Pleasure Principle* (1920). Using the term *Reizchutz*, Freud proposed the existence of a threshold of stimulation by the external environment, the exceeding of which becomes psychologically traumatic. Later psychoanalysts (Mahler, 1958; Khan, 1963; Gediman, 1971; Esman, 1983) expanded Freud's view to include the regulation of internal stimuli also among the function of the "protective shield." Moreover, they traced its origins to mother-infant interactions whereby the mother regulates the extent of stimulation the infant has to face. This function is then internalized by the child who then develops self-regulatory functions with regard to the tolerable amounts of

inner and outer excitement. A strong protective shield forms the structural background of courage.

- *Maternal input*: Besides contributing to the genesis of the "protective shield," the mother helps the child become courageous in three other ways: (i) by playing peek-a-boo, she teaches the child the art and "ego pleasure" (G. Klein, 1976) of survival and bearing hardships (in this case, the momentary absence of mother), (ii) by looking at her child with confidence in his abilities, the mother makes him bolder; this is the essence of the "visual cliff experiments" (Sorce et al., 1985) cited by Bonovitz above,[9] and, (iii) by reliably meeting his developmental needs even if occasionally frustrating his instinctual wishes,[10] the mother creates a fundamental sense of optimism (Benedek, 1938; Erikson, 1950) in the child which, in turn, undergirds courage.
- *Father's role*: Interactions with the father also add to the child's courage. This happens in three ways: (i) by handling the child with greater physical roughness (than the mother) and by playing with him forcefully (e.g., throwing him up in the air), the father conveys to the child that risks can be taken, that danger is not all that it seems and that one can not only survive it but even enjoy it, (ii) by letting the child use his body for testing strength (e.g., arm wrestling) or by playfully asking the child to hit him and then showing no sign of suffering, the father becomes a role model of physical fortitude (Pruett, 1988), and (iii) by helping the child to separate from mother (Mahler et al., 1975), the father enhances the child's orbit of reality exploration and thus confers upon him greater self-confidence and courage. By demonstrating that he is able to bear the "anxiety of distance" that the mother cannot, the father upholds himself as an ideal of courage (Akhtar, 1992a).
- *The games of latency and early adolescence*: These invariably involve scenarios of losing and regaining safety. One has to leave a zone of safety, court danger, and return to the "home base." These games permit the player, rather like a toddler, the vicarious enjoyment of both merger and separateness from the mother (Mahler et al., 1975; Akhtar, 1992a). Phallic-oedipal undercurrents and attempts to master castration anxiety are also implicit in this sort of play (Glenn, 1991). This is nowhere more evident

than at amusement parks. The rides offered there involve high speeds, exposed situations, tunnels, darkness, giddiness and vertigo, and unfamiliar angles. By exposing the thrill seeker to physical danger and then returning him unhurt, such rides serve as counterphobic reassurances against castration anxiety. However, by removing an individual from familiar and safe ground (home, mother) and then returning him to it, these rides also capitalize on libidinization of separation-related fears. In summary, the games played by latency-age children and the counterphobic thrill-seeking of adolescents become developmental milestones toward the structuralization of adulthood courage (which, as has been noted, implies a greater mentalization of the risks involved and a less driven quality to the behavior involved).

- *Identification with heroes*: Finally, courage is also fueled by identification with heroes in late adolescence and young adulthood. A working-through of negative Oedipus complex is essential for such ego-ideal consolidation (Blos, 1967). However, psychic strength is derived not merely from the changed configuration of primary object-relations but also from internalization of fresh and societally-upheld individuals of valor, moral integrity, and intellectual freedom.

All in all, the attribute of courage in an adult is derived from a multiplicity of sources that include hereditary traits, maternal and paternal inputs, child's own re-working of early anxieties via games and thrill-seeking, and late identification with historically and culturally important figures.

COURAGE IN THE CLINICAL REALM

> The psychoanalytic psychotherapist is consistently faced with situations that demand courage, i.e., spirited, lively, vigorous responses in which psychological danger is faced without shrinking. (Prince, 1984, p. 48)

> Even when—and it always is—the story is very complex, a willingness to walk together into the deepest circles of the patient's experiential hell characterizes the attitude of compassion or emotional

> availability that the process of psychoanalytic understanding requires. This psychoanalytic compassion, I repeat for emphasis, is not reducible to moral masochism on the part of the analyst, nor is it to be contrasted with properly psychoanalytic work, usually seen as explicitly interpretative. (Orange, 2009, pp. 135–136)

The concept of courage as elucidated here has many implications for the conduct of intensive psychotherapy and psychoanalysis (Kohut, 1971; Prince, 1984; Olsson, 1994; Levine, 2006; Jacobs, 2008; O'Neil, 2009). This is true for both the patient and analyst in ways that overlap but also differ in certain regards.

The Patient's Courage

The patient shows courage in seeking help. It is not easy to pick up the telephone and call for a psychotherapeutic consultation. One feels embarrassed, anxious, and hesitant. The moment implies admission of weakness and vulnerability; one has failed to master something oneself. Child-like dependence often surfaces, with all its attendant hopes and anxieties. To tolerate all this and yet persist in the desire to seek help requires moral and intellectual courage. The narcissistic risk that the patient undertakes in calling for an appointment needs to be silently recognized and reciprocated by permitting the patient some lee-way in setting up the time for the first meeting. Asking such questions as "how urgent do you think your situation is?" or "when was it that you were planning to see me?" permits the patient to negotiate a realistically needed and feasible appointment. More importantly, allowing the patient to exercise some control subtly emphasizes the mutuality of the therapeutic undertaking and helps restore the patient's self-respect at a time of difficulty and self-doubt. It also acts as a positive reinforcement of the patient's courage.

More challenges await the patient upon his arrival at the therapist's office. Spontaneously or in response to the therapist's inquiries, he has to reveal things about himself that are socially embarrassing. He might be worried about them and might realize that he needs to talk about them but doing so in reality mobilizes the barriers of shame; he fears being mocked, looked down upon, and even denied further help. And yet, the patient chooses to tell what is troubling him.[11] Sometimes this happens as a result of the therapist's interventions or, more likely, due to the therapist's peaceful and understanding stance. At other times, the patient musters courage from within himself. The following clinical vignettes illustrate this point.

Clinical Vignette: 1

Norman Liebowitz, a thirty-two year-old internist from a regional medical center, came to see me for depression.[12] From all external appearances, he seemed successful: he was young, handsome, financially stable, and physically healthy. He was also happily married and recently had become a father. It was this last epoch that I felt had, paradoxically, triggered the depression he was feeling. Support to this line of thinking was given by the account of prior masochistic mishaps associated with his graduation from college and from medical school.

As the interview proceeded, Dr. Liebowitz abruptly stopped and said while all he had said so far was true, there was something else that was troubling him even more. This "something" had been with him for many years but he had never been able to talk about it with anyone. I responded by gently encouraging him to say more about what this hidden problem was and also about the concerns that had led him to keep it a secret. After some hesitation, Dr. Liebowitz revealed that he liked to chew upon cats' nails. He would frequent the houses of friends and acquaintances and, at times, scout the neighborhood to find a cat. Holding the animal up in his arms, he would bite off a chip from its nails. He kept these bits and pieces in a glass vial and chewed upon them at his leisure. As the interview progressed, a second interaction with cats emerged. He liked to bring a cat's face very, very close to his own face and then breathe in the air that came out of the cat's nostrils. Both these acts gave him deep gratification though he also worried about their apparent oddity and did not quite know what to make of them.

The next day, while describing his family background, Dr. Liebowitz came upon the topic of his mother. He sighed, saying, "You don't want to know about her. She is so controlling and so intrusive that I cannot describe. She lives about a thousand miles from here but I constantly feel her claws digging in to me." As he said this, he grabbed the upper part of his left arm with his right hand, making the latter appear like a claw, and dug his nails into the skin. Seeing the connection between the biting off of a cat's nails and the alleged claw of his mother on his arm, I said, "Did you notice what you just said?" He was puzzled, "What?" I said, "What do you make of you using the word 'claws' in connection with your mother and how do you connect her 'claws' with a cat's nails?" He was dumbfounded, but gradually became somber and began to talk about his chronic difficulty of maintaining an optimal distance from his mother. With further elaboration during the session, the biting off of the cat's nails and breathing the air coming out of the cat's nostrils could be seen to symbolize the two sides of this distance-closeness conflict. As this clarification settled in our dialog, I could see him become more animated and curious about his intrapsychic life.

Clinical Vignette: 2

Jack Rheuban, a forty-five year old fledging attorney, sought help for depression, increased drinking, and insomnia. He felt particularly guilty toward his wife (whom he deeply loved) for his recently inability to enjoy their mutual activities. He had lost interest in sex and did not feel like socializing with their friends.

As he recounted all this, what became apparent was that he had kept many aspects of his life secret from his wife and was full of remorse about this. These secrets, on surface, involved the extent of his drinking and the exaggerated reports of his income to his wife. With the progress of our work, however, secrets of his childhood emerged.

Jack had been a lonely child, even though he had a sibling, a sister who was four years older than he. Born with a club foot, he underwent many surgeries as a child and wore special, corrective shoes. More traumatic was the bullying by neighborhood kids and school mates. And even worse was the mocking by his own—rather sadistic—father, who would imitate his awkward gait and laugh. Jack grew up hating him and found little solace from his mother.

The childhood secrets involved his drawing elaborate diagrams outlining his plans to murder his father once he grew up. Another secret, which he had more difficulty revealing, involved his touching his sister's genitals (when he was eight and she twelve) while she was asleep. He claimed that he never understood why he did that except that doing something "weird" made him feel special and powerful. I said that I could understand this dynamic, adding that perhaps as our work proceeded, we would understand more about all this.

Around this time, Jack found himself badly stuck in a session. He finally revealed that he wanted to tell me something but was afraid that I would make fun of him. He also wondered if I would find him disgusting and refuse to see him any longer. I responded by saying that we needed to observe two things here—*one*, that he was already trusting me enough to consider telling me whatever about himself was troubling him so much and, *two*, that by imagining me laughing at him, he was transposing the image of his father upon me.

Jack relaxed somewhat and then, after a long pause, revealed that he often picks his nose and eats the snot gathered on his finger tip. Another pause followed. Then I spoke and said something along these lines, "I think you are relieved that you told this to me because now you are not alone with this secret. I also understand you would fear being shamed by me: this is something that under ordinary social circumstances would be found disgusting and be mocked. However, for the work you and I have undertaken, the question is hardly of shame and ridicule. The question is one of understanding. In other words, how do we understand this behavior? Frankly, it is too early for me to say anything about it but I have a vague sense that it might be akin to one of the so-called 'weird' things you have done in part to keep yourself feeling vital, alive, and something special. What do you think?"

The point of the two clinical vignettes is to underscore that the patient shows courage in revealing aspects of himself (the chewing of cats' nails in the first case and the eating of snot in the second case) which can be found repulsive by others. And yet, a "self-righting" (Lichtenberg, 1989) tendency[13] provides the motive to show those aspects to a trusted other and courage translates this motivation into action.

The role courage plays in the patient's participation in treatment does not end with such bold revelations. The process of intensive psychotherapy and psychoanalysis is long. It takes moral and intellectual courage to persevere in the face of external obstacles, internal resistances, and dysphoric transferences that inevitably crop up during such work. Moreover, the patient has to encounter unpleasant truths about himself and renounce lofty notions of being just, forever loving, and 'good.' He has to acknowledge and accept his own aggression toward others, struggle against forces of habit, renounce familiar instinctual short-cuts, and utilize the freshly-gained insights for new, if a bit uncomfortable, adaptive patterns. Kohut (1971) speaks of the "courage that allows [the patient's ego] to undertake tentative moves toward a humorous attitude with regard to his grandiose fantasies" (p. 326). And Jacobs (2008) emphasizes that the translation of insight into action not only requires working through the major transferences and resistances but also great courage from the patient. This is especially true if the deeper knowledge acquired about oneself as a result of analysis warrants major social changes (e.g., in marital status, employment, sexual orientation).

The Analyst's Courage

The analyst also needs courage in order to meaningfully participate in his work with the patient. This is true from the day he opens his office door to welcome a new patient, for he is not only permitting a total stranger in his physical space but in his inner self as well. The need for courage on the analyst's part persists throughout their work over the subsequent years and remains evident when the analyst lets go of the patient on the last day of the treatment. In Prince's (1984) words, "the psychoanalytic psychotherapist is consistently faced with situations that demand courage, i.e., spirited, lively, vigorous responses in which psychological danger is faced without shirking" (p. 48). Levine (2006), however, feels that a certain amount of "masochism is embedded in the clinician's decision to be creative, to take the risk, to act with integrity in accord with what the clinical situation appears to demand" (p. 545). The tension between Prince's and Levine's stance finds a sophisticated resolution in the following comment by O'Neil (2009).

> If, as psychoanalysts, we do not define courage too generally or superficially, and if we do not always pathologize self-sacrifice or seemingly cowardly behavior as masochistic, if we do not assume to know with certainty which is which, we will learn with our patients and identify with them what is truly courageous and what truly represents a self-destructive, masochistic solution to inner conflict. The "good feeling" of courage, freed from neurotic resolution, can then be experienced. (pp. 61–62)

This is in the spirit of Balint's (1957) recommendation that the analyst be comfortable with "the courage of one's own stupidity" (p. 305), i.e., bear not knowing and take the risk of finding out and learning afresh from interactions with the patient. Any assessment of the analyst's courage therefore needs a nuanced, moment-to-moment, and longitudinal perspective, spanning the entire course of analytic work. Take for instance the very first encounter between the patient and the analyst. At this point, the analyst's courage manifests in his capacity to utilize a differential therapeutic approach. In other words, his refusal to foreclose the possibility that a given patient might need (and, benefit from) some other form of intervention (e.g., psychotropic medication, marital counseling, sex therapy) shows his courage. After all, not all patients appearing at analysts' offices need psychoanalysis.

Further nuance is added by the fact that some individuals seeking consultation might not need any treatment all. And, the analyst should possess the ethical integrity to inform the patient of this. Doing so can involve loss of potential income and giving up the possibility of continued exchange with an intelligent and interesting person. More importantly, turning down a patient for believing that he or she does not need one's help requires tempering one's 'clinical narcissism."

Clinical Vignette: 3

Shahla Modaressi, a sixty-six-year-old, tall and attractive Iranian woman, was referred to me by a family friend who happened to be a research psychologist. While well-meaning, this individual was not clinically informed; his referral was based more upon friendly concern than upon medical need.

During our meeting, I heard that Shahla's oldest son, a thirty-seven year old married engineer, had died in a car accident about a year previous. (Her husband and their other two sons were doing well). The loss had devastated Shahla and though, with passage of time, its intensity had diminished somewhat, the pain was still there. She had begun socializing and had returned to the weekly game of bridge with her friends. She took care of herself and was elegantly dressed, had sophisticated touches of make-up, and wore attractive jewelry. At home, her life had resumed normalcy but, from time to time, she broke down in tears. A framed photograph of her son now adorned the mantelpiece of the living room's fireplace. She looked at it adoringly, often with tear-filled eyes. Her appetite and sleep were fine and the usual pattern of physical intimacy with her husband had resumed.

It became evident to me that she was dealing with a profound grief to the best of her ability and little was needed in terms of psychotherapeutic intervention. When I shared all this with her, she was immensely relieved. I told her that while I would remain available to her should matters get worse, at this point, I saw little reason for her to continue seeing me. "Reminiscing with family, talking to friends, enjoying what you can of life—an occasional drink, a game of bridge and some poetry—is frankly all you need," I said. Shahla left with relief and gratitude at feeling understood.

Besides the measure of differential therapeutic and deferred treatment, there are many other aspects of clinical work that demand courage on the analyst's part. "The core of psychotherapeutic courage is the ability to face and deal with one's inner experience" (Prince, 1984, p.

48) as these unfold over the course of clinical work. Inner experiences that require courage to bear include factual uncertainty, moral ambiguity, and the over-stretched capacity for empathy with thoughts and feelings too foreign to one's native experience. More specifically, the necessity to endure being the target of the patient's transferences calls upon the therapist's courage. Transference-based "seductions" of both erotic and sadomasochistic variety test the therapist's fortitude. Month after month, and year after year, the therapist has to accommodate the patient's transference distortions of him and of the strong affects from the patient's side and within himself (Coen, 2002).

Clinical Vignette: 4

Rebecca Bonowitz, a child-welfare attorney in her early forties, found my book, *Broken Structures* (Akhtar, 1992b), and took the words *Ex voto* in its dedication—"To my brother, Javed Akhtar, *Ex voto*"—to mean that my brother had passed away. Not only was I faced with the task of resisting to tell her that this was not the case, I had to "allow" her this belief and treat it like any other analytic material, i.e., with respect, curiosity, exploration and, if need be, with interpretation and re-construction (not terribly hard in light of her life-long hatred of *her* brother). Even more importantly, I had to bear the discomfort that arose within me due to the re-activation of my ambivalence toward my brother. To sustain a proper analytic attitude and not succumb to enactments required much fortitude on my part.

While circumstances of such sort test the analyst more, a certain amount of courage is integral to the very act of empathizing. After empathy involves the courage to loosen one's psychic boundaries and establish a "trial identification" (Fliess, 1942) with another person's stance. Courage on the analyst's part is also needed to forego the 'parasitic satisfaction' (Fromm-Reichman, 1966, p. 65) that tempt him during clinical work: money, generation of ideas, using the patient as a springboard for one's own fantasy life, and so on. And, needless it might appear to state, the act of interpretation is inherently of courage since it involves (i) trusting one's "conjecture" (Brenner, 1976) while knowing that there is little guarantee that these are correct, and (ii) bringing to the patient's awareness something that the patient does not know (or, does not know clearly enough), hence disrupting him to a greater or lesser degree.

Finally, three situations need to be mentioned which especially call for the therapist's courage.

- *The courage to rupture the patient's pathological hope*: Basically, this involves "having to state that neither analysis nor analyst is an omnipotent rescuer, as the patients in their illusion need to believe" (Amati-Mehler and Argentieri, 1989, p. 301). In a case of "malignant erotic transference" (Akhtar, 1994), for instance, such intervention translates into the analyst's explicit declaration that he would never marry the patient. With those endlessly lamenting a long-dead parent, the analyst might have to literally confirm the irreversibility of the situation. A less dramatic, but essentially similar example is of the patient who "kept crying and saying 'I can't help it', and the analyst who said: 'I'm afraid I cannot help it either'" (Amati-Mehler and Argentieri, 1989, p. 296). Such interventions can be subsumed under the broad rubric of "optimal disillusionment" (Gedo and Goldberg, 1973), which requires that the analysand learn to give up magical thinking. Neither conventional nor risk-free, interventions of this sort disrupt the transference dynamics and have the potential of traumatizing the patient. Indeed, when their "dosage" or timing is inappropriate—and this may not be entirely predictable—the resulting despair and psychic pain might lead the patient to become suicidal. This puts analysis to a most severe test. Temporary departures from neutrality then become unavoidable and adjunct stabilizing measures might have to be employed. On the other hand, interventions of this sort can constitute a turning point of the analytic process in less complicated circumstances, provided, of course, the analyst's "holding" (Winnicott, 1960) function is in place and the effects of such an intervention can be analyzed.
- *The courage to acknowledge mistakes*: Psychotherapists and analysts deal with "soft" and fluid material and therefore it is not surprising they frequently make errors. Some of these arise from the therapist's inexperience and the consequent technical rigidity. Others result from the therapist's failure of empathy (Kohut, 1977) or from specific countertransference lapses which make him lose touch with the patient's psychic reality. Under these circumstances, "the patient feels misunderstood and unable to get through

to the therapist" (Wolf, 1994, p. 93). An honest bit of soul searching on the therapist's part then reveals that he has contributed to occurrence of a disruption. This must be explicitly acknowledged and conveyed to the patient. By so doing, the therapist (a) provides the patient with an experience of having effectively communicated his distress to the analyst; this results in a self-enhancing experience of efficacy, and (b) restores the patient's experience of a positive bond with the analyst. While an acknowledgment of one's lapse in empathy is often sufficient, in situations where the therapist's 'mistake' is gross, an apology might be indicated.[14]

- *The courage to seek consultation*: The analyst must not be cock-sure regarding his way of working. He must retain humility and have the moral courage to seek consultation when faced with difficult and puzzling clinical situations. Celenza's (2007) reminder that psychoanalytic treatment is based upon confidentiality and not "hyper-confidentiality" (i.e., secrecy) and refusal to permit supervisory input or peer consultation is apt here. The treatment bubble must remain porous to corrective input from others. This is especially so when the therapist is ego-compromised (e.g., physically ill, undergoing a divorce) or is making "unusual interventions" (Akhtar, 2011a).[15]

All in all, both undergoing analytic treatment *and* conducting analytic treatment rest upon many ego capacities. Prominent among these are honesty, integrity, empathy, mutuality, patience, generosity (see chapter 4), and, in light of the foregoing discourse—courage.

CONCLUDING REMARKS

> Courage often involves choice, and is activated by a social and historical moment. It is part of one's personal and public destiny, a reflection of one's past experiences and spirit come to a particular expression—one that can be judged by others, by fellow citizens in their way, or social scientists in theirs. (Coles, 1965, p. 97)

In this chapter, I have attempted to bring diverse literature on courage into a harmonious gestalt. After delineating the nature of courage, I have briefly commented upon the phenomenological aspects of counterphobia and cowardice. I have devoted a section to courage's relationship with joy, faith, and wisdom, and a subsequent section to the developmental origins of courage. Finally, I have discussed the role of courage in the clinical situation.

Now, I want to turn to two questions that have remained unanswered so far: (i) are courageous acts always "good" or can these be "bad" as well? and, (ii) how does the culture at large view counterphobia, courage, and cowardice? The first question tends to reflexively elicit an affirmative response. Images of brave soldiers, good Samaritans, and live organ-donors pop-up in the mind and make us equate courage with "goodness." However, careful thought reveals all sorts of conceptual problems here, especially the perspective being used to call something "good" or "bad." Take, for instance, the "9-11" scenario. The gallantry of firefighters, who despite enormous risks, entered the burning towers to save innocent lives, is regarded as both courageous and "good." But what about the actions of Muhammad Atta (and his partners) who hijacked the airplanes and rammed them into the twin towers? To be sure, there exist people in this world who consider these actions to be courageous and even "good." We do not agree but does that automatically make us right and them wrong? Take another example. This pertains to the Yasser Arafat (the President of Palestinian National Authority from 1994 to 2004), who was considered a terrorist by Israel and before him, to Yitzhak Shamir (the Prime Minister of Israel from 1983 to 1984 and 1988 to 1992) who was declared a terrorist by the British (Brinkley, 2012). Do we regard their actions to be courageous? Do we regard their actions to be "good"? The point of these examples is that the link between courage and goodness is forged under the prism of sociopolitical bias. It is not inherent and ubiquitous.

Talking of culture brings us to the second question raised above, i.e., what is the attitude of the culture-at-large toward counterphobia, courage, and cowardice? While little has been said about this in our literature, my sense is that counterphobia evokes amusement, fascination, and mock horror; courage evokes respect, admiration, and awe, and cowardice evokes derision and contempt. Underneath these conscious reactions lie different scenarios. At the deeper layers of the mind, counterphobia evokes a bit of wistful envy (see our reactions to the daredevil Evel Knievel and the escape artist Harry Houdini); we long for such fearlessness ourselves. Our unconscious attitudes regarding courage and cowardice are even more striking. Society valorizes courage and derides cowardice. For the courageous, it erects statues and monuments. For the coward, it spins jokes and slurs. However, a deeper scrutiny reveals that while celebrating courage, the society actually rewards cowardice. Think about it. Cowardice involves renunciation of desire, compromise of authenticity and ascribing at all costs to group cohesion; it is these attitudes that society rewards. Freud's (1930) *Civilization and Its Discontents* goes even further and proposes that cultural institutions that enforce repression of man's instinctual freedom might themselves be the creation of such renunciation.

That being said, the fact seems to be that all three reactions, namely, counterphobia, courage, and cowardice, have a place not only in the societal and cultural life but in the intrapsychic experience of all human beings. Each has its origins, its functions, its place, and time. Each can be put to good and bad use. And, believe it or not, each, in its own way, can contribute to human resilience, an attribute that forms the topic of my next chapter.

2

RESILIENCE

The deleterious impact of psychological trauma manifests in symptom clusters that are so diverse as to be practically innumerable. The most commonly seen pathways, however, are (i) phobic withdrawal from specific situations or from life in general, (ii) masochistic brooding and "injustice collecting" (Bergler, 1961), (iii) chronic anger and revenge seeking, (iv) flashbacks, nightmares, startle reactions, and other signs of "post-traumatic stress disorder" (DSM-IV-TR, 2000, pp. 463–468), and (v) making narcissistic capital out of misfortune and regarding oneself as an "exception" (Freud, 1916) to the ordinary rules and regulations of society. All this is well established. It forms the daily staple of clinical practice in the mental health field. Less recognized is the fact that psychological trauma can, at times, have silently positive effects upon the individual's ego functioning and adaptation. These include vigilance, healthy stoicism, enhanced ambition, perseverance, and pursuit of knowledge about self and others. A posttraumatic increase in altruism is also sometimes evident.

Such Janus-faced consequences of trauma give rise to all sorts of questions. For instance, what determines whether positive or negative consequences will be predominant in the aftermath of trauma? What regulates their proportion? Is the outcome of trauma a once-and-for-all occurrence or subject to psychic elaboration, layering, and modification? Do pre-traumatic ego assets matter more in governing the outcome of trauma than the ameliorative influences that follow it? What is the role of intelligence, inborn talents, imagination, and fantasy here? How and to what extent do societal institutions (e.g., organizations, museums, memorials) and cultural containers (e.g., theater, cinema, poetry) help transform the impact of individual or group trauma? And, so on. From this panoply of curiosity, one question stands out for the clinician: why is it that some individuals crumble in the face of trauma while others can withstand any assault on their system? In other words, what are the genesis, dynamics, and epistemology of resilience?

DEFINITION AND PSYCHOANALYTIC UNDERPINNINGS

> Preclinical and clinical work suggests that moderate childhood stresses that can be successfully managed or mastered are likely to cause stress inoculation and stress resilience to subsequent stressors. —Southwick et al., 2005, p. 280

> Resilience concerns the enigma of survival. Survival means not only physical survival, but implies keeping something intact. Maybe one's morality, that is, keeping one's mind's integrity while others lose their moral anchorage, a belief in something positive in oneself, and potentially also in others. —Varvin, 2009, p. 364

The major psychoanalytic glossaries (Eidelberg, 1968; Laplanche and Pontalis, 1973; Moore and Fine, 1968, 1990; Rycroft, 1968) do not list "resilience" as a recognized term, and the index to Freud's collected works has no entry on it (*Standard Edition*, Vol. 23). Turning to the English language, one finds "resilience" defined in *Webster's Ninth New Collegiate Dictionary* as "(1) the capability of a strained body to recover its size and shape after deformation caused especially by compressive stress; (2) an ability to recover from or adjust easily to misfortune or change" (Mish, 1983, p. 1003). A careful look at this definition reveals that resilience (i) can involve both physical and psychological realms, (ii) is not only a response to trauma but to change in general, and (iii) consists of either a return to the psychosomatic *status quo* or to a more or less harmonious adaptation to the altered inner or outer reality.

The last-mentioned characteristic brings forth the linguistic conundrum involving the relationship between resilience and flexibility. While occasionally used interchangeably (Kay, 1976, pp. 343, 673), the two denote rather different phenomena. *Flexibility* indicates malleability, compliance, and adjustment to changed situations. *Resilience*, in contrast, puts a premium on return to the original state, defiance, and recovery. In Hartmann's (1939/1958) terms, *flexibility* is closer to *autoplastic* and *resilience* to *alloplastic* adaptation.

This brings us back to psychoanalytic literature pertaining to the forces that lead individuals toward self-protection and recovery from mishaps and hardships. Freud's (1905b, 1909, 1915) description of 'ego instincts' is a case in point here. These instincts serve "self preservative" (1909, p. 44), "self seeking" (1908, p. 212), and "self subsisting" (1930, p. 122) aims. The prefix 'self' in this context is usually taken to mean bodily self, and it does have that connotation. However, it also includes the psychic self; thus, the aims of ego instincts were also *psychically* self-preservative and self-seeking. Freud emphasized that self-preservative instincts operate in accord with the reality principle and strive for what is useful to guard against damage to the individual.

A more explicit enunciation of psychological forces that help an individual rebound from suffering is to be found in Nunberg's (1926) paper titled "The Will to Recovery." Nunberg posited that a mind faced with trauma or struggling with neurotic conflict longs for infantile omnipotence. This regressive sleeve of the ego later becomes the source for the energy to overcome the psychic disturbance one is faced with. LaForgue (1929) added that benevolent superego needs to be in place for this transformation of infantile omnipotence into adaptive energy to take place.

Four years later, Freud (1933) specifically mentioned the "instinct for recovery" (p. 106) and traced its phylogenetic origins to the "power of regenerating lost organs" (p. 106) in lower animals. He acknowledged that this force contributed to the success of psychotherapy and psychoanalysis. Temperamentally given to pessimism, which had steadily increased with old age and illness, Freud, however, did not go deeper into the nature of the "instinct for recovery"; instead, he used the idea to buttress his proposals of repetition-compulsion and death instinct.

The concept of an inner force that propels recovery and, by implication, is responsible for human resilience in the face of trauma remained ill-developed in subsequent years of psychoanalysis. Freud's disinterest contributed to this inattention. The fact that over the years psychoanalytic motivation theory went much farther than its early drive-based model also resulted in the "instinct for recovery" to be left behind.[1]

Three avenues of psychoanalytic observation then led to a rejuvenation of interest in resilience and recovery: (i) the study of the experiences of the Nazi Holocaust survivors (Brenner, 2004, 2008; Kestenberg, 1972; Kestenberg and Brenner, 1996; Kogan, 1995, 2007; Valent, 1988) as well as the autobiographical accounts made available by such individuals (e.g., Levi, 1996; Parens, 2004), (ii) empirical observations of children raised by emotionally disturbed (Anthony and Cohler, 1987) or physically impaired (Wagenheim, 1985) parents, and (iii) the infant-observational studies (e.g., Edgcumbe and Burgner, 1972; Emde, Graensbauer, and Harmon, 1976; Lichtenberg, 1980; Parens, 1979) that permitted access to the inner motivational systems pertaining to basic human needs of survival and growth, including the human "self righting instinct" (Lichtenberg, 1989). Together these three sources of information shed light upon the multidetermined nature of human resilience. They underscored the complex interplay of constitutional, intrapsychic, and societal factors in the genesis and sustenance of this capacity.

Equipped with this linguistic and psychoanalytic thesaurus, one might define resilience as an ego capacity to metabolize psychological trauma to the extent that resumption of the original level of psychic functioning becomes possible. However, this does not imply a literal return to the original state since the pre-trauma innocence is neither recoverable nor desirable anymore. Hence the resumption of functioning typical of resilience is an ego advancement; it assimilates the psychological consequences of trauma and is accompanied by deeper insight into the self and its interpersonal context. Needless to add, such advance is inwardly supported by a strong constitution (Anthony, 1987), unimpeded functioning of ego instincts (Freud, 1905b), the achievement of libidinal object constancy (Hartmann, 1952; Mahler, 1968; Mahler, Pine, and Bergman, 1975), a benevolent and kind superego (Nunberg, 1926; LaForgue, 1929) made of good internal objects, and familial and societal support systems.

These complex constituents of resilience have been elucidated in the vast literature on Holocaust survivors. However, since the ground covered has mostly focused upon psychological trauma (individual or group), I offer three striking vignettes where the trauma faced by the individual was predominantly physical (though, of course, with powerful emotional consequences). I hope that the encounter with their histories will illuminate the mystery of human resilience from yet another perspective.

THREE EXCEPTIONAL MEN

> We can access the ego's sublimation potential by such factors as frustration tolerance, the resistance to regressive loss of functional autonomy, the capacity for obtaining substitute gratifications, inborn talents, the capacity for postponement and delay of discharge. Probably, the most important is the degree to which function pleasures can be substituted for instinctual ones. —Sandler and Joffe, 1966, p 355

> To accept oneself within limits is an important aspect of emotional maturity that is in contrast to narcissistic rationalization, to denial, to resignation and cynicism, and to masochistic self-blame. —Kernberg, 1980, p. 127

Stephen Hawking (1942–Present)

Professor Stephen Hawking is one of those scientists who truly broadened our understanding of the universe. Explaining the relativity theory and quantum mechanics to lay public in an interesting and comprehensible manner, Hawking has transformed complexities of physics into enlightened living-room conversation. While his intellectual feats are amazing, one is awed by his ability to accomplish success while battling a degenerative disease; through most of his adult life, he has been confined to a wheelchair.

Hawking does not profess any religious or spiritual sources of encouragement, yet he has transcended a life of suffering. At first glance, the logical thinking that has characterized his professional endeavors would predict a fatalistic and hopeless response to his illness. So what is it about his experiences that allowed him to passionately pursue a scientific career, defy negative prognoses, and captivate us all with his path to find meaning in life? In *Stephen Hawking: A Life in Science*, White and Gribbin (2002) provide a description of both the life and work of

Professor Hawking that gives the reader an understanding of his development from a young boy to a world-renowned scientist.

Stephen Hawking was born in London during World War II. His parents were from middle-class families who valued education. His father was a doctor who specialized in tropical diseases. A remote figure in the family, he spent most of his time abroad doing research. He encouraged the young Stephen in his studies and had high expectations that were not always met. For example, when Stephen was eight years old, his father had hoped he would be accepted to the prestigious Westminster school and was greatly disappointed when Stephen failed the entrance exam. As he entered college, his father discouraged Stephen's interest in cosmology, as it was not a "respected" field. His relationship with his mother was more supportive. She also studied at Oxford, but was subsequently under-employed as a secretary at a medical research unit. Little is known about their early relationship, but her active role in liberal politics and frequent public rising to Stephen's defense provide some clues that she promoted free thinking and supported Stephen's unconventional choices. Their home was described as clean but cluttered with various things collected from around the world.

As a child, Stephen was eccentric, awkward, skinny, and puny. He was teased and bullied, but formed a small group of friends who were at the "top of the class." His superior intellect was recognized by age ten, but the demands of St. Albans private school left few opportunities to develop interpersonal relationships beyond the classroom. The childhood "war" games he invented had rules and objectives so complex that he and his friends would spend much of their time figuring out the consequence of a single move.

At seventeen, he began undergraduate studies at Oxford. His father had advocated for his acceptance but did not express great confidence in his son's abilities. A private tutor by the name of Dr. Robert Berman was retained to help Stephen along. Dr. Berman became an important mentor for Stephen during college, although he relied very little on him for academic help. Stephen's innate aptitude and understanding of physics allowed him to work very little, yet win all sorts of awards for academic excellence. He also developed an interest in rowing and transformed into part of an "in crowd" as an aggressive coxswain. His reputation at this time was one of a gritty, ruthless, accomplished but seemingly lazy student. When he scored at the borderline of first and second honors on final exams, it was his hubris that led to a highest-level degree from Oxford and a chance to study under Fred Hoyle (1915–2001), a top astronomer of the time, at Cambridge. He was placed under the lesser-known Dennis Sciama (1926–1999) instead, who turned out to be a highly suitable mentor.

Stephen Hawkins was twenty-one when he was diagnosed with amyotrophic lateral sclerosis (ALS). He had already begun his studies toward a doctorate in cosmology, and the news of his illness caused him deep depression; he was given a two-year life expectancy by his doctors. He became reluctant to proceed with his studies, which were wrought with their own setbacks, but an encounter with a young boy in an adjacent hospital bed helped him shift perspective. As he watched the boy die, he reasoned, "At least my condition doesn't make me feel sick. There are people worse off than me" (White and Gribbon, 2002, p. 63). While in the hospital, he dreamed he was going to be executed. In another recurring dream, he would sacrifice his life to save others. These dreams turned the helplessness of being terminally ill into acts of persecution by others or of altruistic suicide. Either way, they minimized his passivity. He concluded, "If I'm going to die anyway, I might as well do some good" (White and Gribbon, 2002, p. 63).

Another strong influence in his life was a woman he met at a party during the time just prior to his diagnosis, Jane Wilde. She would become his first wife. She restored his will to live and provided the support he needed to complete his doctorate at age twenty-three, despite his rapidly deteriorating health. They decided to start a family quickly, since there was so little time left. Four years after Hawking's diagnosis, the couple had a son. Contrary to all expectations, Hawking did not die. In fact, he strangely blossomed. His scientific career took off, and by age thirty, he was an established, world-class physicist. At thirty-six, he received the Albert Einstein Award given by the Lewis and Rosa Strauss Memorial Fund; this is one of the most prestigious prizes in physics. The following year he was appointed as Lucasian Professor of Mathematics at Cambridge University, a chair once held by Sir Isaac Newton. He went on to have two other children, and Jane was there to raise them.

His main method of coping with ALS was and has been spending most of his time preoccupied with nature and the origin of the cosmos, what he calls the "game of the Universe" (White and Gribbin, 2002, p. 118). He states that he is not normally depressed about his disability because "I have managed to do what I wanted to do despite it, and that gives me a feeling of achievement" (White and Gribbin, 2002, p. 192). He prefers that others focus on his scientific achievement rather than his physical limitations. In some sense, he has refused to allow ALS to penetrate his psychic structure and define him and his identity. This ego stubbornness in part accounts for his resilience. He has met each challenge to his ability to communicate with others with a creative solution, rejecting the option to remain silent. This has been in the form of technical innovations that allow a computer to speak for him and that allow him to control his own mobility and sometimes express his personality with his computer-guided wheelchair.

The popular success of his books, *A Brief History of Time* (1998), and *The Universe in a Nutshell* (2001), demonstrated his ability to relate to a lay audience and helped launch his international fame. He describes his motivation for these projects as simply to meet the exorbitant expenses involved in his daily care. As a public figure he has advocated for people with disabilities to have access to technologies that facilitate mobility and communication. He has not been free of public controversy; most notable was his divorce from his wife of twenty-five years and subsequent remarriage to his nurse, Elaine Mason, in 1995. Curiously, Mason's first husband, David, had designed the first version of Hawking's talking computer. This naturally led to some raised eyebrows. Despite such lapses, Stephen Hawking has managed to create an overall life of meaning and purposes. He remains confined to a wheelchair and requires twenty-four-hour care. And yet he continues to contribute to the lives of others, travel extensively for work and pleasure, and passionately pursue scientific inquiry.

Christopher Reeve (1952–2004)

Widely known for his successful acting career, especially his role as Superman, Christopher Reeve won even greater respect for his response to a horseback-riding accident that left him paralyzed from the neck down. Struggling toward recovery, he gave a voice and face to those with spinal cord injury. As he regained some function and championed efforts toward stem-cell research, he amazed the world in the process with his heroic efforts and altruism. In his autobiography, *Still Me* (Reeve, 1998), he documented his life prior to the accident and chronicled his experiences afterward. He allowed the reader an intimate witnessing of his journey, revealing his thoughts, feelings, and insights along the way.

Christopher Reeve publicly told a unique story of resilience. He moved beyond the role of survivor and managed to maintain self-esteem, family, and career. His life prior to the accident may hold clues to understanding his internal resources. His story also highlights important external sources of resilience available to him. His way of handling adversity was mediated by both these internal and external factors. It informs a pathway to recovery that does not sidestep one's original goals but allows for overcoming limitations and staying on course.

Christopher Reeve was born in New York, New York, and was four years old when his parents divorced. He grew up in Princeton, New Jersey, mainly with his mother and brother, but had regular contact with his father. His mother, Barbara, was a journalist, and his father, Franklin, was a professor and a writer. This exposed him at an early age to social/societal ideas and the creative arts. He and his father kept regular company with Robert Frost, Robert Penn Warren, and Daniel Patrick Moynihan. His parents greatly valued education; his stepfather funded his tuition at the esteemed Princeton Day School.

His mother was among the first to notice his precocious intellect as well as innate talents, which included sports, theater, and music. By age nine, he was performing in professional theater. In his teenage years he balanced a developing career with his schooling. He also had a love for ice hockey and was a leading goalie in high school. He was also a leader among his peers in theater groups and was very active in school organizations. He went on to simultaneously pursue college at Cornell and study/perform in top theaters of Britain and France. In lieu of a final year at Cornell, he accepted a spot at the renowned Julliard School for the Performing Arts in New York; Robin Williams was his roommate, and they were mentored by the best. His talents brought him many opportunities for contact with extraordinary people, most notably Katherine Hepburn, with whom he shared the stage in a Broadway play. Reeve was diligent and committed to his craft, and his hard work was rewarded. He brought a tremendous amount of talent to the opportunities he was presented, and in this sense his success in acting was experienced as effortless. He was confident, handsome, charming, and principled.

In addition to his professional endeavors, Reeve had strong liberal political beliefs. His activism started with opposition to the Vietnam War in high school and continued with his support of environmental protection in college. Reeve addressed the United Nations regarding the pollution of the Hudson River in New York. He also initiated and supported political groups to address the needs of actors and even risked his life to advocate for the Chilean actors persecuted by the Pinochet government. With this background and tenacity, it is not surprising that he would later advocate for all those with spinal cord injury and reject a defeatist position regarding his own medical prognosis.

At thirty years of age, Reeve landed the leading role in the movie *Superman* (Warner Brothers, 1978). It was a risky career move as the childlike and lighthearted nature of the script had the potential of demoting him from the cadre of serious actors. Reeve was, however, not averse to risk-taking, and the great success of the movie actually furthered his career. It was during the filming of *Superman* in England that he developed a relationship with modeling executive Gae Exton, which resulted in three children. They separated unmarried four years later but maintained an amicable joint custody arrangement much in the model his parents had demonstrated. Shortly after his separation and return to the United States, he met Dana and fell in love. They married, had a son, and maintained a loving relationship that would later prove able to withstand unthinkable hardship.

Reeve was a sports enthusiast. He was an accomplished pilot, avid sailor, and competitive horseback rider. This is important to understand the tragedy of his riding injury, in that it was not a result of recklessness, but a true accident. Werman's (1979) reminder that subscribing to the principle of psychic determinism must not erase the capacity to believe in the occurrence of random events is pertinent in this context.

Reeve's love of sports and the physical skills nurtured over his lifetime may have translated into the athleticism and competitive intensity he showed in his physical rehabilitation. In the moments and days following his accident, he went through a range of emotions that included depression and suicidal despair. He was quite serious about his desire to end his life, and it was Dana who uttered the words that redeemed him, "You're still you, and I love you" (Reeve, 1998, p. 28). The love of Dana, the nurturance of his family, and the support of an extensive social network became complementary to his own sense of determination. They provided an environment that constantly fueled resilience in the face of setbacks, thick despair, and periods of stagnation.

In the course of his physical rehabilitation, Reeve continued his life as an actor with his starring role in *Rear Window* (ABC, 1998). He also realized a dream as director of a television movie *In the Gloaming*, (HBO, 1997), which won an Emmy along with many other awards. He maintained a rigorous commitment to his physical recovery, maintaining the range of motion in his limbs so they would be functional in the event on re-innervation. He used innovative technologies that allowed him to be supported in the upright position and to 'walk' on a treadmill using electrical implants to stimulate his muscles.

He spoke to relevant subcommittees of the United States Senate and advocacy groups in support of political steps to remove restrictions on stem-cell research and to increase federal funding for research. In 1996, he created the Christopher Reeve Paralysis Foundation to help raise money for the American Paralysis Association. The Christopher and Dana Reeve Paralysis Resource Center is now the premier resource center for families and patients dealing with paralysis.

Reeve shared his personal story via speaking engagements and his books. He addressed a wide range of audiences with intent to inform and inspire. In his book *Nothing Is Impossible* (2002), Reeve spoke of significant topics such as humor, mind/body, parenting, religion, advocacy, recovery, faith, and hope. In his self-reflection he presented these areas as paramount to his individual healing. He offered an optimistic perspective to his own challenges and suggested that this perspective is available to anyone in any situation.

Christopher Reeve died of complications related to a sacral decubitus ulcer, a common problem in paralyzed individuals as a result of immobility. But it is unlikely that he will be remembered for the way he died. His refusal to retreat in the face of a life-altering trauma, all that he lost and all he regained, leaves a legacy of a true Superman who reminds one how to live. He showed that dignity can survive, even triumph over adversity. Reeve was posthumously awarded an honorary Doctorate of Letters degree by Rutgers University in 2005 and a Doctorate of Humane Letters degree by the State University of New York at Stony Brook in the same year. The latter degree was received, on his behalf, by Brooke Ellison, a paralyzed young woman on whose life a television movie had been recently directed by none other than Christopher Reeve.

Michael J. Fox (1961–Present)

In *Lucky Man* (2001), Michael J. Fox, the actor turned activist, chronicles his life and battle with Parkinson's disease. When he burst out on television screens across the nation in the mid-1980s, Fox kept America laughing with his serious comic antics and his boyish charm. His successful career in movies and television sitcoms is how most people remembered him until November of 1998, when he disclosed details of his protracted battle with a relentless, incurable disease. Many shared in the shock of the implications for his future, but most did not understand exactly what it meant. His rise to the role of advocate and fund-raiser for parkinsonism helped educate the general public about the illness and its prognosis. Instead of turning to alcohol or drugs, or self-destructing in some other way, he emerged stronger and more vivacious with renewed fight and purpose. He continued to lead a productive life and gracefully dealt with the loss of his career as an actor.

In the first chapter of his book, Fox notes, "An actor's burning ambition, when you think about it, is to spend as much time as possible pretending to be someone else" (p. 16). He describes self-doubt as a "worm eating away at you that grows in direct proportion to your level of success" (p. 16). It is here that one begins to see how Fox struggled with self-esteem, and his life is revealed as hardly exempt from failures and challenges. One learns that his main struggle was to maintain connection to common human experiences in the midst of an extraordinary life. The narrative Fox provides gives parkinsonism a starring role. As opposed to the role of a career-killing villain, the disease becomes the hero that helps Fox maintain a connection with the soft and vulnerable side of humanity.

Michael's father was an Army soldier, but he spent much of his childhood with his brother and three sisters in Burnaby, British Columbia, after his father's retirement. He enjoyed hockey and was quite good, but his short stature limited any hopes of a professional sports career. He was always the family clown, and his interest in the performing arts was not a surprise to those who knew him during his childhood. His Nana (his caretaker) was one person who took it very seriously and saw something special in his future. It was she who predicted, "He'll probably be famous someday." Her influence on his life was profound, and her death when he was eleven years old, devastating. Her belief in him, however, remained a source of encouragement for him long after her years. His mother was very loving and remains a source of support to him. Fox credits both his parents with enabling him to be psychologically strong and resourceful. This close family network was undoubtedly helpful in nurturing his dreams, but his rise to fame was also facilitated by innate talent, perseverance, and serendipity.

He began to explore the creative arts through writing, art, and playing the guitar in "rock-and-roll garage bands" before realizing his interest in acting. At age fifteen, he debuted as a professional actor while costarring on a sitcom. At eighteen he moved to Los Angeles and after three years of playing small roles landed the part of Alex P. Keaton in the popular television sitcom *Family Ties* (1982–1989). This brought him wide recognition and many professional awards, including three Emmys and a Golden Globe. His subsequent success in *Back to the Future* (Universal Pictures, 1985) made him tremendously wealthy and gave him an enduring sense of achievement. However, fame also brought personal challenges.

A blurred distinction between public and private experience, consequent upon fame, led Fox to feel disoriented and inwardly unanchored. His drinking, already on the brink of being excessive, worsened. While the premise of acting includes a mutual suspension of disbelief and taking on of roles, the "being-famous-in-America's-fun-house" has no guidebook or script to govern one's life. His desperate effort to remain grounded in the real world in the face of being famous was taxed by the complex emotions aroused by learning he was suffering from the serious disease of parkinsonism.

His wife, Tracey Pollan, then became influential in his life. Before their marriage, as his costar on *Family Ties*, she had challenged him to evaluate his drinking habits. Their relationship allowed him to see the importance of creating a scared space between them that maintained boundaries with the rest of the world, and she encouraged him to discard his "yes-man" persona and made him accountable for his actions. He reduced his drinking, and she stood by his side through the numerous hospital visits his illness dictated.

For the next seven years, Fox kept his diagnosis a secret from the public and the major of his professional colleagues. During part of this time, he was enduring shock, denial, shame, and fear. The nature of the disease and its available treatment results in oscillations three to four times a day between symptom control and symptom exacerbation. This was a threat to his career; his secrecy kept him further bound. But he also describes his illness as a "gift" that provided him an opportunity to choose between "adopting a siege mentality or embarking upon a journey" (Fox, 2002, p. 5). A "keep-your-head-down-and-keep-moving mentality" (Fox, 2002, p. 17) and frequent reliance on the ability to elude, evade, and anticipate potential obstacles in his way became his self-identified traits of a hearty and adaptive nature.

Fox's personal struggle with Parkinson's disease became public in 1998. Over a series of media disclosures, the news spread, and an unexpected result of this public disclosure was how many other lives were made less shameful by having a connection with him through a shared illness. This observation motivated Fox to begin playing an active role as a public health advocate. In 1999, he addressed the United States Senate Appropriations Committee to seek more federal funding for Parkinson's research. Following his retirement from full-time acting in 2000, he founded the Michael J Fox Foundation for Parkinson's Research. He now frequently endorses political candidates who support stem-cell research that could lead to a cure for parkinsonism. In this transition, Fox has transformed an impossible personal situation into a society movement for change while retaining optimism and gratitude for the opportunities life has given him.

LESSONS FROM THEIR LIVES

> Some of us who encountered adversity in childhood have embraced it as a daemon of creative insight and purpose and lived fully, without too much envy or resentment. Others have become magnets for attracting more pain, always susceptible to recreating what hurt them. The difference seems to lie in the attitude taken towards suffering and pain. —Young-Eisendrath, 1996, p. 61

> The short list of protective factors on which resilience studies have converged include connections to competent and caring adults; cognitive and self-regulation skills and positive views of self; and the motivation to be effective in the environment. —Masten, 2001, p. 234

First and foremost, let us acknowledge that the sketches that I have provided here do not constitute psychoanalytic data; gathering that requires consent, cooperation, closeness, confidentiality, and close process monitoring. I do not have that there. What I have is psycho-dynamically informed ethnography that gives some clues about specific individuals but mostly yields large-scale patterns. Indeed a careful look at the brief histories of these three men does reveal many areas of commonality, which include the following:

- Being born to loving parents (even though Reeve's parents got divorced, they maintained a cordial relationship and cared deeply for their children);
- Possessing exceptional inborn talents that were evident from early childhood onward;
- Encouragement of these talents by loving parents, caretakers (Fox), and mentors (Hawking and Reeve);
- Early conviction of bodily strength and integrity, even superiority, via considerable athletic skills (rowing for Hawking, sailing and riding for Reeve, and ice hockey for Fox);
- A supportive and loving spouse;
- More than ample "efficacy experiences" (Wolf, 1994) in the form of one's efforts producing desired results and even public recognition;
- Solid financial resources.

These seven factors can be seen as essentially belonging to three categories: (1) *constitutional* (talent, physical prowess, good genes), (2) *familial* (loving parents and spouses), and (3) *societal* (mentors, social success, fame, and money). They constitute what Parens (2004), tipping his hat to the originator of this idea and those who expanded upon it, has termed the "Garmezy-Luthar triadic processes." This refers to the three factors (biological, intrapsychic, and social) proposed by Garmezy (1985) as the fundamental substrate to human resilience.

To belabor the unmistakable presence of this triad in the lives of Hawking, Reeve, and Fox is fruitless. More important is to raise the question of whether all three elements of Garmezy's triad are essential for developing resilience. Can a strong suit in one or the other realm (constitutional, intrapsychic, and society) render strength in a second or third area unnecessary? Another question involves the "special" status of the three individuals described here. Are these individuals truly exceptional or do they come across as such due to their being world-renowned? Christopher Reeve's and Michael J Fox's pre-existing fame certainly has played a role in how awesome their stories appear to us. But what to say of Stephen Hawking, who gained international recognition *after* developing his crippling disease? The answer seems to be that while fame and money can help, it is something internal, some fire within that pushes through the night of near-surrender. That such "right stuff," to extrapolate from Wolfe's (1979) phrase for the determined nature of Apollo 11 astronauts, is made up of complex biopsychosocial ingredients goes without saying. Hawking might be an "invulnerable child" (Anthony, 1987), but there also seems to be truth in Settlage's (1992) statement that "the predominance of love is the glue of a unified self-representation" (p. 352). If this is correct, then we can add that it is love (from others, for others, for oneself, and for life in general) that ultimately underlies the phenomenon of resilience. At the same time, there seems to be something elusive here. The need to know more makes itself strongly felt.

SOME NEWER STUDIES

> Like resilient sapling trees that have had to grow at unusual angles in order to bypass obstructions to sunlight, those who at a young age endured genocidal persecution have followed their own twisting and turning paths in order to grow. —Brenner, 2008, pp. 80–81

> While I do not believe that resilience can be induced or indoctrinated, it can be modeled and potentiated. Conversely, resilience can be diminished or lost in states of regression and/or personality damage. Some survivors of severe, protracted, and recurrent traumatization have, nevertheless, been able to rebuild post-traumatic rewarding lives. Not all those who survive manage to thrive, but resilience can make the difference between effective coping and chronic debility. —Blum, 2008, p. 189

More recent studies of resilience have largely supported the views of Garmezy (1985) mentioned above, while adding certain important nuances to our understanding of this phenomenon. In a series of contributions, Cyrulnik (2004, 2005, 2008) has emphasized that a capacity for resilience is greatly enhanced if the traumatized can somehow or the other turn to a fresh attachment figure and establish an emotional bond with him or her. This bond becomes the "tutor of resilience" (2008, p. 24). Another important factor is the capacity to make sense of the chaos that surrounds one.

> Knowing that trauma is bound to reality (starvation, torture), and that traumatism is linked to the representation of reality, we can say it stems from a system of signs, meanings, and expressions of emotion constructed by the group surrounding the child. The meaning ascribed to the event highlights the critical role of narratives to support resilience or prevent it. In the wake of trauma, historization of an event—having made it history—allows a framework toward a vision of the world we perceive (Bruner, 1990). As soon as the event is framed into a meaning and put toward a direction by making narratives and daydreams, the wounded child knows how to behave, how to avoid, how to cajole, and how to attack the stressor or cuddle against his or her secure base in order to learn to face the danger. (Cyrulnik, 2008, p. 26)

Another set of contemporary investigators are Southwick et al. (2005, 2008) who underscored the complex interplay of genetic, neurophysiological, and environmental variables in determining the individual's capacity for resilience. They underscored the importance of humor, altruism, grounding in reality, and good role models.

Hauser et al. (2006), studying the life trajectory of troubled teenagers over the course of many years, emphasized the benefits of conceptualizing resilience in terms of a process rather than a collection of traits. Viewed in this way, the capacity for resilience is open to influence by time and experience. In other words, resilience is a developmental process and, like all such processes, can undergo regressive deterioration or progressive consolidation. Investigation by Hauser et al. (2006) revealed that the three factors of relatedness, agency, and reflectiveness played a great role in consolidation of resilience. According to them,

> *Reflectiveness* is curiosity about one's thoughts, feelings, and motivations, and the willingness to try to make sense of them and handle them responsibly. *Agency* is the conviction that what one does

> matters, that one can intervene effectively in one's own life. *Relatedness*—engagement and interaction with others—may be highly valued even when there are no helpful others around, and these may predispose youngsters to be able to use supportive connections when they are available. (p. 39, italics in the original)

Such matters formed the focus of the 38th Annual Margaret S. Mahler Symposium held in Philadelphia, PA, on April 14, 2007, the proceedings of which have been published in a volume titled, *The Unbroken Soul* (Parens et al., 2008). In addition to the above-mentioned views of Cyrulnik and Southwick et al., this volume contains two other outstanding contributions, namely, those of Henry Krystal and Harold Blum. Krystal, who has made major contributions to the study of the Holocaust trauma (1973, 1981, 1985), stated, in this volume, that under dire circumstances "hidden vestigial optimism permits some limited alertness and initiative, even inventiveness" (2008, p. 55). He emphasized that a special combination of positive personality traits and fortunate circumstances is needed to survive and be resilient. However, in the end, it is the access to good internal objects, love from others, and love for others, that sustains one in the dark passage through massive trauma.

> Most of all, there is the clear indication that one's resilience is proportional to the capacity to mobilize one's love powers. Love outraged is experienced as anger or hate. Love rendered helpless manifests itself as shame. However, love represents the survivor's self-reintegrating and self-healing powers. (p. 62)

Blum (2008) made a distinction between two types of resilience: one that implies resistance to traumatic decompensation, and the other that assures recovery from it. Referring to the first type, Blum noted that some individuals—admittedly a minority—manage to avert being traumatized or have only very mild and transient disturbance when faced with dire circumstances. He cited the observations of Anthony and Cohler (1997) on "invulnerable children," who not only survived extremely chaotic upbringing but thrived and, at times, became quite creative. Referring to the second type of resilience, Blum emphasized the confluence of variables needed to assure recovery from trauma. Talking of the Nazi Holocaust, Blum noted:

> Jews survived by luck, by chance events, by their wits, by the wisdom of their families, and by making use of any opportunity to remain obscure, to hide in plain sight or out of sight, to escape, to befriend those who could provide assistance. Chance played a role in encounters with kindly strangers and those obscure individuals who provided shelter and protection from the murderers. Chance also favored the prepared mind, which could then better cope with emergency situations. (p. 177)

Mention must also be made of the recent memoir of Henri Parens, the distinguished psychoanalyst and child survivor of the Holocaust. Titled *Renewal of Life: Healing from the Holocaust* (Parens, 2004), the profoundly poignant and wise volume provides a first-hand account of massive psychic trauma, valiant struggle to survive and grow, the powerful role of supportive strangers and non-familiar caretakers, the ethical imperative to bear witness, the contribution of superior intellect in adaptively dealing with psychic endangerment, but above all, the ever-sustaining strength of good internal objects (Parens' mother was surely more than "good-enough") in leading to the gestalt of what we call "resilience."

In a commentary upon an abridged version of this autobiography (Parens, 2008), Shapiro (2008) emphasized the healing powers of creating personal narratives, be they in the form of written memoirs or co-constructed psychoanalytic scenarios.

> In the personal narrative, one can slowly sort out the complicated issues of what happened over time; how things evolved; what is one's own responsibility and the accountability of others; what could have been controlled or prevented and what could not; what made others do what they did; why bad things happen to innocent people; the role of the bystander and the helper; the role of outright evil; the role of chance, fate, or predestination; the place for faith and spirituality; and the confusions and parallel worlds—such as being helped by someone who was going skiing in the midst of genocide. We humans are meaning-seekers. Telling a story can be both tremendously comforting and enormously painful. Telling and re-telling stories is central to healing and recovery from trauma. (p. 121)

At the same time, Varvin's (2009) warning against idealizing the concept of resilience must be heeded. Far from being a spontaneously appearing gift, resilience is a labored and bloody achievement, snatched from the jaws of psychic annihilation. Resilience does not imply

> an idealistic view of human nature and certainly not of one's own nature. Resilience is about emotions like courage, love, humor, but also about capacities to deal with, work through, and overcome difficult emotions like hate, wished-for revenge, depression, and wish to destroy. Resilience is, from the perspective from emotions, maybe more about capacities to deal with negative emotions and about strength to implement and be an agent of one's life. (p. 364)

Varvin emphasized that what happens after traumatization is a long drawn-out and complex process. And, that process does not depend only upon variables within the individual (e.g., intelligence, good internal objects) but upon the "holding" function of the culture-at-large as well as upon serendipitous fortunate occurrences. In a tone, the wryness of which is reminiscent of how Freud often spoke about the masses, Varvin concluded

> Thinking about resilience, I also can see more clearly what should not be done when meeting the traumatized and wracked, and which all too often happens due to inhuman bureaucratic routines, xenophobic politics, and mere stupidity. (p. 367)

CONCLUDING REMARKS

> What the state of the individual, what his life conditions are at the time of occurrence, is critical with regard to how the trauma will impact on him or her. The trauma itself will impact the individual according to these parameters. And, recovery from traumatization will depend on the state of the individual after the trauma has seized and the state of his objectal universe, both in the short term and long term. —Parens, 2009, p. 336

In this overview of resilience, I have first highlighted the difficulties in defining the concept and then offered a tentative psychoanalytic definition of it. I have underscored the multiple and complex variables that contribute to human resilience and attempted to demonstrate them with the help of the histories of three distinguished individuals' struggles with devastating physical illness. Having thus set the ground for deeper elucidation of resilience by the contributors to this volume, I wish to conclude by indicating some areas that, in my opinion, strongly require further investigation. I present them in the form of the following questions:

- Does resilience spread evenly across the personality function or exist in combination with brittle islands of rigidity?
- Is resilience after trauma self-limiting or self-perpetuating?
- Do characteristic dreams predict, depict, or accompany resilience after trauma?
- Does the concept of resilience have similar applications in children and adults?
- What is the interplay between resilience and developmental maturation?
- How significant is the cultural context in shaping the resilient outcome of trauma? Harvey and Tummala-Narra's (2007) recent book addresses this issue in depth, leaving one to wonder whether there might be "subcultures of flexibility" and "subcultures of resilience" on a large-group-psychology basis.
- What is the role of belief in God vis-à-vis human resilience?
- Is there such a thing as too much resilience?
- At what psychoeconomic point does resilience acquire "as-if" (Deutsch, 1942) qualities?
- Do traumas caused by family members require help from extra-familiar individuals and vice versa in order to be handled in a resilient manner?
- Does the confluence of constitutional, psychological, and societal factors leading to resilience have a qualitative or quantitative dimension?
- Do creative outlets (e.g., poetry, painting) result from resilience or cause resilience?

As far as this last question is concerned, the answer seems to be "both." In other words, creativity is simultaneously a source and consequence of resilience. This paradox, most likely, is not to be resolved. More important is to recognize what Kogan (2007) has eloquently stated:

> By appearing in the transitional space between re-enactment and representation, creative activity ultimately allows the [individual] to be in touch with mourning and enables its working through. It affirms the forces of life, thus overcoming silence and death. As an act of imagination, it is a path to hope and a profound beginning. (p. 122)

3

GRATITUDE

The preceding chapters on courage and resilience have highlighted the powerful role played by the love and support of early caretakers in the genesis of positive personality traits. Not surprisingly then, individuals with true courage and resilience also have the capacity for feeling gratitude. And it is to this third member of the trio (courage—resilience—gratitude) that I now direction my attention. I will begin my discourse by delineating its phenomenological scope and its developmental origins. Following this, I will describe the psychopathology that exists in this realm. Then I will attempt to show how issues pertaining to gratitude make their appearance in the clinical situation. I will conclude by making some synthesizing remarks and noting areas that might warrant further attention.

DEFINITION AND PHENOMENOLOGY

> No man has ever lived that had enough of children's gratitude and women's love. —Yeats, 1933, p. 12

> Gratitude is an appreciation of desired elements that have occurred among the events and happenings of one's life. Its counterpart, resentment, is the rejection of one's life until certain desired elements appear. —Griffith, 2010, p. 90

The word "gratitude" is derived from the Latin *gratus* and refers to "the state of being thankful" (Webster's Ninth New Collegiate Dictionary,

1987, p. 534). Its synonyms include appreciation, thankfulness, appreciativeness, gratefulness, recognition, acknowledgment, and giving credit. The experience of gratitude follows gratification and includes (i) the acknowledgment of having received desirable and helpful, tangible and intangible supplies from others, (ii) an emotional state of indebtedness and humility, and (iii) a sense that one ought to offer something in return, though not in a hurried gesture of denial. Gratitude is expressed in many ways, with a simple 'thank you' being the most common of them. The omission of such appreciative response to an act of beneficence causes unpleasure in the benefactor. Depending upon the magnitude of the gift bestowed, such unpleasure can go from mild irritation to shock, pain, and rage. Heilbrunn (1972) maintains that the expression of gratitude stabilizes the equilibrium between the donor and receiver.

> Gratitude has the function of a reciprocal gift which symbolizes the extension of a quantum of affection and thus reverses the roles of donor and receiver. Through word or action, the primary donor offers a quantity of love. Its acceptance affords him vicarious enjoyment through identification with the receiver; its acknowledgment provides such satisfaction of his dependent needs. Both signal possible future repetition of the process with the proven love object. (p. 516)

Indeed, gratitude accompanies romantic feelings. The forfeiture of narcissism that Freud (1914) mentioned in connection with falling in love speaks to this very point. A poem of mine titled *Thank You*, written nearly thirty years ago, captures the humility that comes from feeling loved.

How can I thank you
    for awakening me from the venom-filled nightmare my life had become
How can I thank you
    for making it rain on my drought-stricken days and nights
How can I thank you
    for melting my stony heart and growing lotuses in its lake
How can I thank you
    for giving a nightingale's voice to the mute agony of my soul
How can I thank you
    for tickling me, hugging me, shaking me, kissing me, for loving me
How can I thank you
    Except by returning your love with an unsurpassed humility

Feeling gratitude also requires overcoming greed and acknowledgement of others' generosity (see chapter 4, for details on generosity). Gratitude is linked to feelings of gratification but is distinct from it. In Hinshelwood's words, "Gratitude is a specific feeling toward an object and needs to be distinguished from gratification which is satisfaction of a bodily need. Gratitude is brought out and enhanced toward an object by the gratification that the object gives" (1991, p. 313).

The metapsychological components of gratitude can be described in various ways depending upon the psychoanalytic theory one opts to use. *In structural theory terms*, these include: (i) from the side of ego: a sense of being at peace with oneself and with the world, alongside a post-ambivalent appreciation of the goodness that exists in other people, in social institutions, and in external reality at large; (ii) from the side of id: a noticeable diminution in instinctual tension and a corresponding renunciation of sadomasochistic aims, (iii) from the side of the superego: an automatic reduction of defiant and transgressive impulses and a gentle but firm imperative to do good by others, especially by one's benefactor. *In object relations theory terms*, gratitude implies a renewed and robust contact with the good internal object and an ascension of "good" over "bad" self-object ties. The self-representation is suffused not by manic overestimation but by the glow of satiety and desires for reparation. Moreover there is a greater synthesis of libidinal and aggressive self-representations, a deeper capacity for empathy, and a firmer contact with reality. *In self-psychology terms*, gratitude leads to a resurgent sense of self coherence and a vital momentum for sustaining and strengthening one's stabilizing self-objects.

Given this view of gratitude through the prism of contemporary psychoanalysis, it is interesting to go all the way back to the beginnings of the discipline and see what its founder, Sigmund Freud, had to say about the phenomenon. Starting off literally, one notes that the word "gratitude" appears a mere thirty-two times in the corpus of Freud's work (Guttman et al., 1980). Most of these usages are colloquial and do not provide any psychological insight into the phenomenon. A few others refer to situations which lead to gratitude and to the purposes served by gratitude. The following are some examples.

- Freud (1910b) attributed a son's desire to impregnate the mother to his gratitude for her giving him life. As an aside, it is worth noticing that this motivation for a son's identification with his father became eclipsed by the later emphasis upon the oedipal competitive dimensions of this desire.

- In a related vein, Freud (1910b) hinted at the gratitude for being alive in describing the so-called "rescue fantasy." He noted that the child wishes to give back to the parents the life which he or she owes to them by saving them from danger.
- Another context selected by Freud (1917) for commenting upon gratitude was that of artistic creativity. He asserted that the artist earns the gratitude of those who enjoy his work because he has succeeded in presenting unconscious desires for love, power, fame, money, and success in disguised and aesthetically pleasing ways. Those who enjoy his creativity do not have to do the intrapsychic work themselves and can benefit vicariously by his sublimation.
- Freud attributed (1918) the woman's post-coital embrace of her lover to "an expression of gratitude" (p. 201) and a token of her lasting commitment to him. Here, the omission of man's gratitude to his woman is noticeable and in line with Freud's overall phallocentrism.

These ideas are interesting. However, their focus is upon the triggers and outcomes of gratitude rather than upon the nature of the phenomenon itself. Their ontogenetic roots go to the oedipal phase and that too only of the male child. As a result, these ideas do not provide a fuller picture of how the capacity for gratitude originates in the first place. In order to grasp that, we have to turn to the works of Melanie Klein and Donald Winnicott.

DEVELOPMENTAL ORIGINS

> Not only the prohibitions of the parents but also their love survives in the relation of the superego with the ego. In the course of same development, the experience arises of being responsible to oneself. —Hartmann, 1960, p. 27

> No parent is going to provide a secure base for his growing child unless he has an intuitive understanding of and

> respect for his child's attachment behavior and treats it as the intrinsic and valuable part of human nature. —Bowlby, 1988, p. 12

In a seminal contribution titled "Envy and Gratitude," Melanie Klein (1957) suggested that good relations with the "maternal breast" (a metaphor for mother's love and caring capacities) are the bedrock of gratitude. The shift from "paranoid position" with its smug clinging to a "purified pleasure ego" (Freud, 1915) and its disownment of aggression to a "depressive position" with its ownership of uncertainty, internal aggression, and remorse helps the consolidation of gratitude. Arriving at the "depressive position," the child becomes capable of recognizing that, in reality or fantasy, he has attacked the very mother who loves him and upon whom he is utterly dependent. Dawning awareness of one's own aggression and the remorse for its ruthless discharge upon the mother leads—if things go well on all other fronts—to the acknowledgment of her ultimate goodness and to the resulting desire for reparation. However, for this to occur, a satisfactory relationship with the breast (mother) must already be in place. Klein declared, "A full gratification at the breast means that the infant feels he has received from his loved object a unique gift which he wants to keep. This is the basis of gratitude" (1957, p. 118). She added, "a child with a strong capacity for love and gratitude has a deep-rooted relation with a good object and can, without being fundamentally damaged, withstand temporary states of envy, hatred, and grievance, which arise even in children who are loved and well-mothered" (p. 187).

Klein stated that gratitude is closely related to generosity; in fact, there is a dialectical relationship between the two. Generosity (on the mother's part) results in gratitude (on the child's part) and this, in turn, leads to generosity (on the child's part). Klein (1959) reiterated this last point in a later paper, declaring that feelings of gratitude result in one's relations to other people, particularly in the form of generosity and consideration. Still later, she stated, "Enjoyment is always bound up with gratitude; if this gratitude is deeply felt it includes the wish to return the goodness received and is thus the basis of generosity. There is always a close connection between being able to accept and to give, and both are part of the relation to the good object and therefore counteract loneliness" (1963, p. 310).

Klein's ideas were translated by Winnicott (1968) into experience-near terms and also modified to a certain extent. He suggested that true gratitude is not born in early childhood; it is a later acquisition. And, whatever gratitude the offspring can muster has to arise spontaneously. Putting it bluntly, Winnicott (1957) said that "parents cannot expect thanks for the fact of a child's existence. Babies do not ask to be born" (p. 123). Gratitude, for Winnicott is an aspect of concern and does require the awareness of one's destructiveness toward one's love objects. However, meaningful consolidation of the capacity for gratitude takes time and might not happen till late adolescence. Talking of children, Winnicott stated the following:

> If things went well, they never say "thank you," because they did not know that it went well. In families there is this great area of unacknowledged debt which is no debt. There is nothing owing, but anybody who reaches stable adulthood could not have done it if somebody at the beginning had not taken him or her through the early stages. (1968, p. 146)

Few psychoanalysts addressed the origins of gratitude after Klein and Winnicott, except in expository ways (Rappaport, 1998; Chiesa, 2001) that, in all candor, added little to the existing ideas. Erikson's (1950) concept of generativity and Kernberg's (1980) description of healthy narcissism did, however, offer glimpses of how a well-lived life results in an enhanced capacity to give to others during middle age; this, in turn, emanates from contentment and gratitude toward one's inner and outer worlds. In a recent contribution, O'Shaughnessy (2008) made some important points regarding gratitude in the clinical situation, these will be taken up in the "Technical Implications" section below.

PSYCHOPATHOLOGY

> Gratitude looks very nice, and we like the odd bottle of whiskey and box of chocolates that are expressions of thanks from patients. Nevertheless, gratitude is not as simple as that. —Winnicott, 1970, p. 118

> Given that the goodness of what the other has to offer is a source of envy, dependency upon a loved object becomes

> impossible and must be denied; the narcissistic personality needs to be admired rather than loved. —Kernberg, 1995, p. 151

Many sorts of difficulties exist in the realm of gratitude. Some arise out of anxiety about attachment and dependence. Others emanate from pathological narcissism. Still others result from a sense of guilt and unworthiness. One type of problem with feeling gratitude can contain elements of another type or serve as a defensive shield against the latter. The following categorization must therefore be regarded as tentative and open-ended. That said, the psychopathology of gratitude can be divided into four types: (i) anxious deflection of gratitude, (ii) guilty intensification of gratitude, (iii) narcissistic denial of gratitude, and (iv) sociopathic absence of gratitude. The last two frequently overlap and the distinction between them might even be quantitative than qualitative. Indeed, hybrid forms might be the rule rather than the exception, and yet didactic ease prompts a separate consideration of them as well.

Anxious Deflection of Gratitude

Some individuals have great difficulty accepting gestures of kindness from others. They become flustered upon receiving gifts, praise, compliments, and unsolicited assistance. They blush, act clumsily, get tongue-tied or readily "counterpoise a compliment with a protestation that they do not deserve it" (McWilliams and Lependorf, 1990, p. 445). Often they attempt to balance things out by immediately offering to do something for their benefactor. Take a look at the following incidence which is so routine in our lives that its intrapsychic implications mostly go unnoticed.

A Personal Vignette

This happened some twenty years ago. One morning during a professional meeting in New York, I happened to have breakfast with a colleague from California. Two egg omelet, bacon, toast, orange juice, coffee sort of thing. We had not seen each other for quite some time and the little sit-down meal provided us the opportunity to catch up on personal and professional news. As we finished and the waiter brought the check, I—impelled by the old Indian-style generosity—paid for both of us, declining his not entirely feeble offer to go Dutch. I was expecting that he would respond with something like "Thank you very much" or "That was very nice of you." Instead, he said, "Next year, I will buy you breakfast." I mumbled a few polite words in return and we parted. Something did not sit well with me, though. I found myself wondering about what he had said. "Next year, I will buy you breakfast." I found myself repeating the words in my mind. My colleague had most likely uttered them with a benign, if not affectionate, intent but I was left a bit unnerved. Kept wondering whether my friend was expressing gratitude for my gesture or, by bringing up *his* desire (and, capacity) to act similarly, was balancing things out. The anxiety that propelled his behavior was palpable.

Not given to "wild analysis" (Freud, 1910a), I cannot specifically comment upon the causes of my friend's anxiety. However, in a generalized manner, such readiness to shirk or minimize gratitude seems derived from culturally upheld ideals of self-reliance on the one hand and personal nervousness about affection and attachment (and, freshly mobilized greed) on the other hand. In the clinical context, though, the latter variable plays a greater role. Anxious recoil from receiving goodness from others can lead to an appearance of ingratitude and cause interpersonal misunderstandings.

Guilty Intensification of Gratitude

In contrast to the anxiety-laden inability to bear (and acknowledge) gratitude is the situation where the burden of gratitude becomes too much, due to feelings of guilt and unworthiness. Paraphrasing Freud (1916) individuals with such a malady can be termed "those wrecked by gratitude." They have a tendency to remain indebted for life over small favors done by others. They are unable to forget any kindness showed them, any help offered, and any gift given. They thank their benefactors privately and publicly for years after the latter's good deed was done. Such persistent humbling of themselves and un-ending pay-back to their benefactors does not bring anyone happiness, however. They remain forever shackled to this burden and their benefactors find their on-going thankfulness tiresome and even subtly mocking.

This relational resonance reveals the deeper nature of this "syndrome": it is propelled by a heavy dose of unconscious guilt and masochism. Such guilt (regardless of its source) makes it hard to the individual to accept a favor, thank, and be done with it. Instead, he feels that he has received too much, has gotten what he did not deserve. By thanking his benefactors again and again, he consciously hopes to undo the burden of his gratitude. Unconsciously, however, he is seeking to annoy his benefactors (burden them!) and be scolded by them (and thus derive further masochistic pleasure).[1]

Narcissistic Denial of Gratitude

Since the experience of gratitude acknowledges the existence of the Other's goodness (i.e., goodness that does not belong to oneself), narcissistic individuals find it threatening. They are self-absorbed and intensely ambitious. While needing constant admiration from others, they are unable to pay attention to the needs and wishes of the latter (Kernberg, 1975; Kohut, 1971; Akhtar, 1992b). Envy also plays a big role in their lives and, therefore, "they cannot experience gratitude for what they receive from the other, whose very capacity to give freely they may envy. Their lack of gratitude precludes the strengthening of the capacity for loving appreciation of the love received" (Kernberg, 1995, p. 151).

Grunberger (1975) likens the narcissist to the fetus,[2] which exists in a seemingly self-sufficient, oblivious, and parasitic economy where it receives everything but has to give nothing in return. He posits that a fundamental conflict exists throughout life, between the longing to return to such narcissistic bliss and the unavoidable human necessity for emotional dependence on others. The narcissistic individual, more than others, continues to yearn for unconditional indulgence from his world, uniqueness, omnipotence, and unlimited autonomy. Such a person is frequently preoccupied with desires for invulnerability, infiniteness, and immorality. He considers himself the incarnation of perfection, existing solipsistically, and loathes the acknowledgment of his dependence on others.

This last-mentioned feature comes in their way of being thankful to others. To thank someone acknowledges that one needed something and, by implication, that one lacked something till it was provided by an Other. Narcissistic individuals cannot do this. They deploy all sorts of subtle and not-so-subtle maneuvers to repudiate the feelings of gratitude. McWilliams and Lependorf (1990) have outlined three such interpersonal operations: (i) conferring approval, (ii) reversing roles, and (iii) protesting. The first allows the individual to keep his grandiose self unscathed by "approving" the benefactor as if from a position of higher authority than that of the person who has done something deserving of gratitude.

> For example, a narcissistically oriented parent might tell a teacher who has done exemplary work with his or her difficult child, "You did a good job," rather than "I'm very grateful for what you have done." A woman might say to her lover, "I'm pleased to see you're getting better at keeping your temper under control," rather than "I've appreciated your patience with me." A nice example of approval-conferring masquerading as gratitude occurred in the play *Dreamgirls*, when the lead singer turned during the applause to her back-up duo and gushed, "And I couldn't have done it without them!" The audience senses viscerally how by ostensibly complimenting her co-performers, she has managed to minimize completely their contribution to her popular triumph. (McWilliams and Lependorf, 1990, p. 444)

The second narcissistic method to deny gratitude is constituted by responding to a solicitous inquiry (e.g., "would you like something to eat?") with a posture of comparable solicitude (e.g., "if you are going to cook something"). The roles of giver and receiver are thus reversed and gratitude is by-passed.

> The assumed position is, "You're the one with the needs here, not me; but I'm such a good person I'll humor you." The nuances of this transformation of subject and object are so delicate and elusive that it is no wonder that the spouses of characterologically narcissistic people can be frequently found in a state of complete bewilderment about what is wrong in the relationship and how they might be contributing to its disappointing aspects. (McWilliams and Lependorf, 1990, p. 445)

Finally, narcissistic individuals also shirk gratitude by regarding any compliment as unnecessary (since their impressiveness is so ordinary) or as fundamentally insincere (since they project their own tendencies to lie and cheat upon others). The maneuver of 'denial by exaggeration' (Fenichel, 1945; Sperling, 1963) can also come to the narcissist's rescue;

by making a caricature of his gratitude, the narcissist can get away from truly experiencing the burden on his ego.

Sociopathic Absence of Gratitude

This is the most severe type of pathology involving ingratitude. It is one step ahead of the pathology of gratitude seen in the setting of narcissistic personality. Here the issue is not one of conscious awareness, interpersonal acknowledgment, or social expression of gratitude, the issue is of its absence. Having grown up constantly abused, humiliated, betrayed, and abandoned (Schneider, 1950; Stone, 1980; Shengold, 1989), the sociopathic individual mistrusts everyone and uses others as mere sources of money, sex, entertainment, and other sundry favors. In tandem with his profoundly defiled self, there exist powerful feelings of entitlement as well as profound cynicism, if not contempt, for civil and reciprocal relationships between human beings. Each benefactor is measured against the violation of basic human dignity during childhood about which the beneficiary inwardly grieves. The debt is projected upon the benefactor; any act of kindness therefore becomes only a partial payment of an old debt, hence unworthy of gratitude (Bergler, 1945). Impaired empathy with others and pervasive superego defects also lead to the destruction of the capacity for gratitude in the setting of sociopathic personality. Deeper assimilation and accruing of received goodness is not possible. Persistence of hunger intensifies anger and entitlement. All pleasure is transient and one's fate is tied to the inconsolable gluttony of sensual gratification.

TECHNICAL IMPLICATIONS

> From another standpoint, the termination is less a period of mourning than of rejoicing. . . . The patient feels, as Balint has put it, that he is going through a kind of rebirth to a period of new life. . . . He is almost afraid to feel grateful, lest it be construed as an evasion of gratification, as it well may be. But not entirely, for he has gotten more than he bargained for, more than he paid for, and he will pass its benefits to someone else. —Menninger and Holzman, 1973, p. 176

> We would very rarely interpret feelings of love and gratitude where these are deemed to be genuine (i.e., non-idealizing) and to reflect the analysand's appreciation and gratitude for the analysis and the analyst's efforts. The non-interpretative stance in this case reveals that such feelings are of a different order. We regard them as an achievement of the analysis, and as not requiring interpretation.
> —Erlich, 2008, p. 56

The foregoing elucidation of the phenomenological, developmental, and psycho-pathological spectrum of gratitude carries important implications for our work with patients. Such clinical impact is discernible in five different ways, namely, (i) feeling and expressing gratitude in response to the patient's gestures of kindness, (ii) appreciating and accepting the patient's healthy gratitude, (iii) diagnosing and interpreting the patient's conflicts around gratitude, (iv) making developmentally oriented interventions with the gradual enhancement of the capacity for gratitude as a result of analytic work, and, (v) avoiding countertransference pitfalls in this realm.

Responding to Patient's Gestures of Kindness with Gratitude

As clinicians, we are prone to forgetting that the individual in our care has bestowed upon us the gift of his trust. He has chosen us to guide him through the treacherous sojourn of self-discovery and to bear whatever anxieties, pains, and "silent sacrifices" (see chapter 6) are necessary for achieving this task. To put one's mind and soul—and, in some ways, one's life—in someone else's hands is no small feat. It requires faith in the latter's integrity, strength, and good will. We clinicians are thus in ongoing gratitude of our patients; not only do they elevate us by trusting us, they also educate us about the way the human mind functions and, via myriad forms of collaboration and resistance, improve our listening and communicating skills.[3] Feiner (1977) gave voice to what all analysts know but do not "publicize"; he noted that "through the graciousness of our patients, we get to know ourselves a little better" (p. 12). This is a transformative and deep export from our patients' side. On a concrete and plebian level, they give us money, frequently change their schedules to accommodate our exigencies, and, at times, bring us tangible gifts. All this mobilizes—or, should mobilize—gratitude in our hearts and we must not be recalcitrant in giving it expression.

Two caveats need to be entered here. First, the analyst's expression of gratitude must be tailored to the individual idiosyncrasies and sensitivities that exist in each clinical dyad. Some patients can hear "thank you" from their analysts and then go on with the usual free-associative work. Others are unable to retain equanimity in the face of such expression of gratitude; it acquires greater affective valence for them and, therefore, complicates the analytic process. Well-attuned titration of what the analyst says and how he says that is the key here. The display of gratitude by the analyst is not to be done in a shrill and exaggerated way; it ought to be subtle and more or less integral to the "waking screen" (Pacella, 1980) of his discourse with the patient.

Appreciating and Accepting the Patient's Healthy Gratitude

At times, our patients express genuine gratitude for our tolerance of their affective outbursts, our patient with their fumbling, meandering, and inconclusive associations, or merely our reliability over long periods of time. Such expressions of thankfulness tend to follow periods of emotional turmoil and major life crises. Termination also brings forth the patient's gratitude, often expressed in the form of a small but meaningful gift. To be sure, all these behaviors can contain material for analytic exploration. Worse, they might result from the reversal of subterranean hostility, with the avowed gratitude operating as subtle mockery. Underscoring the nearly ubiquitous admixture of "genuine" and neurotic variables in patients' gratitude and in our responses to it, O'Shaughnessy raises some important questions.

> What, then, are our patients grateful to us for? There are some uncomfortable issues for the analyst here. Is it for the bounteousness of our invitation to bring all to us? Is it for the unique gifts we bestow upon them with our interpretations? If we start to think we are the bounteous bestowers of unique gifts, then we are, of course—as Freud warned—forgetting the phenomenon of transference. It is a dangerous area that can recruit our narcissism, seductiveness, tendencies to couple in spurious idealizations, our capacity for self-deception, or our mania. (2008, p. 86)

This does not mean that *all* expressions of gratitude on the patient's part are spurious and *all* responses on the analyst's part to them are countertransference-based. False gratitude rings hollow whereas genuine gratitude has an air of plausibility and conviction. The analyst's emotional response to the two is different: puzzlement and annoyance at the former, tenderness and pleasure at the latter.

In light of this, excessive questioning of the patient's gratitude is not indicated; this is especially true when its expressions are not maudlin (Erlich, 2008). The analyst is better off accepting the patient's thankfulness in a peaceful manner, at times, by judiciously disclosing his own joy in it. This is especially true at the time of termination. It is also applicable to the issue of gifts offered by the patient (see Smolar, 2002, for a thorough discussion of this matter). Categorically rejecting all such offerings used to be the recommended practice in the days when Lowenstein (1958) spoke of having shocked a trainee by telling him that he ought to have accepted the gift offered by his patient. The view that accepting the gift derails the analysis of such a gesture needs to be tempered by remembering that "rejecting presents often prevents analysts from recognizing their true meanings (Thoma and Kachele, 1994, p. 301). Patient's expression of gratitude sometimes need analytic exploration and sometimes plain and simple acceptance. The importance of "the capacity to have pleasure in one's patient's pleasure" (Treurniet, 1997, p. 621) can hardly be overemphasized.

Diagnosing and Interpreting the Patient's Conflicts around Gratitude

As stated earlier, gratitude is not easy to bear. It has the potential of stirring up anxiety (over the wishes for further attention and material indulgence that are mobilized at the moment of receiving something from others), envy (toward the benefactor's capacity to give and hence his inner "fullness"), hostility (since receiving can remind one of how one had been deprived by others in the past), and guilt (at acknowledging that the very world one hates is being generous and helpful). All these subterranean "risks" can come in one's way of experiencing and expressing gratitude. Such inability (or refusal) might be restricted to the realm of transference whereby the patient cannot bring himself to feel thankful toward the analyst. Or, it can be a feature of his overall character style. In that case, the analyst has to interpret outside of the transference though still keeping his and the patient's attention focused upon the here-and-now of the clinical dialogue.

Clinical Vignette: 5

Dan Schwartzman, a forty-five year old piano teacher who had fallen on hard times, was in psychotherapy for chronic feelings of inferiority, irritability, and rage. He loved his wife and acquiesced to seek help since she was becoming concerned about his increasing reliance upon alcohol to soothe himself.

Dan's main difficulty revolved about the rage he felt at his father who had always belittled and mocked him. His father was a hugely successful businessman who had just turned eighty. On one hand, Dan wanted to cut off ties with his father. On the other hand, he kept hoping that the old man would die and leave him a few million dollars. As a result, he sheepishly showed up at the weekly lunch his father arranged in lavish restaurants in town and where he regularly insulted Dan and showed a starkly preferential behavior toward Dan's sister. Their mother had passed away. While secretly hating the cantankerous old man and praying for his death, Dan feared that, at the slightest whim, his father was capable of disinheriting him and leaving all the estate to his sister. He wanted to be nasty to his father but kept his mouth shut. He was thus on a tightrope stretched between pleasure of revenge and the haven of monetary security.

Dan began one of his sessions by telling me that the previous evening, he had received a phone call from his uncle, his father's brother, saying that he was aware of Dan's financial distress and has left him a considerable sum of money in his will. Dan went on to say, "As soon as I heard this, I said to myself, "Shit, Uncle Bob is doing this because he has found out that my father has disinherited me!" Upon listening to this, I said the following to Dan: "It is striking that, when your uncle told you that he has left you a lot of money, your first thought was not about his kindness toward you but about what it might (or might not) have implied about your father's cruelty toward you. For some reason, it seems, you were just not capable or willing to feel grateful to your uncle even for a minute, or, for that matter, enjoy your own sense of relief. Why?

Anxiety seems to play a great role in such 'inability' to register others' goodness since doing so would automatically lead to a changed world-view and tax the ego's adaptive capacities. Moreover, in accepting that others are being good toward oneself, one is compelled to renounce the pleasures of self-pity and the associated sadomasochism. Passively ignoring others' goodness seems a less risky pathway. At times, one goes a step further and tries actively to thwart and spoil others' goodness. Intolerance of compliments from others is often based upon such dynamics.

Making Developmentally-oriented Interventions Regarding Improvement in the Patient's Capacity for Gratitude

Many patients show no capacity for gratitude at the beginning of their treatment. This is especially true of those with prominent narcissistic and masochistic features. The former preclude gratitude since it mobilizes too much envy. The latter inhibit gratitude since acknowledging that one is receiving something good necessitates altering one's world view and renouncing the sadomasochistic "pleasure" of suffering. As these narcissistic and masochistic agendas come in sharp relief and begin to get modified with the progress of analysis, the patient encounters moments of thankfulness toward others in his heart. He remorsefully realizes that, on previous such occasions, he blithely took (narcissistic) or reflexively rejected (masochistic) the "gifts" that were offered him. Now he accepts gifts and compliments with full awareness and grace. He realizes that he should say "thank you" and, given time and opportunity, try to repay the debt.

As this hitherto thwarted tendency emerges, the analyst must not rush to "deconstruct" it, i.e., decipher its meanings, interpret its transference implications, point out motives that might not be known to the patient, and so on. Instead, the analyst should simply underscore its emergence, validate its hard-won consolidation, and empathize with the expected clumsiness of new ego skills. For instance, if after a long period of analytic work, a narcissistic patient begins to show capacity for gratitude, the analyst might respond by saying: "I think we can see that you have now become able to recognize and acknowledge other people's goodness toward you. I know, from our work together, that this is not easy for you but find it encouraging—as I am sure you do—that despite this not being your style so far, you were able to genuinely thank such-and-such good person who did you this or that favor." "Developmental interventions" (Abrams, 1978) along these lines help consolidate ego strength and this, in turn, facilitates the further uncovering of anxieties clouding this particular realm. Keeping in mind that development is a lifelong process and does not reach finality with one or the other maturational epoch (Pine, 1997) is also helpful in this context.

Avoiding Countertransference Pitfalls in this Realm

Themes of gratitude appear in the clinical situation in three different ways, including (i) the patient shows no gratitude, (ii) the patient shows exaggerated, hence false, gratitude and, (iii) the patient shows appropriate gratitude. These possibilities apply to the patient's attitude about important figures in his past and current life or to his feelings about the analyst. Healthy gratitude has to be gracefully accepted, the exaggerated gratitude carefully interpreted, and the ingratitude patiently tolerated before it gives way to remorse and a newly-emergent capacity for feeling thankful. The analyst's emotional response to these expressive patterns on the patient's part depends upon an admixture of variables that include his technical proficiency, his affect tolerance, and the degree of his emotional neediness on a given day. While a lonely or love-deprived analyst is much more vulnerable to clamor for his patient's gratitude, a need of this sort is more or less universal. Feiner (1977), writing more than four decades ago, observed that the on-coming end of an analysis can especially mobilize

> the analyst's need for the patient to express some special kind of gratitude for the analyst's risk-taking. This expected gratitude goes far beyond objective remuneration, the success of the analysis, and the joy of intimacy achieved. Despite the reasonableness of the patient's actual gratefulness, no amount can satisfy our innermost need, a need in all of us (I mean this literally) since no one outside of us knows the painful, hazardous side of our analytic efforts. (p. 9)

Hyperbolic tone aside, the statement does capture an important and potentially problematic aspect of the countertransference experience. During his clinical work, the analyst has to keep a lot to himself, a lot unexpressed, and a lot relegated to wistfulness and mourning. This involves the diverse longings stirred up in him as he faces the distortions, libidinal and aggressive pulls, and pressures for 'role responsiveness' (Sandler, 1976), from the patient. Also stirred up are longings uniquely his own.

> One of these longings is to experience the patient's gratitude for our unique form of dedication. Gratitude implies a specific form of object relationship involving the selfless devoted helper and an appreciative patient who acknowledges having been helped. This much desired mode of relatedness may be designed to repair internal object relations from the past in which we did not feel properly appreciated and validated. As analysts gain experience, they learn that this sought-after form of relatedness may be thwarted at every turn by certain patients. (Gabbard, 2000, p. 707)

Such "disappointment" has to be handled without giving in to the urge of "squeezing" gratitude out of a patient who is resolutely silent on this front. What helps greatly here is the analyst's overcoming his own narcissistic tendencies and renouncing unrealistic expectations from both himself and his patient. This ultimately permits him "to express the conviction that the patient will also be able to accept truths about himself and his life" (Kernberg, 1984, p. 250), including the fact that he has been helped by others to whom he has not paid enough regard in return.

CONCLUDING REMARKS

> Spiritually speaking, everything that one wants, aspires to and needs is ever present, accessible, here and now—for those with eyes to see. It is the old adage all over again: You don't need to see different things, but rather to see things *differently*. —Surya Das, 1997, p. 55

In this chapter, I have elucidated the structural and dynamic constellations of healthy gratitude. I have also traced the developmental roots of the capacity to experience gratitude and highlighted how psychopathology impairs this capacity or precludes its full expression. Bringing these ideas to bear upon the clinical situation, I have delineated the various ways in which issues involving gratitude impact on our work with patients. Now, before concluding, I would like to briefly comment upon two other areas. The first pertains to child-rearing and the second to the larger issue of gratitude to the world-at-large.

Vis-à-vis child-rearing, it is important to acknowledge the role of 'educational' measures in inculcating gratitude and its culturallysyntonic expression. While deeper intrapsychic processes in which love predominates over aggression lay the groundwork for the origins of gratitude, parental instruction shapes its outward manifestation; they tell the child to say, "thank you," when he or she receives something. To be sure, gratitude is not about good manners but good manners do constitute the vehicle for its interpersonal transport. The availability of well-mannered role models both at home and at school especially the kindergarten-first-second-grade level also helps. The argument that what one teaches a child is implanted on a capacity that is already present in him or her does not rule out the importance of moral instruction; it only confirms that importance.

The other issue involving gratitude is on a "macro-cosmic" level. Ordinarily speaking, gratitude refers to thankfulness toward a need-satisfying object; things are better if such satisfaction comes on a reliable basis and if a loving bond exists between the self and the object. Far from the experience of gratefulness within such relational "microcosm" is what I would call "existential gratitude."[4] Think about it. We live in a world that not only provides for our basic needs but offers us fodder for the highest of our strivings. And such gifts come to us free, i.e., without any effort on our part to earn them. What have you and I done to deserve reading Shakespeare, Dostoyevsky, Chekov, Faulkner, Borges, Dickinson, and Rushdie? Can we assume that the pleasure of smelling a rose, watching a sunset, playing with a puppy, hearing the sound of raindrops on a tin roof, and eating a fig are our birthrights? How is it that we are privy to Mozart's symphonies, Van Gogh's art, Baryshnikov's dance, Bradman's cricket, Olivier's acting, Pavarotti's tenor, and Ruth's baseball? We might know nothing about how telephones work, what makes airplanes fly, and how our thoughts are carried on the wings of email to far corners of the world, and yet we smugly partake of these privileges. I can go on and give more "for instances" but the point, I think, is made. This fragmented, random, and violent civilization of ours also contains goodness: poetry, art, music, sports, democracy, sculpture, dance, etc., and we are given a free pass to this theatre of cultural riches. Such privilege produces in all feeling and thinking human beings a sense of gratitude toward the world and toward one's existence in it. And this type of gratitude propels reparative impulses that are not restricted to one's little interpersonal realm. They spread to include the universe at large including its living beings, its cultural landscape, and ecological idiosyncrasies. Erikson's (1982) concept of "care" comes close to what I have in mind here and perhaps this is what Buddha was referring to when he said that wise men try to express their appreciation and gratitude by some return of kindness, not only to their benefactor, but to everyone else in the world.

Part II

POSITIVE ACTIONS

4

GENEROSITY

Donald Winnicott's (1960) statement that "there is no such thing as an infant" (p. 39)[1] is understood to mean that a human infant is invariably accompanied by its mother and therefore has no existence without her. This is true. However, a more accurate rendition might be that "there is no such thing as an infant without a mother's generosity." After all, it is maternal involvement that gives psychological shape to the inchoate biological entity that a neonate is and it is the mother's care that sets the baby on the path to becoming human. Without it, the baby would attach poorly to the external world, withdraw, and become lifeless. Generosity on the mother's part is the welcome-mat for the newcomer to the house of interpersonal relations. And matters do not end here. The growing child and subsequently the adolescent and the young adult continue to benefit from others' indulgence, though with the important difference that gradually the individual himself becomes able to offer such support to those around him. Generosity toward and from others remains a life-long partner of psychic development and stability.

It is therefore surprising to see how little attention has been given to this topic in our literature. The index of the collected works of Sigmund Freud does not contain "generosity" as an entry and the word does not appear in the textbooks of psychoanalysis (Moore and Fine, 1995; Nersessian and Kopf, 1996; Person et al., 2005). And, in all fairness, it should be noted that my own comprehensive dictionary of psychoanalytic terms (Akhtar, 2009b) has no entry on generosity. A search on PEP web[2] reveals only nine entries on generosity over the course of 115 years and four of them have little to say about the topic. The subject remains in-optimally addressed and my contribution intends to fill this gap.

I will begin my discourse by defining the concept of generosity and tracing its developmental origins. I will then delineate its various pathological forms and highlight the role generosity plays in our day-to-day work with patients. I will conclude by making some synthesizing remarks and noting the areas (including the variables of age, gender, and culture) that demand further attention.

DEFINITION AND DEVELOPMENT

> We find in the analysis of our patients that the breast in its good aspects is the prototype of maternal goodness, inexhaustible patience, generosity, as well as creativeness. —Klein 1957, p. 180

> The young infant's proto-altruism is evident when he reaches out to his mother, sensing her moods. We regard such behavior as instinctive and favored by natural selection, because those babies who are able to interact with their mothers in an increasingly attuned manner are more likely than others to have their physical and emotional needs met. —Seeling and Rosof, 2009, p. 77

The word "generosity" is defined by *Webster's Dictionary* as "liberality in spirit or act, especially liberality in giving" (Mish, 1987, p. 510) and by the *Oxford English Dictionary* as "willingness to share with others" (Weiner and Simpson, 1989, p. 787). Noticeable here is the fact that the state of willingness or "spirit" is accorded comparable weight to the act(s) of giving. In other words, the definition contains both emotional and behavioral aspects of the phenomenon. Further light is shed by tracing the etymological origins of the word "generosity." Its Latin root is *genus* (i.e., tribe), which is related to the Anglo-Saxon words *kin* and *cyng*, precursors of the current English word *king*. An implication of such lexical lineage is that to be generous is to be kingly, i.e., to rise above the masses, to be noble (of birth), and to inspire others.

Not surprisingly then—within the psychological context—generosity implies ampleness of psychic content, space, and action. Care and attention can be given to others without depleting oneself, it says. The self is able to re-generate and be filled with imagination, it assures. Action for the sake of others shall beget gratitude and hence be enriching, it promises. Generosity thus has both an external, "public" face and an inner, private face. Under "normal" (i.e., libidinally satisfactory) psychic conditions, generosity is effortless, elegant, and mildly exalting. While "anagogic" (Silberer, 1914) by nature, i.e., geared toward ethical ideals, such healthy generosity remains anchored in reality. As a result, the giving (of time, money, things, service, and knowledge) is appropriate, helpful, and evokes thankfulness from the recipient. But generosity is not restricted to giving. It also involves accepting people as they are and having a charitable view of their motives. The affect associated with generosity is that of tenderness. Generosity thus represents the "affectionate current" (Freud, 1912, p. 180) of love. It also bears a certain similarity with altruism since both benefit others. However, while generosity can be considered a manifestation of altruism, the latter is not restricted to generosity and can appear in many other forms (e.g., self-sacrifice, service to others).

The origins of generosity are traceable to the earliest periods of childhood. Abraham (1924) declared generosity to be an oral character trait and stated that, in being generous, "the orally gratified person is identifying himself with the bounteous mother" (p. 403). Besides such ontogenesis, there might be an innate basis to the trait as well. Observational data from ethology offer evidence that the qualities of concern, cooperation, and altruism are present in animals (Cheney et al., 1995; de Waal and Van Roosmalen, 1979; Hrdy, 1999). And, psychoanalytically-informed infant-observation demonstrates that social referencing, reciprocity, and empathy originate in earliest infancy and emanate from a state of biological preparedness (see Emde, 1991, for a comprehensive survey of this literature). Putting the ethological and infant-observational data together leads to the conclusion that the seeds of generosity are sowed by nature itself. Seelig and Rosof (2009), who have critically assessed the literature on altruism, conclude that, at its base, the tendency is "hard-wired," since it is conducive to the survival of the species.

This foundation finds nourishment from gratifying experiences in the early mother-child relationship. The optimal ending of the "infantile appeal-cycle" (Settlage et al., 1991) in relief from instinctual and ego tension creates the perception of a good and giving object out there.

Identification with this object strengthens the constitutionally given "proto-altruism" and lays the groundwork for more advanced forms of generosity. Greenson's (1960) declaration that central to all human empathy is a "motherly component" (p. 422) is pertinent in this context. From the early drive psychology perspective, Fenichel (1945) also ended up at roughly the same point.

> "The behavior of the person with oral character frequently shows signs of identification with the object by whom they want to be fed. Certain persons act as nursing mothers in all their object relationships. They are always generous and shower everybody with presents and help, under favorable libido-economic conditions in a genuine and altruistic way, under less favorable conditions in a very annoying manner" (p. 489).

Employing a different psychoanalytic idiom, Melanie Klein (1957) traced the origin of generosity to the establishment of a good internal object.

> "Inner wealth derives from having assimilated the good object so that the individual becomes able to share its gifts with others. This makes it possible to introject a more friendly outer world, and a feeling of enrichment ensues. Even the fact that generosity is often insufficiently appreciated does not necessarily undermine the ability to give" (p. 189).

Such emphasis upon early infantile roots should not make one overlook the role later psychosexual phases play in the consolidation of generosity. During the anal phase, the relinquishment of feces and the subsequent pleasure in mother's approval buttresses the notion that giving is "good." Still later, the renunciation of voyeuristic and competitive impulses during oedipal phase results in the more sublime satisfaction of filial belonging and generational lineage. Once again, the benefit of giving (here, giving in) dawns upon the psychic horizon. The periods of latency, adolescence, and young adulthood widen the orbit of one's experiential world. Neighbors, school teachers, and professional mentors now come to serve as role-models for helpful conduct. Ethnic pride in generosity also shapes individual behavior and so do the oft-repeated dictates of religion. While all religions exhort their followers to be generous, Christianity especially emphasizes this virtue. Note the following sayings from the Bible, King James version, for instance: "It is more blessed to give than to receive" (Acts 20: 35), "God loves a cheerful giver" (Corinthians 9: 7), and "Whoever is generous to the poor lends to the Lord and He will repay him for his deed" (Proverbs 19: 7). Internalization of such dictates during the formative years of one's life can assure that generosity would be an integral part of one's ego ideal.[3]

Going back to earlier ontogenetic factors for a moment, it should be acknowledged that an occasional and short-lived absence of the gratifying object—a "lack" (Lacan, 1955)—can also spur or intensify identification with it. However, when its absence becomes frequent and prolonged, the result is the opposite. Identification with a frustrating mother gives rise to the vengeful lack of generosity. This can manifest as refusal to pay attention to others, chronic miserliness, and, by "downward displacement" as sexual disinterest, especially retarded ejaculation (Bergler, 1935). A different kind of pathological outcome results from patterning oneself after the bountiful mother one wishes to have but does not have in actuality. A rigid quality to behavior accompanies such identification with fantasy figures since there is little possibility of tempering such "introjects" by real interactions between the self and the object. In the end, it seems that the balance between normal and abnormal elements in generosity depends upon the ratio between early gratification and frustration, libido and aggression, actual or imaginary identification, and, finally, between the processes of sublimation and reaction formation.

FIVE PATHOLOGICAL VARIANTS

> The spending of money deceives [some individuals] as to the want of freedom of their libido and thus relieves them for a short time of the painful feeling of sexual insufficiency. In other words, they are under an abnormally strict prohibition, proceeding from the parental imago, against expending their libido freely. A compromise between instinct and repression is made by which the patient, in a spirit of defiance, does expend—not his sexual libido but an anal currency. —Abraham, 1917, p. 301

> The affection-buying compulsive spender tries to buy love wherever he can bolster up his own feelings of inferiority.

> His efforts are self-defeating because he often befriends immature individuals who, instead of giving him the affection he craves, are ever insistent for larger hand-outs.
> —Kaufman, 1976, p. 241

Morbid tendencies abound in the realm of generosity. However, such 'syndromes' remain unrecognized because they are ego-syntonic and deeply embedded in the individual's overall character. The one who has them does not complain. The psychoanalyst discerns them on his own in his patients or hears about their existence in the patients' relatives. Either way, the analyst tends to become tongue-tied. The former situation makes him fearful that in declaring someone generous or otherwise he is unduly relying upon his own value system. The latter injects skepticism in his mind regarding the patient's self-interested reporting. Or, it requires from him the bravery of validating what indeed might be noxious in the patients' environment. Facing such internal pressures, the psychoanalyst can develop resistance to seeing what is in front of him. The situation can be helped by making available clearly enunciated accounts of various constellations of pathological generosity. These include (i) unrelenting generosity, (ii) begrudging generosity, (iii) fluctuating generosity, (iv) controlling generosity, and (v) beguiling generosity. The first three are abnormalities in the intensity, nature, and sustenance of generosity. The remaining two are "pseudo-generosities" since the giving in these instances is hardly selfless. Each condition has its own phenomenological nuance and its own intrapsychic and interpersonal agenda.

Unrelenting Generosity

The syndrome of unrelenting generosity involves incessant and excessive giving to others. There is a pressured and driven quality to the behavior. The individual feels helpless in the face of an inward command to provide and be helpful.[4] He is not conscious of his overstepping limits even though what he gives often leaves him depleted and exceeds the needs and expectations of the recipient. The giving itself might be restricted to intangibles (e.g., time, attention, care) or extend to tangible and material products (e.g., money, gifts). Commenting upon this phenomenon in the realm of money, I have noted that such an individual "often does not have much money himself and the recipient is not needy in reality, only construed as such in the giver's mind" (Akhtar, 2009c, p. 73). The dynamics of financial over-indulgence in others is the same as "pseudo-altruism" where "compulsive caretaking and self-sacrifice cloaks and defends against aggression, envy, and a need to control the object. There is generally little or no conscious pleasure in the behavior, although the analytic observer can detect evidence of sadistic glee in the dramatic exhibitions of suffering that aim, generally unconsciously, at coercing others" (Seelig and Rosof, 2009, p. 948). The fact is that the syndrome of unrelenting generosity is multiply-determined. Vectors of love and hate, rescue fantasy, oedipal pursuit, guilt, envy, and sadomasochism can all play a role in it. There is also a genuine "goodness" (Akhtar, 2011b, pp. 3–28) about most such people which is not the result of reaction formation against aggression. Overlooking this fact while making interpretations of their driven attitude can hurt them and adversely affect the therapeutic alliance.

Begrudging Generosity

This syndrome is evident in those who give but do so with reluctance and half-heartedness. Their torment in giving to others is often overt. The forms this takes include: (i) *giving but not giving fully*. For instance, an uncle promises to buy a guitar for his musically-inclined nephew. He tells the young man to find out how much one would cost. Upon being told that the price would be $400, the uncle gives his nephew $300, telling him to come up with the remaining amount himself; (ii) *giving with a declaration of the hardship involved in procuring the gift*. For instance, a father gives his son binoculars as a birthday gift but spends more time on his travails in purchasing them than on celebrating his son's special day and, (iii) *giving but wanting to be thanked repeatedly*. For instance, a forty-year-old woman gives a copy of *Gray's Anatomy* to her friend's daughter, who has just been accepted in medical school. And, from then onwards, each time they run into each other, she reminds the young woman of the gift. This is done in a serious vein (e.g., "was the book helpful?"), crude jokes (e.g., "wow! look at your anatomy"), and jabs, (e.g., "I should stay away from you since you have read *Gray's Anatomy* and can see the imperfections in me"). The young woman is not allowed to forget that she had received a gift. Klein (1957) eloquently described the dynamics of such begrudging generosity. According to her, "With people in whom the feeling of inner wealth and strength is not sufficiently established, bouts of generosity are often followed by an exaggerated need for appreciation and gratitude, and consequently, by persecutory anxieties of having been impoverished and robbed" (p. 189).

Fluctuating Generosity

Some individuals show a pattern of being alternatively generous and tight-fisted. One day they surprise us with a substantial gift, the permission to use their house or car, or an offer to host the company's party at their backyard deck. The next day, they contribute a shockingly paltry sum to a colleague's humanitarian fund-raising, "forget" to buy a gift for a nephew's birthday, or refuse to drive someone home because they want to save gas. The behavior of such individuals puzzles and irritates others; they are simultaneously generous and miserly. Fenichel (1945) suggested that such fluctuations are due to "the ratio between sublimation and reaction formation in the characterological representation of oral drives" (p. 490). In contemporary psychoanalytic parlance, this pattern reflects a "mirror complementary of the self" (Bach, 1977) whereby one self-representation takes hold of consciousness and action while a contradictory representation is held in abeyance, only to express itself at another occasion. Splitting is clearly evident here though it remains unclear—from a behavioral perspective alone—whether (or how much of) it reflects a borderline personality organization (Kernberg, 1975) or is the result of unassimilated identifications with parents with sharply differing attitudes about giving to others (or with parents one had and parents one wanted). Only deeper self-revelation during analysis can permit the distinction to be made, especially if no gross evidences of splitting, ego weakness, and projective identification exist. If it turns out that the oddly appearing and disappearing conflict with generosity is indeed based upon contradicting identifications with parents, then the oscillations between the two extremes are mostly caused by oedipal triggers. However, if the situation is essentially borderline, even if functioning on a narcissistic level (Kernberg, 1984), the switch is mostly affect-based.

Controlling Generosity

While this element is present in some cases of "unrelenting generosity" and "begrudging generosity," it often exists on its own. Individuals with this trait can give and indeed do so. However, there are always strings attached to their "gifts." The need to influence how what they give would be utilized is relentless. Coercion of the recipient is marked and, even when arising from libidinal anxieties, contains a sadistic flavor. A dramatic example of such dynamic constellation is seen among immigrant parents who offer to pay tuition if their offspring promises to attend medical school. Claiming to love their children, they confuse encouraging achievement with facilitating individuation. Unresolved mourning about their own immigrant status contributes to such psychic blindness (Akhtar, 2011c), though a disturbing imbalance in the love-hate economy of object relations also plays a role. This is more clear when such coercive behaviors occur outside of the setting of immigration. Personal wills and estate bequests especially can reveal (posthumously) the inclination toward "controlling generosity." The person receiving large sums of money or valuable property is made to promise to do this or that deed and, upon his or her own death, leave the gift to such and such person or institution. The element of control is unmistakable, even if acted upon post-mortem. At times, however, the indulged party and the controlled party are separate. A dying millionaire might, for instance, leave all his wealth to his beloved daughter and none to his contentious son, thus dictating the two children's fate and perpetuating their conflict.[5]

Beguiling Generosity

This is a more "smooth" version of controlling generosity. The behavior is charming and sleek. The giver is glib and has a heightened but essentially "borderline empathy" (Krohn, 1974) with the receiver; this refers to a transient attunement to others' affect in the absence of deeper and sustained understanding of their character. The giver appears sincere and even maudlin but, at his core, is deceptive. And, he knows this. Under the patina of flattery and material indulgence, he is out to realize his own instinctual, narcissistic, or social aims. The superego corruption that permits such bribery also lets the avowed respect for the recipient to coexist with hidden contempt for him. Gifts offered to gain sexual favors, employment opportunities, and leniency with judicial enforcements are representatives of beguiling generosity. Imposturous tendencies abound in this realm and the characterological makeup is along the narcissistic–antisocial spectrum.

AN ATTEMPT AT SYNTHESIS

> The gift of time can sometimes be more satisfying and more valuable than money, as Americans will tell you who have volunteered at a homeless shelter or center for troubled families, brought meals on wheels to seniors or gone to the grocery store for an elderly neighbor, helped with non-medical tasks in hospitals, tutored young students in reading or math, mentored kids from poor neighborhoods to help them prepare for college and succeed in life, served as an AmeriCorps volunteer, or stacked sandbags during a flood. —Clinton, 2007, p. 32

> Our goodness is the recognition we offer and the thanks we return for the gifts and the love already given us. Rather than a request for something yet to come, it is a response to the abundance of gifts that have already been given and received. It is in our makeup that, having been given, we want to give back. —Tutu and Tutu, 1989, p. 23

Putting together the normative, developmental, and psychopathological aspects of generosity outlined above poses challenges while also yielding new possibilities. To begin with, the distinction between healthy and pathological generosity (see table I) might turn out to be more dimensional than categorical in nature, with, of course, the exception of the extreme ends of this spectrum. On first blush, it appears that normal generosity is characterized by flexibility, realistic grounding, altruism, and the experience of pleasure that is largely ego-based.

Pathological generosity, in contrast, comes across as rigid and driven, unrealistic, narcissistic, and associated with pleasure that is instinctual in nature. However, contrary to what the current psychiatric nosology would have us believe, emotional phenomena are not well-chiseled monoliths; relational context and intensities of drive activation continually shape and re-shape them. No wonder a careful look reveals that most 'mid-line' instances of generosity contain the dynamics of both healthy and pathological types; their difference lies in the degree to which one or the other dynamic predominates and that too at a given moment.

Lewinsky's (1951) delineation of various types of generosity supports this idea. According to her, there are four types of giving: (i) propitiatory giving, i.e., giving in order to feel deserving of respectful treatment, (ii) assertive giving, i.e., giving in order to boast about one's resources, (iii) fetishistic giving, i.e., giving to deflect one's hatred and envy, and (iv) deceptive giving, i.e., giving stolen goods. While appearing distinct from each other, these categories can hardly withstand skepticism regarding their boundaries. Giving pilfered goods (deceptive giving) can certainly serve the aim of disguising one's hostility (fetishistic giving), for instance. In all honesty, my own subtypes of psychopathological generosity (unrelenting, begrudging, controlling, beguiling, and, fluctuating) too are not sacrosanct. Hybrid forms, containing the features of more than one (e.g., controlling and beguiling, or unrelenting and controlling) subtype are frequent, and transitions from one to the other type over time also occur. The following parable attributed to the revered Persian mystic, al Ghazali (1058-1111 AD), captures one such moment of transition.

> I once had a brother in Iraq. I would go to him when times were bad and say, "Give me some of your money." He would throw me his purse for me to take what I wanted. Then one day I came to him and said, "I need something." He asked, "How much do you want?" And so the sweetness of brotherhood left my heart. (al-Ghazali, cited in Fadman and Frager, 1997, p. 222)

Here, healthy and unquestioning generosity has turned into begrudging generosity, owing to the recipient's incessant demands. Such interpersonal dynamics raise the question whether generosity is a "one-person" trait or is a co-constructed, relational phenomenon. What happens to generosity when it is mocked as a weakness or as stupidity by the recipient? Do praise and recognition enhance generosity? Or, in individuals averse to accepting compliments, can they inhibit generosity? Where the value systems of spouses differ, who decides which one is "unduly" generous and who can declare the other "small-hearted"? And, so on.

All in all, it seems that while the pole of sublime, tempered, and helpful giving is far apart from the pole of grotesquely exaggerated, maudlin, and self-serving bribery, the spectrum of generosity remains wide. State-related, context-bound, emotionally-determined, and co-constructed variants populate much of the field.[6] Matters are further complicated by the pathoplastic impact of age, gender, and culture at large. However, before taking these factors up, it is worthwhile to take a close look at the role of generosity in the clinical setting.

Table 4.1. The Spectrum of Generosity

Variable	*Healthy Pole*	*Pathological Pole*
Origin	Identification with the giving aspects of parents (and other important figures).	Identification with the wished-for aspects of parents (and other important figures).
Extent	Realistic	Unrealistic
Behavior	Flexible and context-based	Rigid and driven
Aims	Altruistic-generative	Narcissistic-sadomasochistic
Pleasure	Sublime	Instinctual
Recipient	Thoughtfully selected	Randomly enlisted
Reaction	Gratitude and appreciation	Puzzlement and annoyance

TECHNICAL IMPLICATIONS

> What I would assert is that if one had to choose, one would do better to choose Freud's early latitudes and naturalness over the robot-like 'anonymity' of our own neo-classical period, when it reached absurd heights. —Stone, 1981, p. 165

> Psychoanalysts do now know in advance which new emotional/relational context will transform old meanings into new ones, and it is unlikely that they could set out to create those contexts even if they knew beforehand which ones they were. Spontaneity is required. —Stern, 2010, p. 23

The foregoing elucidation of the phenomenological and psychodynamic spectrum of generosity carries important implications for our daily work. The clinical impact of knowing the nature and significance of generosity is discernable in six different ways, namely, (i) having and maintaining an attitude of generosity towards the patient, (ii) listening and intervening with an attitude of generosity, (iii) recognizing and accepting the patient's healthy generosity, (iv) diagnosing and interpreting the patient's pathological generosity, (v) unmasking and interpreting defenses against generosity, and (vi) remaining vigilant towards countertransference pitfalls in such work.

Having and Maintaining an Attitude of Generosity

The well-functioning psychoanalyst receives the patient with an attitude of generosity. The origins of such inclination are manifold. Identification with benevolent caretakers of his own formative years, with mentors and clinical supervisors, and with his own training analyst's accepting and "forgiving" stance plays a big role here. The analyst's having been the recipient of such care and realizing its transformative role in helping him overcome neurotic obstacles and traumatic formations of his own leads him to carry what Frank (2004) has termed the "obligation of the cured" (p. 55); this, in turn, fuels his generosity towards his patient. Finally, one must not overlook that practicing analysis is a lonely affair and the profession (with all of 13,000 or so members in a world of six billion people) is an extremely small one. A sense of personal marginality, compounded by the current endangerment of the field, is thus the inevitable legacy of analytic training. This, in turn, primes the analyst to locate the Other within himself, resonate with the alienated selves of others, and to become—in the words of Albert Schweitzer (1875—1965)—"capable of accepting the world" (cited in Mairs, 1966, p. 60).

But how does the analyst's generosity manifest itself in the clinical situation? To be sure, judicious accommodation of the therapeutic frame to the patient's cultural idiosyncrasies (Akhtar, 1999a, 2011c), adjustments of fee during periods of the patient's financial difficulty, and of other sundry "silent sacrifices" (David Sachs, personal communication, April, 2001) implicit in clinical devotion constitute generous acts on the analyst's part. Kradin (1999) enters two useful caveats at this point. *First* involves a warning that, with rare exceptions, offers to reduce fees or prolong sessions must follow the patient's request and not offered by the analyst spontaneously[7]; there is a greater chance of the latter being a countertransference enactment. *Second* tells the analyst to be mindful of the "shadow of condescension" (p. 224) that might silently accompany his acts of generosity towards the patient.

More important is the manner in which the patient is psychically represented in the analyst's mind. By resolutely regarding the patient to be a full human being, capable of moral and, yes, therapeutic reciprocity, and by rejecting the view of the patient as infantile and unwanted, the analyst accomplishes his greatest feat of generosity. Subscribing to the perspective that development does not end with such-and-such maturational epoch but is a life-long process (Pine, 1997) also allows the analyst to view the patient as well as himself as forever "unfinished products"; both are capable of further growth and their encounter has the potential of facilitating such movement. Nuanced optimism, carried over long periods of time when the patient might have no reason to feel hopeful, is the hallmark of the analyst's generosity.

In discussing this issue further, both Frank (2004) and Griffith (2010) evoke the writings of the Jewish philosopher, Emmanuel Levinas (1906–1995). Briefly put, Levinas proposed that ethical relatedness to the other is the foundational stone of the psychic self and requires recognition of difference. Erasing self-other distinction leads to totalization and sets the stage for domination and control. Commitment to dialogue, in contrast, endorses a relation between self and Other while accepting the 'strangeness' and autonomy of both parties. No partner in a dialogue has all the answers and each can enrich the process between them. Levinas' commitment to the Other also lies at the core of analytic generosity. In Griffith's (2010) words,

> "For a clinician, this means building conditions for dialogue where dialogue does not already exist. When this proves impossible, a clinician still must go as far as possible in protecting the otherness of his or her patient by interacting respectfully and ethically, as if awaiting the possibility for dialogue" (p. 247).

Listening and Intervening with an Attitude of Generosity

In a forthcoming paper, Crawford (in press) reminds us of how generosity pervades the manner in which we attend to patients. He states, " . . . we *offer* interpretations, we *provide* a setting for the psychotherapeutic work, we *make ourselves available* to work with our patients and to be on the *receiving* end of their projections, and we attempt to process these projections before *offering*, or *giving*, something back to the patient in our comments and interpretations" (p. 2).

Crawford underscores the generosity that is inherent in the therapist's 'accepting' the patient's projections before metabolizing them for the purposes of interpretation (see also Gill, 1982 in this regard). One can add a few more indicators of generosity in the analyst's way of listening and talking to his patient. These include: (i) attempting to listen from diverse perspectives simultaneously, i.e., from objective, subjective, empathic and, intersubjective viewpoints (Akhtar, 2012), (ii) keeping the 'principle of multiple function (Waelder, 1936) in mind and thus allowing the patient's explanations to exist side by side those of the analyst's while leaving space for still unearthed possibilities, (iii) demystifying the process by occasionally sharing with the patient his reasons for making a particular intervention (Thoma and Kachele, 1994) and, (iv) conveying his "conjectures" (Brenner, 1976) and interpretations in a manner that avoids injuring the patient's self-esteem. In summary, both the analyst's attitude and the analyst's activity are suffused with generosity. This, however, does not translate into a pollyanna-ish permissiveness; the analyst must preserve the therapeutic boundaries and retain a healthy dose of counter-assertion in his interpretive activity.

One particular facet of clinical work in which the analyst's generosity makes its clearest appearance is that of termination. Not only does the analyst let go of the myriad gratifications (e.g., the pleasure of analyzing, the assurance of an income) derived from working with the patient, he also renounces certain self-representations that specifically evolve in the course of a particular analysis. Buechler (2012) eloquently makes this point.

> Just as losing my child would mean losing myself as his parent, losing a patient means losing myself as a particular analyst I was able to be with that person. I also lost the reflection of me that I could find in that patient's eyes. The self I could be with am, the person he was able to see in me, is now only a memory. I would never again be exactly *that* kind of analyst. (p. 135, italics in the original)

Recognizing and Accepting the Patient's Healthy Generosity

While maintaining an attitude of generosity towards his patient, the analyst must also be open to recognize and accept the latter's healthy gestures of generosity. The patient's willingness to change his schedule to accommodate the analyst's needs, telling a nice joke, informing the analyst about a good book, and giving the analyst a small gift at an appropriate juncture in their work (e.g., patient's return from his original home in a foreign country, or at termination) all constitute examples of such generosity. The analyst should gracefully accept them. To be sure, all these behaviors can contain material for analytic exploration. However, undue skepticism regarding the patient's generosity is hardly commendable. Too credulously accepting patient's gestures of generosity can by-pass deeper analysis but excessive questioning can also cause unwarranted disruptions. The view that accepting gifts from patients derails the understanding of such a gesture needs to be tempered by remembering that "rejecting presents often prevents analysts from recognizing their true meanings" (Thoma and Kachele, 1994, p. 301). Transference is affected as much by deprivation as by gratification. The important point is to avoid "superfluous introgenic regressions attendant on superfluous deprivations" (Stone, 1961, p. 170).

Another technical consideration is the handling of the patient's generosity when it emerges for the first time as a consequence of analytic work. The following vignette illustrates this point.

Clinical Vignette: 6

Julia Caputo, a college student in her mid-twenties, sought help for feelings of worthlessness and apathy.[8] She suffered from low self-esteem and was painfully thin-skinned; she felt rejected at the slightest shift of attention on others' part and therefore avoided relating to people. Her background revealed an alcoholic mother who, in her drunken stupor, often forgot to feed Julia when she was a little child. Her father was frequently away on business trips and, when at home, talked to Julia about his own depression and even suicidal thoughts. Julia grew up to mistrust anything, regarding everyone "in power" to be self-centered and lacking interest in her welfare.

In the treatment situation, too, Julia revealed marked sensitivity and a tendency to feel ignored and neglected. The analyst's slightest delay in beginning the session sent her into angry withdrawal. She checked and re-checked her watch and matched it to the clock in the analyst's office. If the analyst ended a session thirty seconds earlier, Julia went into a frenzy. The analyst kept working with Julia's reactions patiently. Empathic comments about her inner experience, validation of her mental pain, reconstructions of early neglect, and transference-based interpretations of the disastrous early mothering gradually led Julia to become calmer and more or less realistically tolerant.

In the fourth year of her analysis, the analyst (herself facing a stressful life situation) "forgot" to be there for a session. Julia arrived, waited for quite a while, and then left. The next day, the analyst realized her error and was quite distressed about it. She approached their session with dread. Julia would be really enraged and treat her viciously, the analyst thought. The situation turned out to be just the opposite. Julia said, "Look, I *was* hurt and annoyed at first. But then I thought you have been so reliable and so steadfast with me over the last four years that one mistake should not throw all that out. Come on, you are human. You can make mistakes. It is okay!" The analyst felt deeply touched by Julia's gesture. She responded by thanking Julia, and expressing her pleasure in Julia's new-found capacity for generosity and forgiveness.

Such clinical work illustrates that a dialectical relationship exists between the interpretive resolution of psychopathology and the resumption of arrested psychic growth. Pertinent in this context is Abrams' (1978) comment that when a hitherto unexpressed healthy capacity emerges as a result of interpretive work, the analyst should not deconstruct it or try to decipher its 'meaning.' Instead, the analyst should make an empathic comment underscoring the progressive trend in the patient's gesture. Settlage (1994) also notes that the analyst helps his patient not only by interpretation but also "by establishing a developmental relationship, by expecting development, by encouraging the patient's developmental intuitions, and by acknowledging developmental achievement" (p. 42).

Diagnosing and Interpreting the Patient's Pathological Generosity

Of the various syndromes of pathological generosity described above, some are evident early on, especially if the analyst's practice is to take a detailed history and separate the initial evaluation from the treatment proper. Other psychopathological patterns (e.g., beguiling generosity, controlling generosity) usually remain hidden early on and surface only with the passage of time. In either case, the long-held, multiply-determined and multi-layered nature of pathological generosity becomes fully clear only with the treatment's progress and with their underlying dynamics beginning to seep into the transference relationship. It is then that such material becomes amenable to interpretation.

Clinical Vignette: 7

Marc Aryaratnam had grown up in Sri Lanka and had arrived in the United States almost ten years ago. His presenting complaints revolved around a problematic marriage which he had entered rather impulsively some three years before seeking consultation. Marc's dissatisfaction with his wife centered upon her lack of cultural sophistication and disinterest in having sex. Fascinatingly, these "deficiencies" were known to him before marrying, though he seemed to have minimized them in his mind. The fact that she had been recently abandoned by a man somehow added to his 'rescue mission.' It was evident to me that Marc was afflicted by what Freud (1910) has called "a special type of object choice made by men" (p. 163).

The customary oedipal dynamics underlying men's involvement with down-trodden, needy women with a "faint breath of scandal" (Freud, 1910, p. 166) was amply evident in Marc's case. Son of a renowned father who drank excessively and mistreated his wife, Marc was determined to rescue his mother from the aggressively-tinged primal scene. Matters were made worse by his mother becoming terminally ill and dying when Marc was eight-and-a-half-years old. The oedipal agenda now got condensed with "survivor's guilt" (Niederland, 1968), and led to Marc's hypertrophied desire to take care of those around him.

As treatment progressed, the trait of underlying generosity came to attention. Marc felt compelled to help any and everybody, it appeared. He would offer assistance to his colleagues, his seniors, his juniors, with little distinction between those who did need such assistance and those who could do without it. Out for lunch or dinner with friends, he felt an unstoppable urge to pay for everyone and, much to the chagrin of his wife, he often did so in reality. The pattern went back to his childhood. Marc reported spending his weekly allowance on candies for his cousins and schoolmates as far back as age nine or ten. Even more striking was his buying a rather expensive shirt for his cousin (whom he had idealized) from the first pay he ever received; he bought nothing for himself.

Within transference, Marc viewed me as somewhat depressed, rejected by others, and in need of protection and "entertainment"; he provided the latter (which, in turn, stood for nourishing meals for his dying mother) in the form of compliments, jokes, fascinating anecdotes, and esoteric pieces of information. My own reaction to him was of fondness, tender admiration of his actual "goodness" (Akhtar, 2011b), and, at times, feeling burdened by his excessive and pressured love of me.

The hypotheses of the projection of a needy self into an object (Akhtar, 2009c) and of the need to control that object in order to keep envy and hostility in abeyance (Seelig and Rosof, 2001) were clearly supported by Marc's malady. However, other variables also seem to be operative here. By insistently giving to others, Marc depleted himself. This was his punishment for letting his mother die and a sort of "atonement" (Rosen, 2009) for the guilt at his supposed negligence (at age six!). By his constantly "feeding" others, Marc became the bountiful mother *he* wanted. By his driven helpfulness, he was not only 'rescuing' the projected parts of his own self, he was also bringing his mother back to life. Kind looks of gratitude and acknowledgment of his grandness by others served as salve against his wound; such gestures served a maternal function. Moreover, his unrelenting generosity curtailed his envy of others; after all, *he* was the one giving to them, *he* had more, as it were. Finally, giving to others left him 'poor' and thus he could avoid being the object of other's envy (and the associated aggression), and paradoxically, by being strikingly generous, he stirred up envy in others, a somewhat sadistic scenario that he greatly enjoyed on an unconscious level.

While Marc's inordinate generosity with money was directed at everyone, at times such gestures make their first appearance in the context of a particular transference. The following clinical vignette illustrates this point.

Clinical Vignette: 8

Dr. Robert Purple sought help when he found himself falling in love with "yet another inappropriate woman."[9] A forty year old internist with a mildly apologetic but earnest and decent way of relating, Dr. Purple had been twice divorced, both times having "discovered" that he had married far beneath his socioeconomic and intellectual status. The current situation was different only on surface; the inappropriateness of the choice became readily evident with questioning during the initial assessment.

Dr. Purple had grown up with a father who was preoccupied with his work and a mother who was anxious and clinging to her two sons. Dr. Purple's older brother had been difficult from childhood onwards; local police was often knocking at their otherwise respectable door. Assuming a quiet and passive stance, Dr. Purple grew up to be kind and industrious man who somehow never blossomed fully, either as a professional or as a lover. He accepted a ho-hum job and twice married needy and impaired women.

Soon after beginning treatment with me, he offered to raise the amount he was paying me. Since little evidence could be unearthed that he had misrepresented his financial status at the time when we decided the fee and had not gotten any salary raise, I was intrigued by this offer. My encouragement for him to elaborate on this idea gradually revealed that he viewed me as an immigrant physician with few well-paying patients; he wanted to help me. I was going to be his next rescue project, it seemed. A transferential re-creation of his needy mother (made more rescue-worthy by the condensation of a realistic perception of her character with the primal scene fantasies of her being beaten by the father) was essentially the motivating force behind Dr. Purple's gesture.

A more dramatic example of such transference-based generosity is provided by Rothstein (1986) who describes a patient's offer to donate a huge sum of money in order to establish a research foundation bearing both their names. Exploration of this wish revealed the desire to remain united with the therapist (to undo the traumatic separation from his mother during childhood). Giving money to the therapist also assured his loyalty and helped bypass the analysis of the mistrust that the therapist would not really be there for him when he needed love and support. Money was to serve as glue between them.

Unmasking and Interpreting Defenses against Generosity

It is not uncommon to come across patients who defend vehemently against goodness, regardless of whether it is their own or coming to them from others (Schafer, 2002; Akhtar, 2011b). Such recoil can involve an aversion to recognizing and accepting generosity. The patient might distort his perceptions to not see that those around him—including the analyst—are being kind towards him. Or, he might repudiate his own longing to give, even when these rise to the surface as a consequence of analytic work.

Clinical Vignette: 9

James LeRoy, a highly successful investment banker in his mid-forties, had broken off ties with his only sibling, a two-years-younger brother. James was, by all customary guidelines, diagnosable as having a narcissistic personality disorder. Affluent, clever, and socially prominent, he hid a morose and self-doubting inner life. Nothing satisfied him; money, cars, women, and sex all sooner or later left him bored and empty. He had little to do with his wife though he could be animated about his children. His inconsolability was what brought him to analysis.

James's break-up with his brother had allegedly come about because of the latter's ingratitude for his help. However, as our work deepened, it became clear that it was James who had been exploiting his brother. He had asked his brother to write parts of speeches he delivered at prestigious events without ever giving him the credit for doing so. Even the money he doled out from time to time to his financially needy brother was less than he would promise and was accompanied by a subtle hint that it could be a loan and not a gift. Further analysis brought forth childhood acts of cheating his brother; envy of the latter's 'innocence' and 'simplicity' (which, in turn stood for his mental peace) had propelled such destructive behaviors.

James now began to experience guilt though he would often project it upon me; to his mind, I was *making* him feel guilty. With greater ownership of his own emotional state, he appeared to feel an impulse for reparation. James began to express a desire to do something good for his brother. However, he suspected his motives and reacted to his own generosity with sarcasm and devaluation. Behind this lay his fear/hatred of his own "innocence" and "simplicity," loving traits that he had buried deep in his psychic life. Interpretive and reconstructive work along these lines gradually freed up James to approach his brother for the first time with genuine tenderness and generosity.

Contrary to common sense though it might sound, there are many individuals who habitually suppress, repress, and repudiate all that is good inside them (Akhtar, 2011b). They take pride in being callous and mock their acts of generosity and kindness. They envy others' goodness and fear that expressions of tenderness on their part would be ridiculed by them. Interpretive resolution of such defenses along with empathic validation of the traumatic childhood realities that necessitated their emergence can free them up to act more generously.

Discerning and Utilizing the Countertransference to Generosity

Since generosity, by definition, involves a dyadic scenario, its clinical presence or absence has powerful impact upon countertransference. Having discussed the analyst's emotional reaction to the patient's healthy generosity, I will focus here upon his encounter with the latter's pathological generosity. This can be in the form of too little giving or too much giving by the patient. Faced with an un-giving and anally retentive patient, the analyst can become impatient, irritated, and demanding. Faced with a patient who is not only generous by temperament but is offering 'gifts' that are irresistible, the analyst can get seduced and corrupted. Vigilance towards such propensities and dedicated effort to link them up with corresponding transferences can, however, pave the way for deeper analytic work.

Clinical Vignette: 10

In the process of writing her will, Kathleen Roberts, a wealthy widow in her late-seventies, became anxious and sought consultation with me. Intellectually gifted, artistic, and good looking, Kathleen was nonetheless in considerable distress. She felt torn about how to leave her estate in an equitable manner. She had two children and wanted to leave more money to the one with lesser financial resources. But she felt guilty at such 'unfairness'; dividing the money and property on a fifty-fifty basis also appeared unjust to her. She did not know what to do.

Expectedly, this contemporary scenario of fair-unfair dealing contained echoes from her past. Kathleen was the younger of two sisters and had been known to be "her mother's child." This, however, did not mean that she received more love than her sister did from their mother. It meant that she was trapped, controlled, and possessed by the mother. With further exploration, a history of childhood sexual abuse by the mother came to surface. With great anxiety and shame, Kathleen recounted being asked to take off all her clothes, spread her legs, and then undergo a 'test.' This consisted of her mother rubbing her genitals to make sure that there was "no weakness there, no eczema, or anything." This masturbatory ritual went on from age four-five till thirteen-fourteen years of age. After that, its place was taken by the mother's asking Kathleen to describe her imaginary encounters with boys and, as year went on, by the mother's insisting to hear each and every detail of Kathleen's sexual life with her boyfriend. But why was Kathleen and not her older sister chosen to serve the mother's perverse aims? Was this fair that one child was abused and the other escaped the violation, Kathleen wondered.

As our work deepened and with Kathleen's work in sorting out her enormous estate getting into full swing, material began to appear which suggested that she wanted to leave me a huge amount of money. At times, this appeared in derivative forms, i.e., parapraxes, and dreams. At other times, it was explicitly verbalized. Kathleen was genuinely grateful to me for helping her gather the sequestered parts of her psychic life and feel deeper and more meaningful as a person. Her wish to give me something emanated from gratitude. She wanted my work to be available to more women in her situation; there was thus an altruistic streak to her generosity as well.

However, it was my countertransference experience that told the deeper story. I felt split. At one time, I would feel omnipotent, powerful, and entitled to millions of dollars for my work. At other times, I felt that I was being corrupt, unethical, and greedy in my temptation to seduce her to leave me a huge sum of money. Upon brutally honest self-reflection, I was able to connect my vulgar desire to grab her money with an identification with her sexually abusive mother who grabbed her genitals and my recoil from it with my becoming a mother that she needed but did not have. It was such countertransference vigilance and working through that allowed me to interpret her oscillation between putting herself in a potentially abusive situation and hoping that such exploitation would not happen.

Needless to add that as Kathleen's pressure to give me millions subsided, I felt both relieved and a bit sad. The "loss" I was experiencing seemed akin to the mild pain of "tenderness" (Tahka, 1993) experienced by a generative parent in facilitating the offspring's pleasure and the subsequent leaving of the pleasure for the latter.

The recounting of this successful working-through of countertransference feelings should not make one overlook that failures also occur in this realm. Inability to discern, regulate, and learn from one's emotional response to the patient can lead to major disruptions of treatment. This can happen in the face of the patient's excessive generosity toward the analyst of, at times, as a reaction to the patient's financial over-indulgence in someone else.

Clinical Vignette: 11

Pamela Kasinetz, an elderly woman with extreme wealth sought psychotherapy for depression and anxiety of recent origin. The apparent trigger for this was the worsening relationship with her husband of over three decades. With their children no longer at home, the two had become quite alienated; he was engrossed in his business and she with her social commitments and philanthropic work. Matters became worse when Pamela ran into an "adorable" seven-eight year old Cambodian boy in a shopping mall and "fell in love with him." She took it upon herself to help him and his financially strained family. The boy gradually became her constant companion. Paying huge sums of money to his parents, Pamela pretty much took over his life. She would pick him up from school, bring him home, shower him with lavish gifts, and indulge all his whims and desires; his friends also were welcome at her house and were treated with similar indulgence. While numerous examples can be given, one instance should suffice where she spent in excess of thirty thousand dollars over a weekend entertaining her little 'friend' and his four playmates. All this led to frequent arguments between Pamela and her husband who insisted on putting limits on her expenses.

Seeking symptomatic relief, Pamela appeared unprepared to look into the deeper meanings of her fascination with this little boy. Raised in a family of means, she readily dismissed any inquiry into a childhood sense of feeling deprived and thus blocked the therapist's efforts at linking her run-away altruism with potential unconscious issues pertaining to early trauma. It was all 'real' and rationalized in terms of kindness, and generosity toward the underprivileged, as far as she was concerned. Soon after starting treatment, she expressed a desire to pay a much greater fee for her sessions, quoting what appeared to be truly an exorbitant amount. The situation was complicated by parallel problems in the therapist's countertransference to her and to the financial glitter of the situation. Having suffered a childhood parental loss at about the same age as the Cambodian boy Pamela so adored and being financially strapped himself owing to a recent personal crisis, the therapist was made terribly uncomfortable by Pamela's financial seductions. Reacting defensively, he not only made premature transference interpretations but also sternly rejected her offers. He failed to explicate and explore them in a peaceful manner. Pamela soon dropped out of treatment.

This adverse outcome seems to have been the result of a number of factors the therapist's (i) current financial distress made it hard for him to listen peacefully to his patient's extravagance; it stirred up too much greed, (ii) childhood trauma made it difficult for him to hear about his patient's indulgence in a little boy; it stirred up too much envy; and (iii) not seeking a consultation in what was obviously a difficult clinical situation for him; it led to defensive recoil and over-interpretation. Flying solo under these circumstances was an inappropriate clinical choice.

CONCLUDING REMARKS

> Caring is an attitude, not necessarily anything one does. It is a form of interest in another human being that has its roots in the parents' phase-specifically adequate attitudes towards their children at the latters' changing developmental stages. —Tahka, 1993, p. 345

In this contribution, I have delineated normal and abnormal forms of generosity while acknowledging that often the psychodynamic and behavioral features of the two overlap. I have noted these hybrid constellations and sought to demonstrate that shifting identifications and relational pressures on the love-hate economy of psyche can impact upon the presence, type, and extent of generosity. Unlike Kradin (1999) who declared the analyst's generosity to be "a cardinal therapeutic factor in analysis" (p. 223), I have taken a less euphoric view of this component. While acknowledging its important role in creating respect for the patient's essential Otherness, I have underscored that the ways in which issues involving generosity affect our day-to-day clinical work are myriad, nuanced, and complex.[10] However, even such broad-based coverage has left some aspects of the topic unaddressed. In what follows, I will briefly touch upon these matters with the awareness that many questions will remain unanswered.

The first issue is that of the relationship between age and generosity. While my elucidation of its development has established that rudimentary forms of altruism and generosity are evident from the earliest periods of life, it is unclear when exactly mature generosity (with the associated capacities for whole object relations and empathy) finds ego expression. Are there real differences between children's and adult's generosity and if so, are these quantitative (i.e., more or less) or qualitative (i.e., with different sorts of pleasure) in nature? Does the adolescent's bouts of 'hyper-generosity' toward certain peers or social causes reflect a caricature of adult altruism or is it the last flicker of selflessness which is put off by the move toward conventionality in young adulthood? What effect does the onset of middle age have on generosity? Is "generativity" (Erikson, 1950), i.e., the capacity to nurture the next generation in a self-less manner, merely a form of generosity or are the two phenomena different? Clearly, more thought is needed here.

The next issue pertains to gender. Most studies of philanthropic patterns across genders (see Mesch, 2009, for critical review of this literature) reveal that women are more likely to give money to humanitarian causes, though a few investigations have found the opposite. For a psychoanalyst, however, the mere act of giving is not a sufficient indicator of true generosity; people donate money for all sorts of reasons (e.g., guilt, exhibitionism) which have little to do with generosity. More impressive, therefore, are studies (Hoffman, 1977; Winterich et al., 2009) that find women to be more charitable, more empathic, and, psychologically speaking, more generous. Fascinatingly, this was also found to be true for men with high scores for "feminine gender identity." Observations of such sort lend support to the idea that empathy is predominantly a maternal trait (Greenson, 1975). They also suggest that, regardless of their actual gender, those with deeper identifications with a giving mother tend to be more generous in their attitude and behavior. In other words, the outside/actual gender has less influence upon the extent of generosity than does the inside/psychological gender.

Yet another area pertains to cross-cultural differences in generosity. Rife with the potential for making overly generalized and "politically incorrect" statements, the realm nonetheless invites comment. The first thing to note here is that most ethnic groups—at least in the United States—take immense pride in throwing lavish parties and bestowing upon their children (and especially, grandchildren) all sorts of gifts. One constantly hears of "Southern generosity," "Italian generosity," "Greek generosity," "Indian generosity," "Armenian generosity," and so on. The question then arises whether there are ethnic groups that are less generous? Or, does their generosity manifest in forms that are less "loud" and noticeable by others?[11] The determinants of all this might be anchored more deeply in historical forces than particular regional or religious affiliations. Two other points need to be kept in mind. One, large group characteristics vis-à-vis generosity, even if they exist, might not reflect in all the members of the group; individuals have their own personality make-ups and are not solely dependent upon group identifications. Two, disasters of great magnitude (e.g., earthquakes, tsunamis, and even "9/11") have a way of mobilizing generosity in human beings that often crosses over the ethnic and racial barriers of everyday life. Talking of this phenomenon, Klein (1959) emphasized that when people risk their own lives to save others, it is mostly due to their "capacity for love, generosity, and an identification with endangered fellow being" (p. 259) and not due to guilt.

Finally, no discourse on generosity would be complete without the mention of its opposite. Call it stinginess, miserliness, niggardliness, penuriousness, tight-fistedness, small-heartedness, or whatever else you might, the syndrome *is* a part of humanity and unfortunately seems here to stay. It can manifest as the inability (or refusal?) to devote attention, time, care, and effort for the sake of others. It can also appear in the form of sexual disinterest, ethnocentricism (that sees no other group as having contributed anything significant to human civilization), and, at times, opting to not have children (Kradin, 1999). However, since money can have multi-faceted and powerful emotional significance (Freud, 1908; Ferenczi, 1914; Jones, 1918; Fenichel, 1938; Borneman, 1976; Krueger, 1986), lack of generosity finds it most churlish expression in chronic miserliness. Now, this is a Janus-faced problem with considerable intrapsychic and interpersonal ramifications. Before going into them, however, it should be emphasized that miserliness is unrelated to the actual financial state of the individual. Both the rich and the poor can be miserly and both can be generous. Tight-fistedness is the inverse of large heartedness. It is not about lack of money. That said, the problem of miserliness appears to have two faces. Subjectively, the miser is saddled with terrible anxiety; parting with money stirs up in him the dread of becoming poor and resourceless. Saving money is equated with psychic security and the slightest monetary bleed is felt to be life-threatening hemorrhage. The miser resorts to all sorts of conscious and unconscious measures to avoid spending. Rationalization especially comes to his rescue; it helps stinginess masquerade as prudence. Inner tension nonetheless persists. In contrast to such anxiety-laden inner world, the miser's object relations are permeated with sadism, even though he is consciously unaware of it. His lack of generosity, what to say of his frequent cheating and unfairness in paying his due, become a torture for his friends and relatives. The miser seems to be saying to them "Why should I give you anything when I myself have not been given much?" This brings up the fact that while anal drive derivatives are clearly discernable in it (Freud, 1908; Jones, 1918), "monetary constipation" is, at its bottom (pun unintended), a reaction to early oral deprivation. The miser has experienced a profound and traumatizing lack of nourishment from his early caretakers and, in a move typical of "identification with the aggressor" (A. Freud, 1936), has adapted an ungiving attitude towards others. Yesterday's victim has become today's perpetrator. The miser's self is split; a cruel and withholding adult triumphantly parades outside while a deprived child weeps inside. In sharp contrast to this bleak portrait is the free-flowing pleasure of giving to others. The sweetness of generosity is akin to children's laughter which the great Indian poet Rabindranath Tagore (1861–1941) said constitutes the best sound in the world.

5

FORGIVENESS

Psychoanalysis has had little to say about forgiveness. The topic is neither listed in the index of the *Standard Edition* of Freud's works nor in the *'Title Key Word' and 'Author Index' to Psychoanalytic Journals—1920-1990* (Mosher, 1991).[1] This omission is puzzling since issues closely linked to forgiveness (e.g., trauma, mourning, guilt, need for punishment) have been of utmost concern to psychoanalysis. Reasons for this neglect are unclear though many possibilities exist. *First*, the tradition among psychoanalysts to treat Freud's work as a touchstone before positing their own views creates the risk of topics not addressed by the master being ignored. Forgiveness is one such phenomenon. The word itself appears a mere five times in the entire corpus of his work (Guttman et al., 1980)[2] and then too in a colloquial rather than a scientific manner. *Second*, forgiveness is a hybrid psychological concept with unmistakable interpersonal and social referents. Thus it borders on areas where psychoanalytic theory traditionally has been at its weakest and prone to heuristic omissions.[3] *Third*, originating in clinical concerns, psychoanalysis has devoted greater attention to morbid psychic phenomena (e.g., anxiety, hate) at the cost of positive and life-enhancing emotions (e.g., courage, altruism). This bias, admittedly rectified to a certain extent by the recent writings on wisdom (Kohut, 1971), tact (Poland, 1975), hope (Casement, 1991), and love (Kernberg, 1995a), is also reflected in the literature's inattention to forgiveness. *Finally*, the benevolence implicit in forgiveness gives religious overtones (a la "to err is human, to forgive divine") to the concept. This link, strengthened in the mind if one regards "sin" as the fraternal twin of forgiveness, might also have given psychoanalysts considering the topic a pause.

Nonetheless, the phenomenon of forgiveness remains dynamically, technically, and socially important enough to warrant serious attention from the discipline. My paper is aimed to fill this lacuna. I will begin by highlighting the psychodynamics of giving and seeking forgiveness. I will then attempt to elucidate the evolutionary and developmental correlates of these phenomena. Following this, I will discuss the various psychopathological syndromes involving forgiveness. Finally, I will address the technical significance of these conceptualizations and conclude with some remarks about areas needing further investigation.

DEFINITION AND DYNAMICS

> With the possibility of forgiveness, hate cannot annihilate but can only temporarily anesthetize the loving part of the self in relation to the hated person. With the possibility of forgiveness comes the possibility that the hated person may again become someone to love and thus the experience of hate is more tolerable. Loving behavior following a genuine act of forgiveness may be accompanied by a feeling of joy. —Stolorow, 1971, p. 102

> Like revenge, the fantasy of forgiveness often becomes a cruel torture, because it remains outside of reach of most ordinary human beings. Folk wisdom recognized that to forgive is divine. And even divine forgiveness, in most religious systems, is not unconditional. True forgiveness can not be granted until the perpetrator has sought and earned it through confession, repentance, and restitution. —Herman, 1992, p. 190

Webster (1998) defines *forgiveness* as the "act of forgiving" (p. 458) and the root word, *forgive*, in the following way: "1a:to give up resentment of or claim to requital for (i.e., an insult) b. to grant relief from payment of (i.e., a debt), 2: to cease to feel resentment against (an offender)" (p. 458). The definition indicates that active intent ("to give up . . . ," "to grant . . . ," etc.) is involved in forgiving. It also suggests that forgiveness comprises of two mental operations, namely the resolution of an unpleasant angry emotion within oneself *and* a changed attitude toward an offending party which is then allowed freedom from one's claims over it. While this not made explicit, the change in affect seems to precede the change in object relationship. Another matter of note is that little mention is made of the association between forgiving and forgetting. The widespread colloquial counsel for one to "forgive and forget" notwithstanding, the fact is that forgetting of a traumatic event, especially too early in the course of mourning and forgiveness, betrays defensive distortion of internal and external reality. To be sure, once forgiveness is granted, the injurious event no long preoccupies the conscious mind. However, with a diminished affective charge, the memory of it remains available at a preconscious level; this serves as a potential signal and informs the ego when a similarly traumatic situation is about to arise again.[4] Yet another issue is the distinction between the dynamics of bestowing forgiveness and the dynamics of seeking forgiveness. The first is related to mourning a trauma and the second to the emergence of remorse over one's own hostility.

Bestowing Forgiveness

In dealing with forgiving, one is immediately faced with the psychology of someone who has something (in actual or psychic reality, or both) to forgive, i.e., some trauma, disenfranchisement, or injustice. One is also faced with a perpetrator who is to be forgiven. Thus in order to understand forgiving, one has to take into account the "victim," the "perpetrator," and the trauma that has been inflicted upon the former. This applies equally to whether the scenario of forgiving unfolds in a clinical or a sociopolitical situation (Volkan, 1997, Akhtar, 1999d).

The Rabin-Arafat handshake at the 1995 peace accord between Israelis and Palestinians at the White House is emblematic of mutual forgiveness between fierce opponents, both of whom held themselves to be the victim and the other the perpetrator. Their reconciliation involved diminution of resentment towards each other, letting go of grudges, making compromises, renouncing omnipotent claims, and settling forless than ideal handouts from life. In Kleinian terms, this is a move from the paranoid to the depressive position (Klein, 1948). In paranoid position, "goodness" is claimed for oneself and "badness" is totally externalized. The world is viewed in black and white terms. The self is regarded as a victim and the other as an oppressor. Mistrust, fear, rage, greed, and ruthlessness predominate. In depressive position, it is acknowledged that the self is not "all good" and the other not "all bad." Capacity for empathy appears on the horizon. There also emerge feelings of gratitude for what one has indeed received, guilt and sadness for having hurt others, and reparative longings to redress the damage done. Reality testing improves and the capacity for reciprocal relationships develops.

In clinical as well as social situations of adult life, three factors seem important in making it possible to advance from traumatized victimhood to forgiveness. These are: *revenge, reparation, and reconsideration.* Although "politically incorrect," some *revenge* is actually good for the victim.[5] It puts the victim's hitherto passive ego in an active position. This imparts a sense of mastery and enhances self-esteem. Revenge (in reality or fantasy), allowing the victim to taste the pleasure of sadism, also changes the libido-aggression balance in the self-object relationship. The victim no longer remains innocent and the perpetrator no longer the sole cruel party. Now both seem to have been hurt and to have caused hurt. This shift lays the groundwork for empathy with the enemy and reduces hatred. Forgiveness is the next step.

The second factor that facilitates forgiving is *reparation.* Acknowledgment by the perpetrator that he has indeed harmed the victim is important for the latter's recovery from the trauma (Madanes, 1990; Herman, 1992). It undoes the deleterious effects of "gaslighting" (i.e., denying that anything destructive has been done to someone). To harm someone and then to question his or her perception of it is a double jeopardy, tantamount to "soul murder" (Shengold, 1989). Note in this connection the pain caused to Jews by those who deny the Holocaust and, in a clinical parallel, the anguish induced in a sexually abused child whose "non-abusive" parent refuses to believe the occurrence of such event. Recognizing the Holocaust and acknowledging the sexual abuse, in contrast, improve reality testing and facilitate mourning. Such a move is given further impetus if the perpetrator shows signs of remorse, apologizes, and offers emotional recompense, material reparation, or both.[6] This testifies to the verity of the victim's grievance and functions as a graft over his or her psychic wound. Receiving apology (and reparation) thus adds to the perceptual clarity of the victim's ego. ("I was right in perceiving what was going on to be wrong"). Alongside such cognitive vindication, being apologized to puts the victim in an active position with choice to forgive or not forgive. The passive underdog of yesterday becomes the active bestower of pardon. This improves self-esteem which, in turn, permits further mourning.[7] Yet another manner in which an apology exerts a healing effect is by shifting the psychic locale of the representations of trauma from the actual to the transitional area of the mind. Without labeling it as such, Tavuchis (1991) hints at such a shift when he says that " . . . an apology, no matter how sincere or effective, does not and can not undo what has been done. And yet, in a mysterious way and according to its own logic, this is precisely what it manages to do" (p. 5).

The "mystery" here is that after an apology is made, the trauma begins to get recorded in both the real and the unreal registers of the mind i.e., it acquires a transitional quality. In this realm it can be more easily played with, looked at from various perspectives, and, finally let go.

The libido-aggression shift as a result of taking some revenge, and the rectified perceptual and narcissistic economy as a consequence of receiving reparation, together result in the capacity for better reality testing. This makes a *reconsideration* of the memories of one's traumas possible. Kafka's (1992) view that we repeat not what we have repressed but what we remember in a particular rigid way is pertinent in this context. Its implication for the clinical as well as the social situation is that to let go of grudges we do not need to recall what has been forgotten, but an amplification, elaboration, and revision of what indeed is remembered and re-enacted over and over again. In tandem, these three factors (*revenge, reparation,* and *reconsideration*) improve reality testing, facilitate mourning of earlier injustices, enhance ownership of one's own destructiveness (Steiner, 1993), permit the capacity for concern for the opponent, and allow "mature forgiveness" (Gartner, 1992) to emerge and consolidate.

Seeking Forgiveness

The wish to be forgiven implies that the subject has become cognizant of having done something hurtful (an act of omission or commission) in actual or psychic reality (or both) toward another individual. It also implies that the latter is significant enough for the perpetrator to want to restore the pre-existing relationship with him or her. Seeking forgiveness therefore emanates from not only a capacity for remorse but from a libidinal component in one's feelings for one's victim. Freud (1912) underscored this by saying that "when one forgives a slight that one has received from someone of whom one is fond," the underlying mechanism is "to substract, as it were, the feeling with the lesser intensity [hostile] from that with the greater [affectionate] and to establish the remainder in consciousness" (p. 62). Moses (1999) emphasizes that in seeking forgiveness, the perpetrator must genuinely own the responsibility of the wrong done by him, and express this not only privately but in an explicit and public form;the apology should be highly specific, accompanied by remorse, and a truly felt commitment to avoid doing the harmful act again. Seeking forgiveness thus involves the working–through of narcissistic resistances to recognizing one's being at fault, tolerance of humility (a "one-down" position being inherent in apologizing), and ego resources to offer reparation. This last point is clearly spelled out in various Judeo-Christian and Islamic scriptures; Mishne Torah (HilchotTeshuvah: 2, p. 42), for instance, declares, " . . . someone who injures a colleague, curses a colleague, steals from him, or the like, will never be forgiven until he gives his colleague what he owes him and appeases him" (Maimonides, c. 1200).

Like forgiving, seeking forgiveness is not easy and requires much intrapsychic work. Moreover, once forgiveness is received, the next step is to accept it. To assimilate the new knowledge about the self and the other requires letting go of the masochistic pleasure of guilt, renouncing a debased self-view, and acknowledging the kindness of the hitherto vilified victim of one's own destructiveness.

EVOLUTIONARY AND DEVELOPMENTAL ORIGINS

> Relinquishing vengefulness means forfeiting pride or malice, and perhaps also letting go of an unhealthy attachment. In the psychological sense, forgiveness is not an act which takes place when anger or hurt or revenge are spent. Rather, it involves the introduction of a leavening agent, an amalgamation resulting in something new: a solution.
> —Durham, 1990, p. 135

Empirical research conducted by social psychologists provides insight about how specific kinds of behavior,

> particularly verbal apologies, induce conciliatory effects, forgiveness, and reconciliation. This body of work raises interesting questions about functional similarities between peaceful post-conflict behavior in monkeys, apes, and humans. —Silk, 1998, p. 356

Evolutionary Foundations

In nature, conflicts arise as self-interested individuals compete over limited supplies of food, space, mating partners, social status, refuge from enemies, and other scarce resources. Such conflicts are sharper within the same species since the needs of individual members are similar. However, when the advantages of joint action outweigh the costs of social life, groups and families evolve. Occurrence of conflict between individual members, in such settings, hampers cooperation and threatens to damage social bonds.

To resolve such conflicts, behavioral strategies for conflict-resolution have been evolved by a variety of species ranging from prosimians to great apes. These strategies enable them to repair the damage caused by conflict, restore peaceful contact, and preserve social relationships (deWaal and Aureli, 1996; Silk, 1998). Chimpanzees kiss their opponents after conflicts (deWaal and van Roosmalen, 1979), baboons grunt quietly to their victims minutes after the attack (Cherney et al., 1995) and golden monkeys embrace or groom their former adversaries (Ren, et al., 1991). Such "signals of benign intent" (Silk, 1998, p. 346) serve a socially homeostatic function. While there is risk here of confusing behavioral events with their postulated function, observational studies, both in experimental settings and in natural habitat, suggest that the "peaceful post-conflict signals" (Silk, 1998, p. 347) do have a calming effect upon former opponents by reducing uncertainty whether aggression will continue or is over. Cords (1992) has conducted elegant experimental studies that demonstrate that post-conflict affiliative behaviors from the perpetrator monkeys' side influence the victimized monkeys to feed together with the former. Among baboons, vocalizations serve a similar conciliatory function (Silk et al., 1996). The facilitating effects of such behaviors upon resumption of cooperation after a dispute are more marked (Silk, 1998) than those upon long term social relationships though there is some support (de Waal, 1989) for the latter too. What remains clear is that perpetrators' attempts to make amends are responded by their victims by resumption of contact and "forgiveness" in non-human primates.

Individual Psychic Development

In light of the ebb and flow of aggression within the mother-infant dyad, it is imperative that forgiveness exist on the part of both if the loving and nurturing aspect of their relationship has to be safeguarded. The mother has to forgive her baby's aggressive assaults upon her and the child has to forgive the mother for her empathic shortcomings and actual limitations. This might seem self-evident, yet the fact is that few psychoanalytic investigators invoke the concept of forgiveness in discussing the metabolism of aggression within the mother-infant dyad.

Klein (1937) is an outstanding exception in this regard. She noted that the infant develops pleasant phantasies involving the mother in consequence to satisfaction and hostile fantasies in response to frustration. The latter are tantamount to death wishes. Moreover, in his omnipotence, the baby feels that what he does in phantasy has really taken place; that is to say, he feels that he has actually destroyed the object. Initially such destructive phantasies alternate with pleasant phantasies, each being aroused in affectively charged circumstances of corresponding unpleasureable and pleasurable states. Gradually, however, the child can hold both views of his mother together in his mind. Conflict between love and hate now develops. Guilt enters as a new element into the feeling of love. Klein noted the following:

> even in the small child, one can observe a concern for the loved one which is not, as one might think, merely a sign of dependence upon a friendly and helpful person. Side by side with the destructive impulses in the unconscious mind both of the child and of the adult, there exists a profound urge to make sacrifices, in order to help and to put right loved people who in phantasy have been harmed or destroyed. (Klein, 1937, p. 311)

Klein stated that generosity towards others arises from identification with kindness of one's parents but also from a desire to undo the injuries one has done to them in phantasy when they were being frustrating. She termed this dually determined attitude as "making reparation"[8] (Klein, 1937, p. 313). Implicit in her views is the idea that the one who has attacked in a hostile fashion (i.e., the child) now comes to recognize his hostility, recover his love for his objects, and experience a wish to repair the damage done to them. He forgives them (for their having frustrated him) while simultaneously seeks their forgiveness (for his aggression towards them). Klein traced the source of the child's aggression to both preoedipal, especially oral, and oedipal frustrations. She also elucidated the mother's "drive to reparation" (p. 318), tracing it to her identifications with generative parents as well as her own feelings of guilt over aggression toward them and her child. She emphasized that the desire to make reparation diminishes the despair arising out of guilt and enhances hope and love in life. In this context, the value of forgiveness becomes paramount. "If we have become able, deep in our unconscious minds, to clear our feelings to some extent towards our parents of grievances, and have forgiven them for the frustrations we had to bear, then we can be at peace with ourselves and are able to love others in the true sense of the word" (Klein, 1937, p. 343).

Besides Klein, Winnicott and Mahler have contributed, albeit indirectly, to understanding the ontogenetic origins of forgiveness. Winnicott's (1971) notion of the "survival of object" speaks to this matter. The "ordinarily devoted mother" (Winnicott, 1960, p. 60) allows herself to be used (and, in the infant's mind, even used up) by her essentially ruthless and cannibalistic infant. His "destructiveness" comes from both the nature of his robust hunger and from his rage at her inevitable failures. She nonetheless survives such rage and destruction, remaining available to be discovered again and again. Going through such use-destruction and re-finding cycles of the object, the child begins to sense the forgiving attitude of the mother and thus learns to accept forgiveness. Also, in identification with her, he begins to develop the ego capacity for containing and metabolizing aggression, a necessary preliminary step in forgiving her and, by extension, others. Winnicott's (1963) views on the development of the capacity for concern further elaborate these issues. According to him, there are actually two sets of experiences that contribute to the development of concern, healthy amounts of guilt, and a desire for reparation. One is the "survival" of the object-mother in the face of the child's oral sadism. The second is the continued interest in the child's spontaneity on the part of the environment-mother.

Just as Winnicott's ideas illuminate forgiveness-related phenomena without actually using the term itself, Mahler's (1975) description of the maternal resilience during the child's rapprochement sub-phase touches upon this issue. The child's maddeningly contradictory demands for closeness and distance, protection and freedom, and intimacy and autonomy, are met by the mother with a non-retaliatory stance. Her containment of the aggression mobilized within her allows the child to gradually see her as neither engulfing nor abandoning and himself as neither a passive lap baby nor an omnipotent conqueror of the world. A deeper, more realistic view of mother is now internalized. With this, external dependency upon her diminishes. The contradictory self images are also mended; growing object constancy is accompanied by self constancy. It is this capacity for object constancy that allows for accommodating (and forgiving) the aggression stirred up by frustrations at the hands of the object.

In essence, Klein, Winnicott, and Mahler, all seem to suggest that the metabolism of aggression in the crucible of mother-infant dyad lies at the root of forgiveness versus vengeance. If the aggression is well-metabolized and love predominates in their relationship, forgiveness would be experienced and identified with. If not, seeds of revenge-seeking tendencies are sowed.

However, such emphasis upon the "oral" foundations of the capacity for forgiveness should not be taken to mean that developments during later developmental phases do not contribute to the ontogenesis of forgiveness. Indeed, they do. In the anal phase, the child is faced with the monumental discovery that something belonging to oneself, namely feces, is 'not good' and has to be renounced. Passage through this developmental turmoil consolidates the capacity to 'let go' in general. Later, in the oedipal phase, the child has to sooner or later forgive the parents for their sexual betrayal of him or her[9] and they, in turn, have to forgive him or her for the desires to intrude. The compensations received by each party (protection, love, guidance by the child; narcissistic and generative pleasure of helping an offspring by the parents) are crucial in letting go of the pain caused to the child and parent by exclusion and rivalry respectively.

Relationship between the Evolutionary and the Individual Origins

There exist striking parallels between the "peaceful post-conflict signals" (Silk, 1998) of non-human primates (e.g., grunting, grooming) and the conciliatory behaviors of children after they have had a fight with their peers. These behaviors, including verbal apologies, gift-giving, and affectionate physical contacts (e.g., hugs, gentle touches), enhance the probability that former opponents will reestablish contact following aggression and might also contribute to preserving the long-term relationship between the opponents.

While the similarity between the conciliatory gestures of non-human primates and those of children is indeed significant, the heuristic path from this observation onwards is fraught with difficulties. The risk of circular reasoning, reductionism, and tautological leaps is great.

Unanswered questions abound. Is it reasonable, for instance, to equate the two behaviors owing to their superficial similarities? Could what the monkeys and apes show be labeled *proto-forgiveness*, an archaic prototype of human forgiveness? Since the complexity of peaceful post-conflict signals increases as the monkeys approach anthropoid proximity, say in the form of great apes, is it possible that human forgiveness is merely the next step in this evolutionary ladder? Or, could the move from paranoid to depressive position, which is supposed to underlie human infantile reparation, also exist in non-human primates? Since in attributing such processes to preverbal human infants we are largely in the realm of speculation, could similar processes be hypothesized to exist in animals? While such matters await exploration, one thing seems certain: the purpose of all forgiveness, *mentalized* (Fonagy and Target, 1997) or not, is to assure cooperation. This was something the primitive man, with his relative weakness vis-à-vis the larger forces of nature, badly needed. In order to establish groups and, later, families, he needed to overlook ("forgive") minor conflicts with other members of his species. And, in an ontogenetic repetition of phylogeny, the human infant, dependent as he is upon other's care of him, needs to be forgiving; holding grudges against mother would not get a child very far!

All in all, therefore, it seems that the attitude of forgiveness has survival value and might have acquired a "hard-wired" status from this evolutionary imperative. The ritualization, complexity, and psychic elaboration of forgiveness, however, is greater in human beings than in non-human primates, though both show evidence of such capacity. The evocation of this capacity seems to have its own prerequisites (e.g., maternal love in case of human beings). Without them, the intrinsic capacity might atrophy or develop along pathological lines.

PSYCHOPATHOLOGICAL SYNDROMES

> At times the superego, which had its origin in the introjection of an external object, is reprojected onto external objects for the purpose of getting rid of guilt feelings. Compulsion neurotics often try to avoid a sense of guilt by appealing to others to forgive them. —Fenichel, 1945, p. 165

> Forgiving and being reconciled are not about pretending that things are other than they are. It is not patting one another on the back and turning a blind eye to the wrong. True reconciliation exposes the awfulness, the abuse, the pain, the degradation, the truth. It could even sometimes make things worse. It is a risky undertaking, but in the end it is worthwhile, because in the end dealing with the real situation helps to bring real healing. Spurious reconciliation can bring only spurious healing. —Tutu, 1999, pp. 270-71

Psychopathological syndromes involving forgiveness include (i) inability to forgive, (ii) premature forgiveness, (iii) excessive forgiveness, (iv) pseudo-forgiveness, (v) relentless forgiveness-seeking, (vi) inability to accept forgiveness, (vii) inability to seek forgiveness, and (viii) imbalance between capacities for self-forgiveness and forgiveness toward others.

Inability to Forgive

Some people just cannot forgive. They continue to harbor resentment toward their offenders for months, years, and often for their entire life-time. They hold on to a grudge (Socarides, 1966) and are given to chronic hatred (Kernberg, 1992; Blum, 1997; Akhtar, 1999c), though they might not be overtly vindictive. Diagnostically, this group includes individuals with severe personality disorders, especially paranoid personality, severe antisocial personality, and those with the syndrome of malignant narcissism (Kernberg, 1989). When given to overt revenge-seeking, such individuals disregard all limits in their destructive pursuit of their offender. Melville's (1851) Captain Ahab is an example-par-excellence of such unrelenting "narcissistic rage" (Kohut, 1972), including its self-destructive consequences. Toward the end of his vengeful saga, Ahab puts his hatred into words:

> Towards thee I roll, thou all destroying but unconquering whale; to the last I grapple with the; from hell's heart I stab at thee; for hate's sake, I spit my last breath at thee. Sink all coffins and all hearses to one common pool! and since neither can be mine, let me then tow to pieces while still chasing thee, though tied to thee, thou damned whale! (Melville, 1851, p. 575)

Premature Forgiveness

A second syndrome is characterized by individuals who seem too readily prepared to forgive and forget injuries afflicted upon them. Obsessional neurotics, with their characteristic reaction formation against aggression, tend to fall in this category. They quickly "forgive" others since not doing so would force them to acknowledge they feel hurt and angry. Such conflict-based premature forgiveness is a compromise formation (between aggressive impulses and superego prohibitions against them) and can be clinically analyzed as such. A more severe form of premature forgiveness is defect-based. Individuals with such a malady feel no entitlement, lack a "healthy capacity for indignation" (Ambassador Nathaniel Howell, personal communication, April 1996), and can not hate (Galdston, 1987). They do not adequately register that they have been wronged. Their object-hunger is intense and their dependence upon others great. Hence, they are all too willing to let go of hurts and injustices. Diagnostically, this group includes weak, unentitled, schizoid, and "as-if" (Deutsch, 1942) personalities with a childhood background of multiple and unreliable caretakers.

Excessive Forgiveness

Excessive forgiveness is seen in masochistic individuals. They repeatedly forgive traumas inflicted upon them by their tormentors and never seem to learn from experience. They live in a state of near-addiction to those who are sadistic or can easily be manipulated in becoming sadistic (Berliner, 1958; Kernberg, 1992), repeatedly submitting to them for further humiliation and torture. States of "co-dependency" in the partners of addicts also depict the masochistic dimension of excessive forgiveness. The addict continues to be self-destructive while hoping that the drug will somehow magically solve intrapsychic problems, and the codependent individual remains relentlessly optimistic that a terrible relationship will, through their ever-forgiving attitude, become all right. The following poem of mine (titled "The Second Poem") portrays this very dimension of masochistic pathology.

Undoing
    the psychic truth,
(Or, speaking from a second room
    within the self?)
Something destructively large-hearted
    took him by his hand,
    led him to the balcony of forgiveness
Again and again.

Pseudo-Forgiveness

Yet another psychopathological group is constituted by individuals who practice *pseudo-forgiveness*.[10] On surface, they reconcile with their "enemies," but inwardly they maintain ill-will and do not mourn (Sohn, 1989). Some of them are genuinely split into parts. One part of their mind accepts reality and is able to let go of previous hurts and injuries while the other, a mad part, holds on to omnipotent dreams of reversing history altogether (Bion, 1957). In a further split within itself, this mad part, on the one hand, maintains that the glorious "pre-trauma" days can actually be brought back,[11] and, on the other hand, ruthlessly carries on vengeful attacks on the (alleged) offender.

Alongside such individuals are those with pronounced antisocial trends and where *pseudo-forgiveness* emanates from calculated lying and hiding of true psychic reality for strategic advantages. Joseph Stalin's wry remark that "revenge is a dish that is best eaten cold" and Joseph Kennedy Sr.'s advice to his son John that he should "not get mad but get even" are examples of such perversions of forgiveness.

Relentless Forgiveness Seeking

Some individuals are relentlessly apologetic about ordinary errors of daily life. They betray a heavy burden of unconscious guilt. Apologizing for their actions does not relieve them of the prohibited and morally repugnant hostile and sexual intentions that lurk in their unconscious. However, the act of repeatedly seeking pardon itself can come to have hostile aims and a hidden sexual discharge value. One of Abraham's (1925) patients gave a very instructive example of this from his childhood.

> His behaviour at that time, even when he seemed to be full of guilt-feelings and repentance, was a mixture of hostile and tormenting drives. These feelings were secretly closely linked with masturbation, whilst externally they appeared to be connected with other small misdeeds in the nursery. Any trivial wrong-doing was invariably followed by the same reaction. The boy would cling to his mother and say in endless repetition: "Forgive me, mother, forgive me, mother!" This behaviour did in fact express his contrition, but it also expressed far more strongly two other tendencies. In the first place, he continued in this way to torment his mother, whilst asking her forgiveness. Furthermore, it was apparent then, as also in later years, that instead of trying to reform himself, he always preferred to repeat his faults and to obtain forgiveness for them. This was also a disturbing factor during his psycho-analytical treatment. We found, moreover, that the rapid rattling-off of the formula of atonement had been devised in imitation of the rhythm of his masturbation. Thus the forbidden sexual wish contrived to break through in this concealed form. (pp. 323–324)

Inability to Accept Forgiveness

Closely akin to those who repeatedly apologize are individuals who remain tormented, often for months and years, despite having been forgiven by others. They seem unable to accept pardon and continue to suffer from remorse and its depressive and persecutory consequences. A striking example of this is to be found in Chekov's (1927) story, *The Death of a Government Clerk*. Vicissitudes of anally regressive hostility, and the defense of reaction-formation against it, are illustrated there via the tale of a Russian postal-clerk who spends his life savings to obtain a highly expensive seat in the Bolshevik opera only to sneeze and squirt his nasal secretions on the bald head of the man sitting in front of him. The protagonist apologizes and is forgiven. However, he cannot settle and remains remorseful. He apologizes again and again. Each time, he is forgiven although with ever-increasing annoyance by the bald man. The clerk writes to him, visits him in the latter's work place, to seek forgiveness just one more time. Finally, the bald man gets enraged and throws him out of his office. That evening the clerk comes home, sits on his living room sofa, and dies!

Unconscious guilt clearly plays a big role in the dynamics of these individuals. In talking about those involved in such endless self-condemnation, Cooper (1995, quoted in Akhtar, 1999c, p. 222) pointedly speaks of their "ferocious superegos and masochistic inclinations."

Inability to Seek Forgiveness

Individuals who lack empathy with others often do not seek forgiveness. They seem oblivious to the harm and injuries they have caused to others. Such oblivion is often the result of severe superego defects, lack of love for others, and the associated incapacity for remorse. At other times, it originates from a tenacious denial of blemishes in oneself. Such denial is aimed at managing paranoid anxieties (e.g., the fear of being severely shamed by others upon apologizing to them) and keeping a shaky self esteem intact. Antisocial and narcissistic personalities are thus especially prone to such behavior (Kernberg, 1984; Akhtar, 1992b).

Imbalances in Forgiving Others Versus Forgiving Self

Psychopathology is also evident when there is a gross discrepancy in one's capacity to bestow forgiveness upon others and oneself. Narcissistic, paranoid, and antisocial individuals readily absolve themselves of responsibility of having caused any harm. They either deny it totally or see their hostile actions as justifiable responses to other's unfairness towards them. They readily forgive themselves but do not forgive others with the same ease. Masochistic individuals are prone to do just the opposite. Repeatedly, they turn a blind eye to their (real or imagined) tormentors, remaining devoted to them. They forgive others but continue to punish themselves relentlessly.

TECHNICAL IMPLICATIONS

> Only when the super-ego becomes less cruel, less demanding as well of perfection, is the ego capable of accepting an internal object which is not perfectly repaired, can accept

> compromise, forgive and be forgiven, and experience hope and gratitude. —Rey, 1986, p. 30

> The ability of the therapeutic relationship to endure hate and aggression serves as a living contradiction to the notion that either the patient or the therapist is 'all bad'. It is this living witness to the reality of ambivalence that makes the capacity for forgiveness possible. —Gartner, 1992, p. 27

Concerns around forgiveness surface in the course of psychoanalytic treatment in many ways. With severely traumatized individuals, *forgiving* (or not forgiving) those who have hurt them (and the transferential reactivations of such objects) sooner or later occupies the center stage of clinical dialogue. With individuals who suffer from remorse over real or imagined injuries caused to others, *being forgiven* by actual external figures (and, in transference, the analyst) becomes a concern.[12]

Individuals who have suffered from severe trauma in childhood (e.g., sexual abuse, physical violence and cruelty, massive and sustained neglect) bring with them an internal world rife with split self- and object representations with a predominance of hate over love and of malice over concern for their objects. Internally they cling to a retrospectively idealized "all-good" mother representation of early infancy (Mahler et al., 1975) while simultaneously holding a contradictory and aggressively charged image of her (and other early objects). The former substrate gives rise to idealizing transferences of varying forms and tenacities. The latter results in guiltless, destructive attacks against the analyst. The patient claims (often, correctly) to have been hurt, abused, and deprived of what was an inalienable right in childhood i.e., having love, an intact family, benevolent guidance, etc. Taking a victim stance, the patient feels justified in attacking the offending parties and the analyst who inevitably comes to represent them. He or she displays an unconscious striving for totally undoing the effects of the childhood trauma or even erasing its occurrence in the first place. Suffering from pathological hope and harboring a malignant "someday" fantasy (Akhtar, 1991, 1996), the patient strives to obtain absolute satisfaction from the analyst without any concern for the latter. He demands that the analyst provide exquisite empathy, love, sex, treatment with reduced fees, access to his or her home, sessions on demand, and encounters at all kinds of hours. As the patient finds the analyst to be lacking in this regard, he berates him or her as useless, unloving, and even cruel. The patient attacks not only the analyst's concern and devotion, but also those parts of his own personality that seem aligned with the analyst and can see the inconsolable nature of his own hunger. It is as if the patient has an *intrapsychic terrorist organization* (Akhtar, 1999d) that seeks to assassinate his observing ego because it is collaborating with the analyst and is willing to renounce the lost, dimly remembered, and retrospectively idealized "all-good" days of early infancy in favor of realistic satisfactions in the current life. This internal destructive agency also renders the patient enormously stoic. Recourse to infantile omnipotence makes any amount of waiting bearable (Potamianou, 1992). For such individuals, the present has only secondary importance. They can tolerate any current suffering in the hope that future rewards will make it all worthwhile.

What, under such circumstances, can move the patient towards forgiveness? As discussed earlier, the factors of revenge, reparation, and reconsideration working in tandem can facilitate mourning of trauma, permit acknowledgment of one's own destructiveness, release the capacity for concern for the opponent, and allow forgiveness to emerge. *Revenge* is taken by the patient in the form of relentless sadistic assaults on the analyst. Continued hostility towards those viewed as offenders (e.g., patient's parents in actual adult life), even if the latter are trying to make amends, is another form of grudge-holding and revenge. *Reparation* is available to the patient in the form of the analyst's lasting empathy and devotion that "survives" (Winnicott, 1971) despite the patient's attacks upon it. *Reconsideration* results from recontextualization and revision of childhood memories (Kafka, 1992); negative images of early caretakers now come to be supplanted with the recall of hitherto repressed positive interactions with them.

However, for such advance to occur, resistances to acknowledging love for the analyst's tolerance as well as to recognizing one's own contributions to the current (and even, at times, childhood) suffering must be interpreted. Defenses against the awareness of sadomasochistic pleasure in ongoing hatred (Kernberg, 1995a) as well as the defensive functions of the unforgiving attitude itself (Jones, 1928; Fairbairn, 1940; Searles, 1956) need to be interpreted. The fact that giving up hatred and forgiving others also opens up newer, less familiar (e.g., oedipal) psychic realms for exploration also makes the patient anxious and regressively cling to a simplistic victimhood[13] which, in turn, fuels continuing warfare with the analyst along the lines mentioned above. While work along the lines mentioned above usually occurs in a gradual, piecemeal fashion, occasionally a firm confrontation with an alternate way of being becomes necessary.

Clinical Vignette: 12

Patricia Brennan, an unmarried Catholic librarian in her mid-thirties had felt immensely rejected by her mother as a child. Her sense was that she was all but forgotten following the birth of a brother when she was nearly three years old. Over the course of a long analysis, the patient incessantly talked of her despair at this rejection. She wanted (a desire she was able to reveal only after painstaking defense analysis) me to mother her, thus making up for all what she needed and did not receive during her childhood. She wanted on-demand sessions, love, physical holding, special status, adoption, travel together, everything. Her despair at not receiving all this was thick and she slowly turned me into a highly desired but ungiving and rejecting figure. She began to hate me.

Condensed with such split maternal transference was a powerful sexual component emanating from her childhood relationship to a deeply admired father who fluctuated between flirtatiously rescuing her and abruptly dropping her from attention. Not surprisingly, this led to an addictive bond with father where idealization was tenaciously maintained and all aggression was shifted to the mother. In this mental set, the patient wanted to have sex with me, be my beloved, marry me. Lacking any countertransference resonance and replete with a desperate, coercive quality, the situation was actually one of a *malignant erotic transference* (Akhtar, 1994).

Analytic work with Patricia would fall apart again and again. Desperate longings for the pre-traumatic, "all-good" mother and the idealized father (and their substitute the "all-giving" analyst) would vehemently surface. At the same time, vicious attacks upon the rejecting mother/and oblivious father (and their recreation in form of the 'bad' analyst) would begin. In such hours, the patient often compared herself to Captain Ahab and me to Moby Dick, his nemesis. She felt her attacks were totally justified. After all, wasn't I depriving her of what she felt she needed? "What would you do if someone was threatening to cut off your oxygen supply?" she would retort. Attempts to help her see that marrying me was hardly akin to needing oxygen would be felt as further humiliation from me and fuel her hostility. Psychological-mindedness would be lost and previously gained insights would be put aside. Reconstruction of events that might have triggered the regression would be sometimes helpful in dislodging the impasse, sometimes not.

In one such session during the tenth year of her analysis, with Patricia going on berating me, I firmly said to her "Look, since you are so fond of metaphorically likening us to Captain Ahab and Moby Dick, permit me also to introduce a metaphor. Tell me, what do you think made it possible for Yitzahk Rabin and Yasser Arafat to shake hands with each other?" The patient responded in a fashion that was typical for her in states of regression. "What does that have to do with anything? Besides, I am not interested in politics anyway." I then said "No, I think what I said is of serious significance to us. Your metaphor has to do with revenge and mutual destruction. Mine has to do with letting go of grudges, however justified, and forgiveness."

Of course, this intervention in of itself did not give rise to an immediate shift from hatred to forgiveness. It did, however, lay the groundwork for such advance and became a landmark in her analysis to which we would return again and again in subsequent months and years. Before deeper mourning of childhood trauma (and the built-in analytic deprivations that had become condensed with them) became possible, there was a protracted transitional phase. In that phase, she developed a collaborative, and mournful mutuality with me, "forgiving" me for not marrying her on the one hand and retaining a hostile and unforgiving, even if less vitriolic, stance towards me on the other hand. The latter, often worked as an *intrapsychic terrorist organization* (Akhtar, 1999d) which sought to destroy not only the external peacemakers (i.e., me) but also her own internal functions aligned with the former. It was only after a protracted transitional period of this sort that the patient became able to see her own destructiveness (and recall her childhood hostile manipulativeness toward her mother). Remorse and forgiveness followed.

Throughout such work, the analyst has to remain respectful of the patient's need for apology from those who have hurt him.[14] He must demonstrate to the patient the awareness that being apologized for a wrong does improve reality testing and that such perceptual clarity is useful for the patient since often the original abuse was denied by the perpetrator or other family members. It also puts the recipient of apology in an active position, undoing the humiliation of passivity and lack of control.

At the same time, the analyst has to remember that not all trauma might be forgivable. The hurt, pain, and rage felt, for instance, by a Holocaust survivor in encountering a Nazi camp guard is hardly subject to ordinary psychic metabolism (Hooberman, 2010). There might be other individual circumstances of torture, abuse, and humiliation that are less public but nonetheless equally unforgivable. Upon encountering such scenarios in the clinical situation, the analyst must not uphold a manic ideal of kindness. Indeed, he might even help the patient feel not too guilty about his lack of forgiveness.

Premature forgiveness should also draw the analyst's attention. Here the analytic task[15] is to bring the patient's attention to it so that the roots of his too readily forgiving others (including the analyst) may be explored. If the tendency is based upon splitting and denial, then the sequestered aggression needs to be brought into the treatment; this is what Kernberg (1992) means by attempting to change a *schizoid* or *psychopathic* transference into a *paranoid transference*. If, however, the tendency is owing to a genuine lack of entitlement then the roots of that should be explored. Similarly, pseudo-forgiveness, based upon maintaining two mental registers and secretly holding on to grudges, needs to be exposed by confrontation and defense analysis. The same holds true if the analyst notices gross discrepancies in the patient's capacity to forgive himself versus others or vice-versa. Underlying narcissistic-masochistic proclivities are what seem to deserve attention in such instances. Issues of unconscious guilt over real or imagined childhood "crimes" (including separating from a needy parent, surviving a deceased parent or sibling, and the more usual oedipal transgressions) need to be kept in mind while listening to those who are chronically apologetic and cannot forgive themselves despite other's having forgiven them.

Besides such patient-related scenarios, the analyst has to deal with forgiveness from his own side in two ways. One involves the controversial matter of apologizing to the patient and seeking forgiveness. The other, perhaps even more contested and heuristically elusive, is the analyst's providing the patient an opportunity to apologize and seek forgiveness from him. Here is an example of the former stance.

Clinical Vignette: 13

In the throes of a regressive transference, Charlotte Boyd entered my office enraged and waving a finger. Approaching the couch, she said, "I have a lot on my mind today and I want to do all the talking. I don't want you to speak even a single word!" A little taken aback, I mumbled "okay." Charlotte shouted, "I said 'not one word' and you have already fucked up this session!" Now sitting on my chair behind her, I was even more rattled. Had I done wrong by speaking at all? As the patient lay on the couch, angry and stiff, I started to think. Perhaps I thought she is so inconsolable today, so intent on forcing me into the role of a depriving person, that she has found a way to see even the gratification of her desire as its frustration. Not entirely satisfied with this explanation, I decided to wait, and think on it. It then occurred to me that maybe she was rightly angered by my saying "okay." In my very act of concession, I had asserted my will and thus paradoxically deprived her of the omnipotence she seemed to need. I was about to make an interpretation along these lines when it occurred to me that in so doing I would be repeating my mistake. I decided to say only "I am sorry" and left the remaining thought unspoken. Charlotte relaxed, and the tension in the room began to lessen. After ten minutes of silence, she said, "Well, this session has been messed up. I had so many things to say. "After a pause, she said, "Among the various things on my mind . . . ," and thus the session gradually "started. " By the time we ended, things were going pretty smoothly.

Now I am aware that a novice too could have said, "I am sorry," but I believe the underlying discernment of ego needs would be missing there. In saying I was sorry, I was acknowledging that I had failed her by not understanding that she needed omnipotent control over me and to have no boundaries, as it were, between us at all.

In discussing the place of apology in psychoanalysis, Goldberg (1987) delineates two possible stances. One stance, exemplified in the clinical material above, emanates from the analytic perspective which suggests that via empathic immersion, the analyst may attain an ability to see the patient's world as he or she does *and* the major burden of achieving and sustaining such intersubjective agreement rests upon the analyst. In this view the failure of intersubjectivity would largely be the analyst's responsibility and thus necessitate an apology from the analyst. The second stance, mentioned by Goldberg, holds the analyst to be more informed about 'reality' and thus viewing transference, however plausible its content might be, as a distortion of that reality. In this perspective, the differences in perception between the patient and the analyst never call for an apology from the analyst. Deftly and convincingly, Goldberg argues the untenability of either extreme position, concluding that while the wish to apologize may be countertransference-based, it does have a place at certain times in certain treatments. Of course, the patient's experience of the analyst's apology needs to be then explored and handled in a relatively traditional way.

Next, as mentioned above, is the question of analyst's providing the patient an opportunity to apologize for his erstwhile destructive attacks upon the analyst.[16] Kernberg (1976) approaches this point when he describes the appearance of intense remorse in the later phases of analysis of narcissistic patients. They become aware of how badly they have treated others in their life, including the analyst, and wish to seek their forgiveness. However, it was Winnicott (1947) who most directly addressed this matter. He declared that a patient who has been hostile for a long time during treatment must, when he or she becomes better integrated, be told how he has burdened, the analyst throughout their work.[17] Winnicott says that this is " . . . obviously a matter fraught with danger, and it needs the most careful timing. But I believe an analysis is incomplete if even towards the end it has not been possible for the analyst to tell the patient what he, the analyst, did unbeknown for the patient whilst he was ill, in the early stages. Until this interpretation is made the patient is kept to some extent in the position of infant—one who cannot understand what he owes to his mother"(p. 202).

Ideally, the patient should arrive at such understanding by himself and as a result of diminishing hate and growing empathy for others. However patients who are too narcissistically vulnerable to sincerely "apologize" to the analyst and seek forgiveness might actually benefit by their analyst's providing them an occasion to do so by acknowledging his having felt burdened by them as the treatment was going on. Such intervention should not emanate from hostile countertransference. It should come from a depressive working-through of the reality that the analyst has indeed felt put upon, at times even abused, by the patient during the course of their work.

MORE RECENT CONTRIBUTIONS

> Apologies' symbolic power could be compared to the power of transference love. Like the case of transference love, one may argue that their effect is superficial and that the resentment would eventually reappear, as old symptoms do in transference cure. Apologies by themselves are not adaptive. The neutralization of aggression—by-product of the

> analytic process—is what makes them adaptive. —Tylim, 2005, p. 270

> While almost any single act may be forgivable, it may become unforgivable in the context of a negative psychological climate. Forgiveness takes place most readily in the context of a mutually respectful relationship. I would go so far as to argue that no intimate relationship can survive unscathed without the patience of undeserved forgiveness. —Person, 2007, p. 396

A PEP web search for papers containing the word "forgiveness" in their title reveals twenty-three publications following the first appearance of my paper on this topic (Akhtar, 2002). Three analysts, namely Melvin Lansky, Shahrzad Siassi, and Henry Smith, have contributed more than one paper each; Roy Schafer and Peter Fonagy, two stalwarts of our field, have also written on the topic and deserve inclusion here. In what follows, therefore, I would largely focus upon the work of these individuals while referring to others only in passing.

Melvin Lansky has made many significant contributions to the psychoanalytic understanding of forgiveness. In a sophisticated psychoanalytic study of Sophocles' *Philoctetes*, Lansky (2003) proposed that the letting go of grudges and chronic hatred happens via overcoming the felt danger of being mocked and shamed by one's betrayers. This, in turn, takes place due to the modification of one's ego ideal by identification with a freshly idealized other. Extrapolating such dynamics to the psychoanalytic treatment situation, Lansky made a bold suggestion: experiences and occurrences in external reality might be necessary to consolidate the result of psychic growth due to working through major transferences. He stated the following:

> Just as Neoptolemus' influence on Philoctetes is essential but not sufficient for Philoctetes'[18] capacity to forgive and carry on, so does psychoanalytic work involve a lacuna between our work and the end state of change. We often do not know the exact connection between the end results of our psychoanalytic work and our best efforts to explain it. The connecting experience is made possible by psychoanalytic treatment, but not always in its control. Just as Heracles' appearance is something for which Philocetetes' relationship with Neoptolemus prepared him to receive, but nonetheless

> lies outside of that relationship, so do we depend, even in the best analytic work, on external circumstances, "divine interventions," to complete the process of working through. (pp. 438–439)

Lansky (2005) again addressed the topic of forgiveness—or rather, unforgiveness, via an investigation of Euripides' *Medea*. He highlighted the transformation of a deep sense of shame into diabolical vengefulness that, in turn, makes forgiveness impossible. His subsequent contribution (Lansky, 2007, 2009) furthered this theme while adding the splitting of self along the shame-rage oscillation in such cases. Forgiveness, within this perspective, arises from the resolution of such splitting. Linking his new insights with his earlier proposals, Lansky (2009) declared that "working through of the splitting underlying the retributive emotions involves the increased bearability of shame, often with the help of an identification with the analyst" (p. 374). Forgiveness toward one's real or imaginary tormentors might then become possible.

Another major contributor to this realm is Shahrzad Siassi. In a series of contributions (2004, 2007, 2009) and in a recent book (Siassi, 2013), she has addressed the ties between bitterness, loss, mourning, acceptance, and forgiveness. Anchoring her proposals in the vivid, poignant, and convincing account of her analytic work of a man in his mid-sixties who had lost his father at age eight months, Siassi (2004) demonstrated the salutary impact of belated mourning on the capacity for forgiveness. Thawing of unresolved grief and the associated affect of bitterness led to awareness of deep ambivalence toward the lost father, at first, and then, gradually, to forgive the heretofore despised parent and even his own self for holding such feelings. Siassi noted that forgiveness is a more active process than mourning, and is "directed toward the unconscious psychic reorganization initiated by the work of mourning" (pp. 930-931). Moreover, while mourning consolidates separation from the object, forgiveness brings me back to it. In Siassi's words, "In forgiveness, the letting go of bitterness and vindictiveness is motivated by the unconscious wish to repair a powerful narcissistic injury, and to become reconciled with someone whose absence or negative presence has been felt as an impoverishment, and, in fact, as a partial loss, of one's very self" (2004, p. 934).

In subsequent contributions, Siassi (2007, 2009) emphasized the relational foundations of forgiveness while acknowledging that "some wrongs seem to preclude the possibility of forgiveness" (2007, p. 1424).

She also differentiated forgiveness from mere "acceptance," since the latter does not involve the re-establishment of an internal bond with the wrong-doing object. Forgiveness, in contrast, seeks to salvage the positive that remains in the relationship after the betrayal of expectations. To quote Siassi herself on this point,

> I hold that it is precisely when the bond is intrapsychically significant that there is a wish to reinstate it and so reconstitute a damaged narcissistic equilibrium. At such times of decision, forgiveness is an unconscious expression of the need for human relationships, and of the preference for quality over quantity in the experience of life. The lessening of anger and the lowering of primitive defenses that follow successful mourning allow for a softening of the superego—this is both a prerequisite and a consequence of forgiveness. Ultimately, forgiveness allows for the renewal of an accepting and potentially more loving relationship with oneself and the world, as well as the other. It is this restitution of the narcissistic balance of personality through the realignment of internal relationships that gives forgiveness its psychodynamic importance and its potential for developmental gain. (2007, p. 1424)

In contrast to Lansky and Siassi, Henry Smith (2002, 2008) questioned the usefulness of the concept of forgiveness, saying that the concept (i) is too seductive and can be readily idealized, (ii) can serve defensive functions, (iii) does not exist in the unconscious and, (iv) can blunt the analyst's appreciation of the aggressive dimensions of psychoanalytic work. These objections have respective counterpoints: (i) any psychoanalytic concept can become idealized, (ii) any concept can serve self-defensive functions, (iii) how does Smith know it to be "the *fact* that in the unconscious, there is no such thing as forgiveness" (2008, p. 919, italics added). Moreover, to deny the validity of a concept because it might not exist in the unconscious is to unreasonably minimize the significance of conscious phenomena. And, (iv) rather than blunting the appreciation of aggression, the concept of forgiveness and its twin, 'un-forgiveness' (Lansky, 2001), primes us for a deeper appreciation of it during psychoanalytic work.

Back then to our discourse on forgiveness. We note the contributions of two most outstanding psychoanalysts, namely, Roy Schafer and Peter Fonagy. Schafer (2005) takes Shakespeare's *King Lear* as the starting point of his discussion and questions the possibility of total forgiveness when one has been grievously injured. He believes that even when the perpetrator earnestly apologizes, some un-forgiveness persists in the victim's heart. Schafer notes that the issue of forgiveness usually arises during the later phases of analysis. Having withdrawn projections, mended splitting, and strengthened reality testing, the analysands can no longer maintain a self-righteous or self-condemning view of themselves.

> Now better prepared to see the self and others as whole, complexly motivated persons with distinct life histories, they realize that what is at issue, at least in relation to their own past and present, destructive feelings, fantasies, and actions, is not so much forgiveness as the need for reconciliation with their own life histories, some hard reparative work, and the need to keep a watchful eye on regressive moves towards persisting unconscious un-forgiveness. (p. 390)

Schafer's perspective differs from that of Smith (2005), who declared forgiveness to be merely the sense of well-being that results from good analytic work. Instead, Schafer suggests that analysis puts one in touch with one's own destructiveness and one's own contributions to their suffering, forces one to questions the desire to forgive or be forgiven. His views seem akin to those of Steiner (1993) who had earlier stated,

> The wish to exact revenge must be recognized, and responsibility for the damage you have done to our objects has to be accepted. This means that to be forgiven, bad elements in our nature have to be accepted but sufficient good feeling must exist for us to feel regret and the wish to make reparation. (p. 83)

Schafer concludes that a deep psychoanalytic understanding of oneself and one's relationships can make forgiveness appear altogether irrelevant; waiving the question of forgiveness might then seem the wiser course to follow.

Fonagy (2009) underscored the dialectic between forgiveness and attachment by stating that "libidinal cathexis is the seed of forgiveness but also its primary product. Forgiveness and the growth of love go hand in hand in a mutually facilitative, benign cycle" (p. 442). Fonagy noted that true forgiveness assumes mentalization, without the capacity to attribute mental contents to oneself or others (as happens in severely schizoid and narcissistic characters), the working-through of aggression necessary for forgiveness can not take place.

> From the mentalizing perspective, forgiveness demands not only sufficient reflectiveness to depict the experience of the other with clarity adequate to prompt the process of reappraisal implied by genuine forgiveness, but, even more importantly, it entails the capacity to be able to reflect on one's own motivations with clarity sufficient to appraise oneself and one's destructive intent. Within this frame of reference, anything other than an accurate and full review of one's state of mind in relation to having damaged someone is tantamount to pseudo-forgiveness. (p. 446-447)

To reiterate, understanding the mental state of the other is both a prerequisite for and a product of empathy and this, in turn, can facilitate forgiveness. It is equally important to become fully aware of one's own motivations and the consequences of one's actions. Forgiving others and seeking forgiveness from others then are processes that require not only the metabolism of self and other directed aggression but a conscious registration of that metabolism.

Now, in putting together the contributions of Lansky, Siassi, Smith, Schafer, and Fonagy, a spectrum is revealed. Lansky and Siassi clearly subscribe to the validity of the concept, elucidate its ties to other affects (e.g., shame, bitterness), and differentiate it from other psychic processes (e.g., acceptance, mourning). Fonagy's views are akin to those of Lansky and Siassi insofar as he also holds forgiveness to be a complex process related to attachment and, more importantly, to mentalization. However, by concluding that "genuine forgiveness is an elusive experience and that the label is more often used in relation to pseudo-manifestations" (p. 450), he leaves the space for some doubt here. Enter Henry Smith. He vehemently discards the concept and does not regard it as useful. Schafer, in contrast, recognizes forgiveness but suggests that upon deep psychoanalytic work (and the resulting contact with the ultimately ambivalent nature of all human relationships, and the ubiquitousness of aggression), the issue of forgiveness can appear irrelevant; the choice is then of acceptance and going-on or non-acceptance and discontinuity.

This survey of the psychoanalytic literature on forgiveness that has emerged since 2002 is far from exhaustive. Many contributions have remained unaddressed and the reader would benefit by looking up Gottlieb's (2004) re-appraisal of Sophocles' *Philoctetes*, Wangh's (2006) essay on revenge and forgiveness in the wake of gay student, Matthew Shepard's, murder in Laramie, Wyoming, Tylim's (2005) discussion of the role of apology in spurring forgiveness, especially in the sociopolitical realm, and Lafarge's (2009) paper on forgiveness in Charles Dickens' *David Copperfield*, to name a few.

CONCLUDING REMARKS

> The idea of a group or its leader asking for forgiveness from another group or its leader may be a potentially powerful gesture if the groundwork has truly been laid. Forgiveness is possible only when the group that suffered has done a significant amount of mourning. The focus should be on helping with the work of mourning and not on the single (seemingly magical) act of asking forgiveness.
> —Volkan, 1997, p. 226

Despite covering considerable ground, I remain aware that many important areas pertaining to forgiveness have remained unaddressed in this paper. The *first* such area pertains to gender. Little is known about the qualitative or quantitative similarities and/or differences in the two sexes in this regard. Women's deeper capacity for commitment in love relations and for making context-based decisions in the moral sphere (Gilligan. 1982) suggest that they might possess a greater capacity for forgiveness than men. However, further clinical and empirical data is needed to confirm or refute this impression.

The *second* such area pertains to the sociopolitical realm. The importance of a perpetrator apologizing and making reparation to its victim is emphatically clear in the recent German apologies and reparations to the victims of Holocaust, the North American expression of remorse for the tyranny of slavery, the offer by the United States of recompense to the Japanese Americans interred in camps during the second World War, and the work of Bishop Desmond Tutu's Truth and Reconciliation Commission in South Africa. At a less dramatic level is the prayer written by Archbishop Renbert Weakland of Milwaukee which builds on Pope John Paul II's request that Catholics observe this year's Ash Wednesday by reflecting upon the pain inflicted on Jews by Christians over the last millennium. To quote one out of the eight stanzas of this prayer, "I ask for forgiveness for all the statements that implied that the Jewish people were no longer loved by God, that God had abandoned them, that they were guilty of deicide, that they were, as a people, being punished by God. Amen"(Weakland, quoted in Gallagher, 2000, p. 17).

Interdisciplinary studies, where sociopolitical processes inform psychoanalysis and psychoanalysis informs the latter (see Volkan, 1997 in this connection), are thus badly needed to enrich the understanding of phenomena related to mourning, apologizing, and seeking and receiving forgiveness.

The *third* area pertaining to forgiveness that needs closer examination is that of cross-cultural variations in the patterns of remorse and reparation. Many questions arise in this context. Are all cultures equally forgiving? Are there transgressions and faults that are selectively more or less forgivable in a given culture? Do some cultures provide socially recognized forgiveness rituals while others do not? Is forgiving faster in the former cultures? Little data exists to answer such questions. It does, however, seem that cultural factors shape the use and formal characteristics of apologies. Barnland and Yoshioko (1990), for instance, have demonstrated that while Japanese and American subjects agree on the kinds of situations that require apologies, they differ to some extent in the kind of apologies that they regard to be appropriate in such situations.

Finally, the application of psychodynamic insights regarding forgiveness to the justice system at large and forensic psychiatry in particular merits further inquiry. Comparing the justice system in the United States to that in Japan and Korea, Harding (1999) finds the former to be characteristically retributive and the latter to have a greater restorative bent. Not unaware of the limitations of the restorative justice, Harding nonetheless feels that it is important that opportunities be provided to the offender to understand the significance of the victim's experience and to make appropriate gestures of remorse and atonement. Chase (2000) reports upon the "victim-offender-conferencing" program (developed in the United States during the mid 1970s) in which the court brings offenders and their victims together with a neutral facilitator. During the meeting the offender is offered an opportunity to apologize to his victim. Overall, however, the legal system remains somewhat ambivalent about the offender's expression of remorse. More work is needed in this realm.[19]

While these areas await further exploration, one thing appears certain from the material covered in this essay. Forgiveness is an integral element of mourning and therefore necessary for psychic growth. Forgiving others for their hurtful actions and forgiving oneself for one's causing pain to others, are integral to moving on in life and to opening oneself for new experiences. Inability or unwillingness to forgive keeps one tied to past and impedes development. Nowhere this fixating element of an unforgiving attitude—here, regarding oneself—is better described than in the following parable from the life of Buddha.

A man approached Buddha while he was sitting, eyes closed, under a Banyan tree, meditating. Amidst sobs and tears, the man reported that his son was very ill and the local healers had given up on the child. The boy was about the die. The man pleaded for divine intervention from Buddha. He cried, wailed, touched Buddha's feet. Buddha, however, sat motionless and neither opened his eyes nor said anything in response. The man left, only to appear the next day filled with rage. His son had died and he held Buddha's inactivity responsible for it. He shouted obscenities, cursed Buddha, and still finding no visible response, spat at him in disgust and left.

Time passed and a day came, a few years later, when the man returned to visit Buddha again. Now he was very remorseful. He said that, over time, he had gradually realized that by remaining silent, Buddha was conveying to him two important messages, that there is little he could do in situation if those who knew about physical ailments had given up, and that there are no words to offer solace to a man whose son is about to die. The man was guilt-ridden for his having spat on Buddha. Crying and holding Buddha's feet, he begged for forgiveness. It was then that Buddha opened his eyes and spoke. He said, "You spat on a river and the water flowed away. The man I was then is gone with time. I am different. You did not spit on me and hence I have no authority to forgive you. But it makes me sad that while you have learnt many things, you are still standing on the same spot on the riverbank. You are being consumed by a moment that has long departed. It is not I, but you, and only you, who can release yourself from this bondage!"

6

SACRIFICE

Aside from a mythopoetic discourse in *Totem and Taboo* (Freud, 1913) and an occasional passing reference (Ehrenfels, 1908; Money-Kyrle, 1930; Carcamo, 1943; Fenichel, 1945), psychoanalysis has paid little attention to the concept of sacrifice. This indifference is curious in light of the field's fervent interest in phenomena (e.g., narcissism and greed) that seem almost exactly contrary to sacrifice. The disinterest in sacrifice perhaps reflects the customary recoil of psychoanalysis from positive attitudes and emotions, especially notions that have a faintly religious flavor to them. Such a trend is beginning to show a reversal, however. Novel papers have been published on altruism (Seelig and Rosof, 2009), atonement (Rosen, 2009), courage (Levine, 2006), forgiveness (Akhtar, 2002; Siassi, 2007; Smith, 2008; Lansky, 2009), and resilience (Parens, 2009). The International Psychoanalytic Association's Publications Committee recently sponsored a comprehensive, edited volume on positive attitudes and emotions (Akhtar, 2009a).

My contribution takes these developments a step further and offers an elucidation of the concept of sacrifice and, in particular, its phenomenological (e.g., etymology, definition, and forms), dynamic (e.g., instinctual, self-based, and moral), sociocultural; and clinical aspects. The aim of this discourse is to enhance knowledge in this inoptimally studied area, and to enlarge the mental space in which clinical and cultural meanings of sacrifice can be explored and beneficially utilized.

ETYMOLOGY AND DEFINITION

> Altruism is more than just a feeling of sympathy. It includes a sense of responsibility, of taking care of one another. When we consider the other as someone precious and respected, it is natural that we will help them and share with them as expressions of our love. —The Dalai Lama, 2008, p. 20

> Normal altruism, the ability to experience sustained and relatively conflict-free pleasure from contributing to the welfare of others, is distinguishable from a need to sacrifice oneself for the benefit of others. In the absence of pathological forms of altruism, the altruistic individual can gratify drives directly, delay immediate gratification, and also enjoy enhancing the good of others. —Seelig and Rosof, 2009, pp. 84-85

The thirteenth- century Latin word for sacrifice, *sacrificium*, has its roots in *sacer* (sacred) and *facere (*to make); thus, sacrifice is defined as an act that makes sacred (Skeat, 1993, p. 411). The Italian and Spanish (*sacrificio*) as well as French (*sacrifice*) words for sacrifice are fairly straightforward derivations from Latin. Corresponding expressions in four other languages spoken by a large proportion of the world's population—namely Arabic, Chinese, German, and Hindi—are, however, more nuanced. In Arabic, there are three different words with the connotations of sacrifice: *Tadhia*, standing for the ritual offering to God, *Nadr*, standing for the promised gift to God or to poor people if one's prayers (e.g., on behalf of a sick child) are fulfilled, and *Isteshad*, standing for the surrender of self and seeking martyrdom in the name of religion and nationalism. The Chinese language uses complex terminology to represent sacrifice-related phenomena. *Xiànshēn* refers to a dedication of life and body to a higher cause and is often used to describe suicide bombings. *Gòngwù* and *jìpēn* refer to devotional offerings, i.e., placing fruit at the feet of a deity and ritual animal sacrifice, respectively. These connotations are distinct from the more commonplace term for sacrifice, *xisheng* which denotes a renunciation for the sake of loved ones. The German word *opfer*, derived from the Old High German *opfar*, has multiple meanings including sacrifice, victim, casualty, prey, and even laughingstock. In contrast to such potentially derogatory connotations, the Hindi term for sacrifice originates from a combination of the expressions *bali* (offering) and *daan* (donation). The resulting word, *Balidaan,* has broad meanings that extend from everyday sacrifices through religious offerings to suicide—and even murder—for a political cause.

Such disparities between linguistic representations of sacrifice are given further texture when placed in the provocative framework of the Sapir-Whorf hypothesis, or the principle of linguistic relativity (Whorf, 1956). It proposes that while culture shapes language, language in turn encodes cognition; the spoken and written words implicitly affect people's thoughts and behavior. A wider incorporation of sacrificial ideals into the language of a people thus contributes to cultural reverence for sacrifice. This reverence can get engrained into the shared cultural psyche of a community and modify human behavior by outlining contexts in which sacrifice could be, and perhaps should be, given.

Two aspects seem fundamental to an act of sacrifice: (i) there is a voluntary surrender of something precious, emotionally significant, or intensely desired; (ii) this renunciation is intended to achieve a purpose of higher value. As far as the first criterion is concerned, the object of renunciation might be a material possession like jewelry or money; sensual pleasure such as food or sex; or their symbolic substitute such as an animal. Sacrifice might also involve the self and/or its interests, as when a parent foregoes personal dreams for the sake of children's advancement. An extreme next step might involve giving up one's life for a presumed higher cause. Freud (1910) hinted at such dynamics in the context of suicide. He wondered what causes "the extraordinary powerful life force to be overcome: whether this can only come about with the help of a disappointed libido or whether the ego can renounce its self-preservation for its own egoistic motives" (p. 232).

These so-called "egoistic motives," which constitute our second criteria for sacrifice, often involve religious, political, and cultural ideals. Religiously dictated acts of self-deprivation are commonplace during the celebration of such holidays as Lent, Yom Kippur, and Ramadan. Politically motivated sacrifices occur in the context of resistance movements which often necessitate the renunciation of personal comfort and safety. Their truly dramatic versions occur as giving up of one's life during war and acts of "terrorism." To be sure, not all terrorist acts are sacrifice-based; motives of revenge, narcissistic rage, and omnipotent fantasies of reversing real or imaginary group trauma often play a greater role in such events. However, if one can take the courageous stance of empathy with the Other's perspective, one might discern an element of sacrifice in some "terrorist" acts. Finding himself trapped in humiliating and dehumanizing circumstances that preclude authentic self-expression and generativity, a suicide bomber, for instance, might be emitting his "last hurrah" in the service of a cherished political cause. The drive to forfeit one's life arises from a higher calling on one hand, and from a grievous threat to dignified life on the other. Winnicott (1960) most likely had the latter dynamics in mind when he stated,

> The False Self has as its main concern a search for conditions which will make it possible for the True Self to come into its own. If conditions cannot be found then there must be reorganized a new defense against exploitation of the True Self, and if there be doubt then the clinical result is suicide. Suicide in this context is the destruction of the total self in avoidance of annihilation of the True Self. When suicide is the only defense left against betrayal of the True Self, then it becomes the lot of the False Self to organize the suicide. (p. 143)

Not all self-sacrifices are so "nobly" motivated. Variables of narcissism and sadomasochism also come to play here. Moreover, personal motivations—no matter how varied—do not exhaust the factors leading to sacrifice. Societally enforced ideals can also induce self-sacrifice. *Sati,* the ancient Hindu practice of a widow's self-immolation on a husband's funeral pyre, constituted a striking model of such culturally upheld—an, in remote past, enforced—sacrifice. Widows who committed *sati* had internalized the misogynous religious and cultural ideals that dictated this appalling practice.

RELIGIOUS PROTOTYPES

> We know a sphere that is ruled by a similar conception [fearful deferral of gratifying one's desires]: the religious sphere. That is where the voluntary submission to sacrifice and privation, the renunciation of instinctual gratification and frequent self-injuries, become preconditions for the attainment of the prospective goal. —Reik, 1941, p. 319

> Sacrifice is admissible as religious ritual but has become reprehensible to the conscious mind of modern man. Christian worship preserves a sacrificial memory, severely repressed, which returns as Communion rites, while the Jewish Passover memorializes the ritual cannibalism of pastoral Semites who devoured the slaughtered sacrifice hurriedly before the break of dawn. —Skinner, 1961, p. 72

The Hebrew Bible narrates the *Akedah*, or "The Binding of Isaac" (Genesis 22:1–24). God asks Abraham to give up his son Isaac as a "burnt-offering" upon a mountain (Genesis 22:2). Abraham decides to fulfill God's wish despite his love for Isaac, who was miraculously born to him when he was one-hundred years old. Abraham journeys up the mountain, builds an altar, binds his son to a pyre, and raises his hand to kill his son with a knife. An angel stops him from committing this act of sacrifice, saying: "now I know that thou art a God-fearing man, seeing thou hast not withheld thy son" (Genesis 22:12). Abraham, then, does not harm his son and instead sacrifices a nearby ram.

Several Rabbinic scholars including J. H. Hertz, the former Chief Rabbi of the United Kingdom and Commonwealth, maintain that the story's primary message opposes mistreatment of children as in human sacrifice (cited in Kimball, 2007). In Jewish tradition, however, the *Akedah*is evoked on Rosh Hashanah, where the blowing of a ram's horn is reminiscent of the ram Abraham sacrificed to God. This blowing of the *shofar* symbolically alerts the listeners to the coming judgment by God of the deeds of the people, and signifies the beginning of a ten-day period of reflection and repentance (Maimonides, *Yad*, Laws of Repentance 3:4). The *shofar* and a prayer read on Rosh Hashanah, on the other hand, serve as reminders to God Himself of Abraham's merit and willingness to sacrifice his son. This memory is evoked to entreat God to forgive the Jewish people for their sins. The *Akedah*is then revisited on the second day of repentance to remind the Jewish people of God's mercy, the ideal commitment to God as exemplified by Abraham, and may be further interpreted as an endorsement for Jewish martyrdom. The ultimate act of *Kaddish Hashem,* or sanctification of the divine name, occurs as self-sacrifice of life as an alternative to converting to another religion.

In the New Testament, Abraham is portrayed as willing to perform the sacrifice of Isaac due to his belief: "that God was able to raise him

[Isaac] up, even from the dead" (Hebrews 11:17–19). Due to this passage, many Christians lend significance to the Old Testament promise God makes to Abraham: "In Isaac your seed shall be called" (Genesis 21:12); Abraham trusts this assurance even as he undertakes the task to sacrifice his son. Christian Biblical commentators popularly view the "Binding of Isaac" as an allegory to God's plan for Jesus. Just as God's Son, Jesus, dies as substitutional atonement for humanity, the ram God provided for Abraham dies as a substitute for Isaac. Abraham moreover mirrors God's willingness to give up his Son, Jesus, for a higher purpose. Furthermore, both Jesus and Isaac carry the wood for their own sacrifices up a mountain.

Jesus' atonement on behalf of humanity is essential to most denominations of Christianity. Christians believe that Jesus is the Savior through whom men can escape from retribution for their sins, and even be granted eternal life in Heaven. "For the wages of sin is death, but the gift of God is eternal life through Jesus Christ our Lord" (Romans 6:23). According to this doctrine, God sacrificed Jesus as a martyr to receive the penalty for all men's sins. "God made him who had no sin to be sin for us, so that in him we might become the righteousness of God" (2 Corinthians 5:21). Jesus in turn accepted crucifixion so that sinners can be reconciled with God rather than themselves being punished. "He himself bore our sins in his body on the tree, that we might die to sins and live for righteousness; by his wounds you have been healed" (1 Peter 2:24).

In the Qu'ran (37: 99–113) too, the tale of Ibrahim's (Abraham) sacrifice occupies a significant place. Called the *Dhabih* in Arabic, the saga is interpreted in a different manner. Muslim scholars believe the elder son of Abraham, Ishmael, is an ancestor of Muhammad and the Muslim people, while Isaac is the progenitor of the Jewish and Christian people. The Muslim view of Ishmael is positive, as opposed to the contrary Jewish and Christian views, and the predominant Muslim interpretation of the *Dhabih* considers Ishmael as the son that God calls upon Abraham to sacrifice. The episode is considered a trial of God that Abraham and Ishmael pass by submitting to God's will and therefore revealing their awareness that God is the true owner and giver of everything. *Eid al-Adha*, or the Festival of Sacrifice, commemorates this occasion every year. Traditionally, Muslim families sacrifice a domestic animal such as a sheep or goat, and this meat is distributed in thirds among the family, friends of the family, and the needy.

Moving on from the three great religions of the Middle East to the Indian subcontinent, one encounters Hinduism. Here, the prototypical sacrifice involves the tale of Shravan Kumar and is detailed in the great epic *Ramayana* (circa 400 BC). Shravan spends his days in devotion to God and in service to his poor, blind, and aging parents. When his parents wish to visit various sites of Hindu pilgrimage before their impending deaths, Shravan fashions a basket-apparatus that he hoists upon his shoulders to carry them. Unfortunately, their pilgrimage is short-lived. Shravan is fatally wounded while trying to fetch water for his parents when a local King mistakes his sound at the stream as that of a deer and shoots him with an arrow. When King Dasharatha tries to tend to Shravan, Shravan instructs him to instead quench the thirst of his parents, and dies. Shravan's parents are stricken when they receive King Dasharatha's confession, and express their lack of desire to live without their cherished son. They curse the King to meet his death, too, from the sorrow of separation from a son. The King does indeed meet this fate, when his son, Rama, later sacrifices his crown and kingdom to go into exile at the bidding of a jealous stepmother. Shravan's sacrificial devotion is thus 'reincarnated' in Rama's selfless renunciation of an opulent life in the palace.

While all four religions touched upon here (i.e., Judaism, Christianity, Islam, and Hinduism) have iconic figures embodying the trait of sacrifice and are imbued with the sentiment of filial surrender to the Divine, each of these traditions portrays the parent-child bond as the crucible of self-abnegation. Each tradition therefore leaves mental space for considering sacrifice from a largely human perspective. This perspective involves both interpersonal and intrapsychic dimensions. The prophets of Old Testament, for instance, declared that it is the disposition of the offerer that determined whether a sacrifice will be "accepted" or not. A psychological dimension was thus introduced into the equation. Later, Jewish thought and, even more emphatically, the Christian tradition placed service to community and fellow human beings as parallel and even equal to material offerings to God. Islam, by requiring that one give *Zakat*, i.e., donate forty percent of one's income to the poor, and by recommending that the meat of the animal sacrificed on *Eid-al-Adha* must also be given to the needy, also underscored the interpersonal and objected-related aims of sacrifice. And, finally, Hinduism, via its tale of Shravan Kumar, clearly spelled out that filial love is often the impetus for sacrifice acts. An implicit subtext of psychology thus runs through the sturdy mythological veins of all four traditions. And, it is this psychological dimension that forms our next focus of attention.

PSYCHOANALYTIC CONTRIBUTIONS

> In the moment when one must cease to use the environment as material for one's own security and well-being (i.e., when the environment does not consent any longer to accept the role of being incorporated in this way), one accepts the role of sacrifice, so to speak, with sensual pleasure, i.e., the role of material for other, stronger, more self-asserting, more egoistic, forces. —Ferenczi, 1930, p. 225

> If the unconscious hatred of fathers, which psychoanalysis has demonstrated was present from the beginning, it must have been responsible for the killing of father-symbols; and, if the present conscious repudiation of this hatred was also present, it must have concealed from the sacrifice the true motive of his act. —Bunker, 1933, p. 155

In elucidating the psychoanalytic perspective on sacrifice, I will first address Freud's views. Following this, I will discuss the contributions of subsequent analysts under three headings: (i) triadic and hostile foundations, (ii) dyadic and loving foundations, and (iii) putting the oedipal and preoedipal together.

Freud's Views

The earliest mention of sacrifice in Freud's writings is found in *The Psychopathology of Everyday Life* (1901). Rather than paraphrase, we'll let the reader encounter the Master's words directly.

> One morning, when I was passing through a room in my dressing-gown with straw slippers on my feet, I yielded to a sudden impulse and hurled one of my slippers from my foot at the wall, causing a beautiful little marble Venus to fall down from its bracket. As it broke into pieces, I quoted quite unmoved these lines from Busch: "Ach! Die Venus istperdu—Klickeradoms!—von Medici." This

> wild conduct and my calm acceptance of the damage are to be explained in terms of the situation at the time. One of my family was gravely ill, and secretly I had already given up hope of her recovery. That morning I had heard that there had been a great improvement, and I know I had said to myself: "So, she's going to live after all!" My attack of destructive fury served therefore to express a feeling of gratitude to fate and allowed me to perform a "*sacrificial act*"—rather as if I had made a vow to sacrifice something or other as thank-offering if she recovered her health! The choice of the Venus of Medici for this sacrifice was clearly only a gallant act of homage towards the convalescent. . . (p. 169, italics in original)

Freud followed this passage with a shorter but similar example of accidentally breaking a recently-acquired Egyptian figure while writing a conciliatory letter to an outraged friend. Both these illustrations of sacrifice have been taken on face value by the subsequent analytic contributors. I, however, feel that Freud's parapraxes are open to other interpretations. The expression (in the first example) "So, she is going to live after all!" has a ring of disappointment and the acknowledgment (in the second example) that he had hurt his friend ("I had to admit that he was in the right," p. 170) sounds begrudging. Looked at this way, Freud's actions appear propelled by displaced hostility, not by reparative atonement. It is also to be noted that both the acts of so-called sacrifice were inadvertent and given that meaning only in retrospect.

Another mention of sacrifice by Freud is in *Civilization and Its Discontents* (1930). Noting that human beings renounce their selfish interests only to maintain group cohesion, Freud declared that "civilization is built upon a renunciation of instinct" (p. 97). The sacrifice of personal interest in such a course of events is voluntary only on the surface.

> Human life in common is only made possible when a majority comes together which is stronger than any separate individual and which remains united against all separate individuals. The power of this community is then set up as "right" in opposition to the power of the individual, which is condemned as "brute force." This replacement of the power of the individual by the power of a community constitutes the decisive step of civilization. The essence of it lies in the fact that the members of the community restrict themselves in their possibilities of satisfaction, whereas the individual knew no such restrictions. (p. 95)

Freud wryly notes that the "civilized man has exchanged a portion of his possibilities of happiness for a portion of security" (p. 115). Putting this portrayal of reluctant, if not enforced, sacrifice together with his personal recollections of inadvertent sacrifice leaves little space for considering that acts of sacrifice might, at times, not be accidental or enforced but deliberate choices made by a mature and thinking individual.

The only place Freud came close to the idea of someone deliberately offering sacrifice is in *Totem and Taboo* (1913). He noted that in observing taboos, one gives up certain wishes. And, if and when one breaks a taboo, one has to atone for it by renouncing some possession or some freedom to appease the higher power that had established that taboo in the first place. Such renunciation—a sacrifice—is intended to diminish guilt and restore good relations with the higher power.

Freud went on to speculate a "pre-historic" murder of the father of the primal horde by his sons. They killed him to seize his powers but their doing so mobilized guilt and a need to restore the father.[1] In the totemic sacrifice that followed, an animal was killed, offered to the god, and devoured. The god was represented twice in this ritual; as a victim and also as a recipient of the victim's flesh. The animal victim was killed (re-enjoying the hostile destructiveness towards the god-father), eaten (consummating the incorporative urges towards god-father), and offered to the god (replenishing the harmed god-father). Freud stated that the hypothesized murder of the father of the primal horde by his sons was not crucial for his formulations since the basis of sacrifice could be the ambivalent fantasies of sons towards their fathers; these, in his view, were ubiquitous anyway.

Freud's ideas on sacrifice as a repetition of parricide as well as an expiation for the guilt associated with it were illustrated by Money-Kyrle (1930), who provided an encyclopedic account of sacrifice in many lands and among many peoples. He emphasized that sacrifice was originally and primarily pre-deistic, having nothing to do with a god as such and was essentially a psychological phenomenon. In other words, the prime motivators for sacrifice were the hostile oedipal fantasies of sons towards their fathers. Needless to add, these 'classical' formulations paid no heed to women making sacrifices and, by their insistent focus upon the oedipal-triangular dynamics, also overlooked the potentially dyadic roots of sacrifice.

Subsequent contributions to psychoanalytic understanding of sacrifice took three different paths. The first continued to explore the triadic (oedipal) and hostile foundations of sacrifice even while giving a new twist to them. The second looked for the origins of sacrifice in dyadic (preoedipal) and loving early relationships. The third attempted to synthesize the preceding two perspectives.

Triadic and Hostile Foundations

Freud's (1913) emphasis upon the parricidal fantasies and the oedipal dimension involved in the phenomenon of sacrifice was further elaborated by Fodor (1946), Nunberg (1947), and, more recently, Bergman (1992). The last mentioned gave a new twist to the Freudian notion of the murderous wish of the sons against the father as underlying paradigm for sacrifice. He proposed that the central dynamics of sacrifice arose from the murderous wish of the father against the sons. He proposed that the Laius complex precedes and provokes the Oedipus complex. By providing numerous illustrations from history, mythology and religious doctrine, Bergman made his proposals credible. In a review of his work, Meissner (1996) invoked the related contributions of the literary critic Rene Girard.

> Girard's (1977) thesis is not that far removed from Bergman's, but the chords follow a different set of harmonics. He argues that sacrifice has its basis in the threat of reciprocal violence in the body of the community; the disaster of mutual destruction is averted by directing the violence towards a single object, thus protecting the community from its own violence. Thus, violence is at the heart of the sacred, and the function of religion in any society is to subdue and control violence. The gods assume their sacred function insofar as they protect the community—sacrifice is meant to guarantee this outcome. (p. 295)

This argument clarifies the rationale behind the Judeao-Christian proposal of divine love as an antidote to the aggressive themes implicit in sacrifice.

Dyadic and Loving Foundations

While acknowledging the castration-related themes inherent in sacrifice, Fenichel (1945), Feiner and Levenson (1968), Andresen (1984), and

Carveth (1992) underscored its dyadic and loving foundations. Fenichel (1945) emphasized that sacrifice avoids separation. Unduly self-sacrificing individuals turn out to be excessively dependent on external supplies of love and have a greater need for psychological merger for remaining stable. Their sacrifices are tinged with masochism. However, the self-object glue provided by sacrifice can also emanate from genuine concern and love. Searles (1958) emphasized this dimension of sacrifice in the genesis of psychotic character organization; the growing child sacrifices his individuality and perceptual integrity for the psychic sustenance of an emotionally disturbed mother. Feiner and Levenson (1968) studied college students who had dropped out and discerned that, in many cases, there was a sacrificial aspect to this behavior; it was necessary to maintain family integrity. To avoid a sacrifice in such context would have entailed facing unbearable separateness and the threat of psychological disorganization.

Andresen (1984) declared that the "higher power" to whom one offers a sacrifice does not have to be divine; it can refer to a deeply loved human object. He then described fantasies of the "sacrifice complex" with three nodal points: "(1) The offerer's concern for the state of the deity or beloved; (2) the offerer's interpretation of his strivings and the events of his life as determiners of the fate of the deity or the beloved; and, (3) the offerer's intention to have the deity or beloved profit from an offering which in some fashion depletes the state of the offerer" (p. 542).

In other words, acts of self-abnegation can arise out of the concern for an object. Andresen's ideas thus come close to Klein's (1940) concept of "reparation." A somewhat different view is presented by Carveth (1992) who observed that sacrifice of the self can at the same time be the affirmation of its core values and ideals. He proposed the concept of "empathic identification," which, contrary to Klein's (1946) "projective identification," refers to the capacity to feel for others and help them by invoking a consciously held (and not split-off) view of one's deprived child self. Carveth proposed that many acts of sacrifice emanate from such healthy actualization of one's self; it is through conscious and loving empathy that one can "receive" what one gives to a needy other.

Putting the Oedipal and Pre-Oedipal Together

In a set of richly textured papers linking the concepts of innocence, spirituality, and the sacred, Grotstein (1997a, 1997b) offered a perspective on sacrifice that attempted to bring together the theories based upon Oedipus complex and castration on the one hand and reparative longings towards the mother on the other. Reading the oedipal saga from a Kleinian-Winnicottian viewpoint and combining it with the Christ theme, Grotstein thus shed new light on the phenomenon of sacrifice.

> Oedipus, the psychoanalytic "everyman," represents the infant who has a destiny to "use the object" with autoerotic and autosadistic vigorousness, acts that were destined ultimately (in the depressive position) to bring him to the awareness of deeds to which he had to blind himself in order to undergo these life-honing rituals of normal development. The infant, like Oedipus, is on the horns of a dilemma: He *must* use and imaginatively destroy his subjective object (Winnicott, 1969, 1971) and thereby place his objects and his innocence in jeopardy. Yet if he does not undergo this ritual of inexorable development and avoids his fate, he defaults into ontological guilt for being untrue to his destiny. He becomes self-branded as a coward.
>
> In some uncanny and numinous way, Christian theology seems to have gone to the heart of this profound matter by instituting not only the act of the confessional where sinners could be properly "shriven" (in anticipation of psychoanalytic "exorcism") but especially the ceremony of the Eucharist in which the sinful participant (from object usage and misusage) experiences absolution (the transfer of his sinfulness unto the image of Christ) *by actually drinking His symbolic* (believed by some to be actual) *blood and eating His symbolic flesh. In ritualistically recommitting the destructive act on Christ, the synedcochic sacrifice for all mankind, the sinner becomes absolved and is restored to innocence.* Conclusion: Our innocence is jeopardized when we relate to our needed objects. We must allow ourselves to risk feelings of guilt toward our objects and jeopardize our innocence by living our lives to the fullest—as long as we pay authentic homage to contrition and never lose sight of the most fundamental truth of object relations, that our very lives are predicated on the sacrifice of others for us, beginning with the placenta, whose death initiates our birth. (p. 202, italics in the original)

Grotstein's emphasis upon the hostile-reparative sequence in the rivalrous dyad (even if, oedipal) paved the way for linking the triadic and dyadic substrates of the sacrificial tendency in the human mind.

THE TRIAD OF ALTRUISM, MASOCHISM, AND NARCISSISM

> The traits that reflect overdependency on support, love, and acceptance from others also reveal, on psychoanalytic exploration, a tendency to excessive guilt feelings towards others because of unconscious ambivalence toward loved and needed objects, and an excessive reaction of frustration when their expectations are not met. These patients show an abnormal vulnerability to being disappointed by others, and they may go out of their way to obtain sympathy and love. —Kernberg, 1988, p. 63

> Just as all altruistic behavior cannot be reduced to a "masochistic surrender" without exploring normal and pathological narcissistic needs and concerns, for the same reason one cannot explore narcissistically driven normal and pathological altruistic behavior either without attending to the level of differentiation of masochistic components and the potentialities to hate. —Garza-Guerrero, 2009, p. 97

By now, it has become clear that a myriad of factors are interwoven into the psychodynamics of sacrifice. These include defenses against hostility, love and devotion, the desire to relieve guilt, moral narcissism, and the desire to diminish anxiety about the future by "bribing" the deities (and their intra-psychic stand-in, the superego). Most of these variables have been addressed by Freud and the psychoanalytic contributors who followed him. Others need further explication.

Altruism and Sacrifice

The concept of altruism defined, in Darwinian sociobiology, as behavior that "promotes the fitness of the recipient at the expense of the provider" (Badcock, 1986, p. 116) comes pretty close to that of sacrifice. Within psychoanalysis, however, altruism has largely been seen as a vicarious way of deriving the gratification which seems forbidden to oneself (A. Freud, 1946) or "an adaptive outgrowth of reaction formation" (Vaillant, 1977, p. 110). Such "pathologizing" of altruism implied a similarly skeptical stance towards sacrifice. However, more recently,

Seelig and Rosoff (2001) have elucidated normal and healthy forms of altruism, tracing their origin to the "hard-wired" self-effacement that is conducive to the survival of the species. This "proto-altruism" is later enhanced by identification with the kind and caring attitude of one's parents.[2] The outcome of such intermingling is "generative altruism," i.e., the ability to experience conflict-free pleasure in fostering the success and/or pleasure of another (Seelig and Rosof, 2009).

This becomes clearer as one moves to the realm of parental or filial love. Denuded of sexual edge, such love builds largely on what Freud (1905) termed the "affectionate current" of love life. Concern, respect, mutuality, optimal distance, and tenderness contribute to this current. Bearing real hardships (e.g., physical, financial) in the course of rearing children shifts this current closer to the stream of sacrifice. Tahka's (1993) observation regarding feelings of tenderness is apt in this context. According to him, such feelings result from "empathic sharing of the object's pleasure and subsequent leaving of the pleasure for him. In a loving relationship, this letting the object keep the pleasure for himself is followed by a second re-pleasure in the subject for the loved person's feeling good and for the knowledge of having contributed to that oneself" (p. 244).

In plebian terms, "tenderness" refers to the sweet and sour affect accompanying the facilitation of one's children's individuation. For instance, the parent might want his or her child to follow a certain professional path but comes around to accept and even support a different choice on the latter's part. Such malleability for the sake of one's offspring is the stuff of sacrifice. A related concept in this realm is that of "generativity" (Erikson, 1950) or the capacity to nourish and guide the next generation, to treat them with benevolent care, and to encourage them in their pursuits. This also carries subtle echoes of sacrifice. Loving one's children might not require overt and gross sacrifices but a modicum of self-surrender is integral to it.

Even romantic love that is dependent upon sensual excitement involves the coexistence of humility, tenderness, and concern for the other. While the word 'sacrifice' is generally not mentioned, phrases such as "capacity to give" (Kernberg, 1995, p. 58), "renunciation of alternative possibilities" (Altman, 1977, p. 48) do make an appearance in psychoanalytic writings on mature romantic love. Benedek's (1977) observation that the distinction between "narcissistic" and "anaclitic" love (Freud, 1914) diminishes within a couple over time and Chasseguet-Smirgel's (1985) comment that the pain over remnant longings for oneness with the primary objects and for incestuous gratification is set aside in the favor of attachment to the couple's unity also hint that elements of sacrifice are inherent in love.

Masochism and Sacrifice

Since sacrifice involves renunciation of property or pleasure, it is tempting to equate it with masochism. Indeed, there *can* be overlaps between the two. Both involve self-deprivation and both yield a certain kind of pleasure. Both reflect ego's obedience to the superego. This can make one regard all sacrifice as masochistic. Reflecting such tendency is the following comment by Anna Freud: "Why one should be good if one gets nothing out of it. I mean there has to be a reward for this enormous renunciation" (cited in Sandler and Freud, 1985, p. 457). But the question is what sort of reward that might be? Is it an id-reward or an ego-reward or even an ego-ideal reward? Clearly, the reward in masochistic surrender to a "bad" object is id-based, i.e., intense, affect-laden, and, at least, in part, somatically anchored. The reward in sacrifice is in the form of an "ego pleasure" (G. Klein, 1976), i.e., milder in intensity and not affectualized.

I therefore propose that sacrifice and masochism are not synonymous and can exist independently of each other. Masochism is associated with unconscious rage at the other, sacrifice is not. Masochism can propel sacrifices but not all sacrifices grow out of masochism. One can make a sacrifice (e.g., give up an employment opportunity so that one's children would not have to move to another city) without exalting it into a maudlin act of self-deprivation and without drawing self-pitying pleasure from it. And, one can be masochistic (e.g., unconsciously choose indifferent and cold lovers) without any element of sacrifice in the behavior. Finally, the suffering associated with sacrifice does not have 'instinctual' qualities (i.e., urgency, intensity, repetitiveness) while this is typically the case with masochism.

Narcissism and Sacrifice

On surface, the coupling of narcissism and sacrifice seems strange. The two seem polar opposites. Narcissism, at least in its exaggerated and pathological form (Freud, 1914; Kernberg, 1974; Kohut, 1977) is characterized by self-absorption, inability to love, greed, search for glory, and a readiness to cut ethical corners in the pursuit of wealth and fame. In contrast, sacrifice implies a premium on morality and a well developed capacity for renunciation. Narcissism and sacrifice thus appear poles apart till the time we stumble upon the concept of 'moral narcissism' (Green, 1986) which forms a bridge between the unlikely duo. Pride drawn from the yearning to be pure and above ordinary human beings is the essence of 'moral narcissism' and can contribute to making sacrifices. An illustration of such vanity comes from Gandhi (1940) who, in attempting to become "absolutely passion-free" concluded: "I must reduce myself to zero" (pp. 504, 505).

I hasten to add, though, that Green's (1986) description of 'moral narcissism' emphasizes a striving to impoverish object relations in order to restore the infantile megalomania of self-sufficiency. My use of the term is softer and implies that renunciation of one's desires can, at times, deepen ties with loved objects. Whether Green's version is better termed "malignant moral narcissism" and mine "benign moral narcissism" is debatable but it is clear that a certain amount of narcissistic gratification is integral to sacrifice. It is the extent of such personal benefit that distinguishes a true sacrifice from an exhibitionistic gesture masquerading as renunciation.

AN ATTEMPT AT SYNTHESIS

> All cultures at all times have idealized heroes whose achievement involves painful and dangerous feats, if not actual martyrdom. The achievement is not valued unless it is fired in pain. No culture choses to live without inflicting pain on itself; even cultures seemingly devoted to nirvana-type ideals have painful rituals. —Cooper, 1988, p. 125

> Mature religiosity includes an integrated value system that transcends the individual's interest and has truly universal validity that applies to all human beings. It is a comprehensive and harmonious system, and its fundamental principles are love and respect for others and of the self. . . . Such a mature religiosity includes the capacity for reconciliation, forgiveness, and reparation on the basis of understanding

the unavoidable ambivalence of all human relationships.
—Kernberg, 2012, p. 372

By pooling together the various notions and different aspects of sacrifice delineated above, I seek to draw a composite and nuanced profile of the phenomenon. This profile accommodates the polarities of altruism versus narcissism, masochism versus a conscious choice to bear pain for the sake of a higher cause, and appeasement (of gods and/or externalized containers of the superego) versus atonement (finding relief for personal remorse). I define sacrifice as a deliberate act that results from putting self-interest aside for the benefit of someone else. The relationship between sacrifice and compromise is complex. On the one hand, acts of sacrifice are invariably multi-determined and hence represent a particular form of compromise formation. On the other hand, sacrifice is distinct from what is colloquially called a compromise. The former involves renunciation of an id pleasure for an ego ideal gratification while the latter involves trading one id pleasure for another or seeking the two in some sort of half-hearted combination. Sacrifice has a moral dimension and benefits others whereas compromise does not necessarily possess these attributes.

Sacrifice is inevitably accompanied by some discomfort. In fact "a sacrifice without suffering is no sacrifice" (Gusdorf, 1948, 182). However, the attitude toward such suffering can range from silent stoicism (healthy) to gloating masochism (pathological). Religious undertones might contribute to sacrifice but are, by no means, necessary. Our view of sacrifice therefore extends beyond ordinary offerings made during religious rituals to include a broad array of acts that range from a family putting off vacations to pay college tuition of a child to a politically-inspired self-immolation. Possibilities of self-satisfaction via benign forms of "moral narcissism" (Green, 1956) as well as those of self-harm are included as is the extent to which the act of sacrificial renunciation is anchored in reality.

Taking such diverse variables into consideration has led me to conclude that it is difficult to describe their each and every permutation and combination. What appears realistically possible is to delineate the two extreme ends of the spectrum of sacrificial acts and practices, with the hope that such shedding of the light on the periphery would automatically illuminate the center. In other words, only a few acts of sacrifice would fall on either extremes of this spectrum; most sacrifices would belong somewhere in between what we have termed the "healthy" and "pathological" poles of the continuum (see table 6.1).

SACRIFICE IN THE CLINICAL REALM

> Some of the factors inherent in analysis create the conditions for moral change, and affect only indirectly the moral aspects of personality. It has often, and rightly, been stated that analysis frequently enhances man's capacity to realize more fully his potentialities. If moral inadequacy is due to neurotic causes, successful analysis can remedy it. —Hartmann, 1960, p. 86

> The act of sacrifice, either ritualistic and obligatory on one hand, or altruistic and self-suffering on the other, is obviously a complicated issue. Obligatory acts are either acts of communion, or propitiation, or they are covenants. Altruistic acts have been seen as offerings of love for purposes of redemptive value. . . . What is essential in the difference between ritual and altruistic is the apparent possibility of choice in the latter. —Feiner and Levenson, 1968–1969, p. 560

It is well known that anonymity, neutrality, and abstinence characterize the proper psychoanalytic attitude, even though occasional departures from them might be inevitable and clinically necessary. Of this "trio of guideposts" (Pine, 1997), abstinence is the one that approaches the conceptual and affective hues of sacrifice. Freud (1915) evoked the notion in the context of technique vis-à-vis transference love and sternly declared that "the treatment must be carried out in abstinence" (p. 165). By this, he meant that the analyst must not succumb to the patient's demands for erotic indulgences. While initially restricted to libidinal pressures in transference, the rule of abstinence applies to negative transferences also. In other words, the analyst must not be tempted to disprove that he or she is not as 'bad' as the patient thinks. All in all, the principle of abstinence requires that we neither attempt to modify the transference by indulging the patient nor by changing our behavior toward him. Subsequent analytic contributions (Greenson, 1967; Schlesinger, 2003) clarified that abstinence affects both the analysand

Table 6.1. The Spectrum of Sacrifice

Variables	*Healthy Pole*	*Pathological Pole*
Primary motivation	Generative concern	Defense against aggression
The subject of deprivation	Self	Self/Other
Presence of suffering	Yes	Yes
Enjoyment of suffering	No	Yes
Bodily harm	Absent-minimal	Possible-serious
Life-threatening	Almost never	Frequently
Renunciation	Realistic	Unrealistic
Socioculturally acceptable	Yes	No
Cognitive functioning	Intact	Narrowed
Pleasure in life	Retained	Compromised
Exhibitionistic quality	Absent	Present
Rigidity of behavior	No	Yes
Demonstrable benefit	Yes	No

and the analyst; the former has to tolerate some deprivations and the latter has to sit on his or her impulses to gratify the patient. On a concrete level, abstinence might involve not eating, drinking, or smoking during the sessions by both parties (Akhtar, 2009c, p. 1).

The essential point here is that in conducting clinical work, the analyst has to put aside his desires, curiosities, and, to a certain extent, his personal comfort for the sake of the task that the dyad has undertaken. The analyst might experience upsurges of hostile, affectionate, tender, or erotic interest in the patient but he does not act upon the resulting impulses. Instead of gratifying them through motor (or even verbal) discharge, he subjects them to the searching curiosity of his "psychoanalytic work ego" (Olinick et al, 1973). By gaining deeper understanding of their origins within the transference-countertransference matrix, he hopes to subjugate these impulses and, in turn, help the patient gain further access his inner world. And, insofar as the analyst does not trade one temptation for another, but renounces the instinctual component of his desire for the 'higher' purpose of advancing someone else's development, his abstinence contains a flavor of sacrifice. This truth of everyday clinical practice is eloquently expressed by Grotstein (1997a).

> The analyst undergoes many sorts of volitional suffering in the course of doing analysis, that is, the ascetic and celibate posture in abandoning sensual desire—like the priest. In the depressive position,

> suffering may either be redemptive in terms of felt or actual damage done to others, or it may be "realistic" in terms of the vicissitudes of the "cosmic lottery" if the traumatic stimuli causing the suffering are not personally causally connect with the self. In other words, the person in the depressive position is able to experience the difference between *persecutors* and *enemies*. The concept of sacrifice is also intimately involved with the phenomenon of suffering, especially the putative purpose of the suffering; one may suffer persecutorily and must therefore resign to be sacrificed for the purpose of others (e.g., Schreber, 1903), or one may sacrifice oneself as a martyr in order to control others, or one may undergo voluntary sacrifice in the state of *agape*. (p. 205, italics in the original)

It is from such a loving position that the analyst draws his or her capacity to commit more overt sacrifices called forth by special occasions. Agreeing for phone or email contact from a severely ill patient during one's vacation constitutes one such example. Not charging for a session missed by the patient for religious holidays, especially if these are different from those of the analyst's is another. Not publishing the clinical material—however compelling—gathered in the treatment of psychoanalytic trainees and fellow mental health professionals forms yet another illustration of such sacrifices. Most analysts act in this manner habitually though the stern legacy of "classical" training can, at times, make them less forthcoming in acknowledging such benevolence.

A Personal Anecdote

During a brief teaching stint in a distant country some years ago, I was staying in a hotel along with some fellow analysts. Having the afternoon off from academic work, we were enjoying ourselves at the swimming pool. Soon, however, I was approached by a bellboy who said that there was an urgent phone call for me from the United States. Alarmed, I rushed to the hotel lobby and found that my secretary had called, asking me to immediately check my office voice mail. It turned out that one of my patients was in acute crisis and was imploring me to call her right away. I went to my hotel room and called her back. We talked for about twenty to twenty-five minutes and she gradually calmed down (incidentally, she had no idea *where* I was calling from). We agreed to pick up the thread upon my return to work in a few days.

When I returned to the pool, David Sachs, a distinguished (and senior) colleague asked me where I had been for so long. I told him that I had a clinical emergency and had to talk over the phone with a patient in distress. He calmly listened to this and then asked me how long was the phone call? I told him. He asked if I knew the amount of money that the call would cost me. I said that I did not but would estimate in the range of $20—$30. Fixing his glance upon me now, he asked, "Would you add this money to the patient's bill?" A momentary regression took over me; he was an older man, my senior as an analyst, and certainly more clinically experienced. I felt like I was facing an oral exam (with its unmistakable association, though mentalized only later, with visit to a dentist). I quickly searched for the 'correct' answer and then equally quickly recovered from the regression and said what I knew all along what I would do. I said, "No, I will not." He broke into a big, sunny grin and said, "You know, I just wanted to see whether textbook psychoanalysis has totally consumed you or do you retain the basic, simple humanity we all need in doing our work." Then, turning serious, he added, "You know, we are physicians. Our work involves many silent sacrifices."

My colleague's remark that 'silent sacrifices' undergird the therapeutic attitude and fuel the capacity for 'survival' (Winnicott, 1962) in the face of the patient's transference-based seduction and attacks turns out to be true. And, when the analyst's capacity for making such sacrifices gets compromised, the risk of boundary violations increases.

The scenario involving sacrifice in the clinical situation extends beyond such considerations, however. It also involves the countertransference reactions to the patient's actual or claimed sacrifices. Here, the analyst's character and cultural background can come to play a significant role. Analysts who are temperamentally generous and have been raised in cultures that uphold self-effacement can better discern and empathize with their patients' sacrifices; the risk of automatically equating such actions with masochism is thus reduced. The opposite is true of analysts who are of frugal temperament and have been raised in what the Russian poet, Joseph Brodsky calls "the republic of ends/ and means that counts each deed" (1973, p. 136). It is true that the former's credulous stance and the latter's skeptical stance can both yield important data about the patient. It is also true that both orientations have their clinical limitations. The former risks leaving masochism unanalyzed, the latter risks labeling healthy altruism as sick. A balance between the two perspectives is needed. This, too, is not a once-and-for-all measure; it requires individualized calibration with each given clinical situation.

Now, it must be added here that all that looks like sacrifice is not sacrifice (and vice versa). A narcissist, for instance, might label the "compromises" he makes as "sacrifices." In contrast, a masochist might deride his "sacrifices" as "compromises." Clearly, one cannot go by spoken words alone; it is the placement of ideals over desire rather than the barter of one desire for another that characterizes sacrifice. Nonetheless, the therapist's emotional response to sacrifice matters since it can alter the course of subsequent treatment.

Cultural factors might also affect the countertransference experience, especially if the analyst and patient come from different ethnic, religious, racial, and economic backgrounds. The following reminder by Klauber (1968) is pertinent in this context.

> Analyst and patient are not only analyst and patient; they are also individuals with highly integrated, and to a large extent unmodifiable, system of values, and the attitude of one to another expresses not only transference and countertransference but views which remain ego-syntonic and firmly held on reflection. A theory of technique which ignores the immense influence on the psychoanalytic transaction of the value systems of patient and analyst alike ignores a basic psychic reality behind any psychoanalytic partnership. What has to be taken into account is what the Greeks might have called the *ethos* of the patient and analyst—a word meaning originally an accustomed seat—in addition to the *pathos* of more labile reactions. (p. 128, italics in the original)

A sustained perspective of this sort helps the analyst become aware that while "sacrifice" does not figure in his lexicon, it might in that of the patient. The two perhaps think differently about certain matters and such difference is not always reducible to resistance or lack of insight. Going further, the analyst might become able to distinguish sacrifice from masochistic self-deprivation and help this patient tease out this difference as well. "Anagogic" interpretations (Silberer, 1914) of this sort might free the patient to choose which sacrifice (and how much of it he wishes to undertake) and which he would rather let pass.

CONCLUDING REMARKS

> Just as a caterpillar must shed its familiar cocoon in order to become a butterfly and fly, we must be willing to change and shed the cocoon or hard armor of self-centered egotism.
> —Das, 1997, p. 104

In this contribution, I have elucidated the psychodynamics of sacrifice. Acknowledging that tributaries of altruism, narcissism, and masochism can all contribute to acts of sacrifice, I have attempted to distinguish healthy and adaptive forms of sacrifice from their pathological and problematic counterparts. Throughout this discourse, I have maintained respect for the complex and multi-faceted nature of the phenomena under consideration. I have paid attention to the large number of variables operative here; these include: evolutionary imperatives, "hard-wired" brain propensities, ontogenetic experience, and adulthood transformations of intrapsychic life.

Although I have cast a wide net, certain issues have eluded my reach. On a 'macro' level, these include the influence of historical era and politico-economic climate on attitudes about sacrifice. Many questions arise in this context. For instance, have there been times in man's history when the practice of sacrifice was widespread? If so, was it limited to the God-appeasing context or were the interpersonal dimensions also evident then? Do people become more or less self-sacrificing during the times of economic hardship? Is the concept of martyrdom (i.e., the ultimate sacrifice) equally prevalent in all cultures? And so on.

On a "micro" level, these unanswered questions involve the influence of gender and age upon the capacity to make sacrifice. For instance, are women more capable of making sacrifices than men? If so, does their greater capacity emanate from the childhood change of object (i.e., giving up their primary love object, the mother, and turning to the father) or from their inherent maternal instinct? Can children make sacrifices or are their accommodations to their parents' characterological idiosyncrasies and odd thought patterns (Searles, 1958) solely need-based? Are there shades of sacrifice in what Fairbairn (1952) termed "moral defense," i.e., a child's taking the blame for parental misdeeds and exonerating the latter? Does the capacity to make sacrifices appear on the horizon only in middle age or does it simply get more consolidated at that time? And so on.

It is my hope that answers to these questions would one day be provided by interdisciplinary studies with a mix of history, anthropology, sociology, and psychoanalysis. I do, however, dare provide an answer to the question that was raised at the very beginning of this paper, namely, why has psychoanalysis paid meager attention to the phenomenon of sacrifice? Andresen (1984) notes, "It is my thesis that Freud's original insights into the ubiquity of sacrificial fantasies were correct, and that his findings on sacrifice have won little popularity in analytic thinking, not because they have been refuted by accumulated evidence, but because their importance has gone largely unrecognized" (p. 526).

The tautological bent of this explanation leaves us with no answer as to why the importance of sacrifice has not been recognized by psychoanalysis. And, it is here that I enter the answer to this riddle. I believe that to accord sacrifice the status of an object-related aim that existed de-noble in the mind (and was not merely the result of a defensive alteration of another aim) would necessitate viewing human nature as containing some inherently "good" qualities. Keeping in mind that Freud declared the idea of human goodness to be an "evil illusion" (Freud, 1933, p. 104) and regarded vast swathes of humanity as basically "antisocial and anticultural" (Freud, 1927, p. 7), such acceptance of human goodness could have been a hard pill to swallow for his early followers. Current analysts, however, have begun to take a kinder view of man's nature and address positive emotions and attitudes alongside the usual psychopathological ones. This contribution on sacrifice is one more reflection of this salutary development in contemporary psychoanalysis.

NOTES

CHAPTER 1: COURAGE

1. "Moral courage" must be distinguished from "moral narcissism" (Green, 1980). The former uplifts and the latter destroys the capacity for object relations. More importantly, moral courage permits self-expression and authenticity and moral narcissism, by attacking one's dependent longings and intellectual desires, creates a falsely exalted self.

2. See also Poland's (2007) elucidation of courage in the life of the psychoanalyst Muriel Gardiner in this context.

3. Edward's abdication speech in 1936, though short and terse, conveys the strength of his convictions in no uncertain terms.

4. See in this connection, Casement's (1991) thoughts on "unconscious hope," which pertains to the search for development-facilitating objects and experiences.

5. A curious overlap seems to exist between cowardice and procrastination. Biswas-Diener (2012) observes that not finishing a task that one undertook is associated with a kind of "minor cowardice" (p. 7) in many people's minds.

6. I classified the experience of happiness into four types: pleasure-based (elation), assertion-based (joy), merger-based (ecstasy), and fulfillment-based (contentment), while acknowledging the existence of hybrid forms and transcultural variations (see Akhtar, 2010).

7. Curiously, "renewed faith," i.e., faith found after having been transiently lost, is even a greater inspirer of courage (Ashton, 2007).

8. Committing suicide is frequently seen as an act of cowardice. I beg to differ. I believe that to end one's own life is a very courageous act. However, I hasten to add that what motivates or drives such courage is very often a morbid state of mind. At the same time, one must remain open to the possibility that some suicides do result from a rational preference of dignified death over

a life of indignity and shame. Such suicides are acts of pure courage. Freud's physician-assisted suicide (see Gay, 1988, for details) is an example *par excellence* of it.

9. Essentially, this experiment consisted of one-year-old children crawling on all fours on a glass floor with the mother standing across the room facing the child. A checker-board design had been glued from below to the first half of the floor while the remaining half was left "naked." The latter gave the impression of sudden depth (termed "visual cliff" in the study) and therefore evoked fear in the child. The observers noted that if the mother maintained an affectively-neutral face, the child stopped and did not cross the visual cliff. However, if the mother smiled and encouraged the child, he or she became able to crawl over the transparent glass floor. The conclusion of this experiment was that the child's trust in his or her ability to take risks and bear some tension is enhanced by the mother's faith in him. In the terms of our discourse here, we might call the child's enhanced capacity as "borrowed courage."

10. For a detailed discussion of the distinction between needs and wishes, see Akhtar (1999b).

11. It is this sort of useful "regression" that Winnicott (1955) most likely had in mind when he declared that "it takes a great deal of courage to have a breakdown" (p. 21).

12. This case has also been included in my book, *Turning Points in Dynamic Psychotherapy* (Akhtar, 2009c). Moreover, the name used here is fictitious, just as are the names of all the patients reported in this book.

13. Borrowing the term from the renowned embryologist, Conrad Waddington (1947), Lichtenberg elucidated the concept of 'self-righting' in the context of child development. According to him, "self-righting refers to an inherent tendency to rebound from a deficit with a developmental advance when a positive change in an inhibiting external condition occurs" (p. 328). Once the environmental conditions have become friendlier, children try to make up for lost time by seeking and creating positive experiences and interactions. Lichtenberg emphasized that "self-righting" is not restricted to childhood and continues to be an important psychic attribute throughout the lifespan.

14. The controversial matter of an analyst apologizing to the patient is taken up in detail in chapter 5 on forgiveness.

15. In a recently edited volume (Akhtar, 2011a), I have gathered clinical examples of "unusual interventions," such as gratis treatment, variable duration of sessions, physical contact with the patient, giving advice, deliberately conducting psychotherapy outside the office, giving gifts to the patient, refusing to listen to kind of material and so on. The book also discusses the theoretical rationale, indications, contraindications, risks, and benefits of such measures.

CHAPTER 2: RESILIENCE

1. The "instinct for recovery" resurfaced in the form of the drive for self-actualization implicit in the works of Winnicott (1960), Balint (1968), and Kohut (1977). Lichtenberg's (1989) notion of "self-righting" also contains heuristic echoes of this concept.

CHAPTER 3: GRATITUDE

1. Procci's (1987) concept of "mockery through caricature" is pertinent in this context. The element of excess in the submissive attitude of such individuals exposes to the world the unconsciously registered unfairness of the benefactor (he gave so little!). Pseudo-compliance with the imagined anti-instinctual attitude of the benefactor to the point of caricature serves to discharge repressed aggression towards him.

2. Grunberger's stance must be taken as largely metaphorical. Freud, it should be noted, considered all scenarios involving intrauterine life to be "retrospective phantasying" (1918, p. 103) and declared that the idea of "intrauterine happiness is far-fetched" (1926, p. 136).

3. Analysts invariably thank their patients for such gifts in the 'Acknowledgments' section of their books. However, they rarely write about their gratitude in scientific papers. O'Shaughnessy is at least one step ahead of most since, in her recent contribution to the topic, she openly acknowledges having left "untouched the question of the analyst's gratitude to the patient" (p. 2008, p. 86).

4. The Christian practice of saying grace before meals creates a bridge between the 'microcosm' of childhood moral instruction and the 'macrocosm' of what I have called 'existential gratitude' here.

CHAPTER 4: GENEROSITY

1. Winnicott himself recalled having made this statement at a scientific meeting of the British Psycho-Analytical Society in 1940. However, 1960 was the first time it appeared in print.

2. The PEP Archive (1871-2008) contains the complete text of *46* premier journals in psychoanalysis, *70* classic psychoanalytic books, and the full text and editorial notes of the 24 volumes of the *Standard Edition*as well as the 18 volume German *GesammelteWerke*. PEP Archive spans over 137 publication years and contains the full text of articles whose source ranges from 1871 through 2008.

There are approximately 75,000 articles and 8,728 figures that originally resided on 1449 volumes with a total of over *650,000 printed pages.*

3. In his book, *Giving* (2007), Bill Clinton, former President of the United States, notes that being taught to tithe during childhood was foundational for his civic-mindedness and work on behalf of others.

4. It is tempting to call this condition "compulsive generosity," a temptation to which Meltzer (1975) did fall prey. However, the prefix "compulsive" is inappropriate in this context since compulsive acts are, by definition, reluctantly performed and undertaken solely to seek relief from the anxiety produced by underlying obsessions.

5. At times, the "controlling" and adverse impact of generosity is inadvertent. For instance, one of Oprah Winfrey's numerous beneficiaries underwent divorce, with her husband blaming Oprah publicly: "She did not mean to hurt us, but she ruined our marriage with her generosity and insistence on taking up so much of Gayle's time" (cited in Kelley, 2010, p. 258).

6. Tongue-in-cheek though this may sound, one also has to consider a nosological entity like "absurd generosity." Otherwise, where would one put the wealthy heiress Leona Helmsley's (1920-2007) leaving millions of dollars to her Maltese dog, "Trouble"?

7. I have elsewhere (Akhtar, 2009b, pp. 91-93) discussed the complex issues involved in conducting gratis treatment.

8. Two things should be noted about the clinical material included in this paper. First, all names in clinical vignettes are fictitious. Second, cases 1 and 6 have been "lent" to me by two colleagues, both of whom prefer to remain anonymous.

9. This case and case 5 have also appeared in my earlier discussion (Akhtar, 2009b) of psychotherapy and money.

10. Casement (1999) and Anderson (2000) also take exception to Kradin's exaltation of generosity as a "cardinal" therapeutic principle. Anderson goes a step further and suggests that, at times, the analyst's generosity can pose problems for clinical work, especially if the patient is not receptive to such gestures.

11. The finding that in the year 2010, America's 308.7 million contributed $290.98 billion to charity while China's 1.3 billion people gave $16.4 billion (Von Bergen, 2012) has the initial impact of making the Chinese seem less generous. However, their generosity might manifest via taking better care of their elderly and infirm relatives.

CHAPTER 5: FORGIVENESS

1. A computerized update extending up to 1998 fares no better in this regard.

2. In contrast, "punishment" finds 253 mentions. This speaks volumes not only to Freud's own "punishing" (Gay, 1988, p. 140) conscience but to a certain puritanical bent of the classical psychoanalytic theory itself.

3. The term "identity" has had a checkered history in psychoanalytic theorizing for the same reason (Akhtar, 1999a).

4. An alternate view is voiced by Hunter (1978) who states that "forgetting is an almost invariable accompaniment of forgiving, and forgiving leads to it, the process not being complete unless forgetting results. This is literally forgetting and not repressing, and is analogous to the letting go and forgetting that takes place through mourning. " (p. 167). Interestingly, it is a Dutch novelist, Cees Nooteboom, who brings the two views (i.e., what is forgiven should be forgotten *and* what is forgiven should be remembered) together in a deliciously paradoxical manner. Nooteboom (1980) says that the injury that has been forgiven should be forgotten but the fact that is has been forgotten should be remembered!

5. Note Nietcshze's remark that "a small revenge is humaner than no revenge at all" (1905, p. 71), and Heine's (quoted in Freud, 1930, p. 110) witticism that "one must, it is true, forgive one's enemies—but not before they have been hanged."

6. Material reparation (e.g., giving gifts following a dispute) alone, however, is far less effective in eliciting forgiveness than a sincere apology with no offer for tangible compensation (Sanders, 1995).

7. Empirical research has demonstrated that apologies, when they are constructed appropriately, reduce the victim's motivation to blame, punish, or retaliate against the transgressor (Darby and Schlenker, 1982, 1989; Ohbuchi et al. 1989); improve the victim's perception of, and empathy with, the transgressor's character (McMillen and Helmreich, 1969; Scher and Darley, 1997; O'Malley and Greenberg, 1993); and increase the victim's willingness to forgive the transgressor (McCullough et al. 1997; Sanders, 1995).

8. Klein (1937) demonstrated the dynamics of 'reparation' in not only mother-child relationship, but in father's relationship to his children, childhood and adolescent peer relationships, adult friendships, and choice of a mate as well.

9. At first, of course, the child "does not forgive his mother for having granted the favor of sexual intercourse not to himself but to his father" (Freud, 1910, p. 171). Such "forgiveness" arises only with passage of time and with the above-mentioned compensations to the child.

10. A parallel phenomenon is that of "caricatured modesty" (Jones, 1913, p. 244) seen in conjunction with a narcissistic personality.

11. See also the related descriptions of "someday . . ." and "if only" fantasies (Akhtar, 1996) in this regard.

12. Such phenomenological division, reminiscent of Kohut's (1977) "Tragic Man"—"Guilty Man" dichotomy, is admittedly simplistic. In the flow and flux of analytic clinical material, we are always in the world of "both/and. " Thus trauma-based revenge fantasies gradually leading to forgiving the "enemy," almost always co-exist with guilt over one's own ruthlessness and the consequent need to be forgiven. Yet, separating the two configurations does afford a didactic ease in elucidating the dynamics of respective events in the transference-countertransference axis.

13. Forgiving early offenders (and the analyst who embodies them in the transference) also mobilizes fears that the treatment might come to an end. See Grunert (1979) and Akhtar (1992) for negative therapeutic reactions emanating from this dynamic.

14. The sexual abuse literature pays special attention to this issue, with some family therapists (e.g., Madanes, 1990) requiring the perpetrator to actually, even ritualistically, apologize to the victim in front of other family members.

15. Some might question such agenda-based approach to clinical work. After all, the aim in psychoanalytic listening involves "not directing one's notice to anything in particular" (Freud, 1912, p. 111) and dealing with all material alike. At the same time, there is also a legacy of "strategy" (Levy, 1987) in psychoanalysis that dictates measured, deliberate tracks of interventions in certain circumstances. It is my impression that most clinicians strike an intuitive balance between a free-floating and strategic approach to clinical listening and interventions.

16. In work with children, such attacks might involve the analyst's office and even his body.

17. Blum (1997) has recently raised questions about Winnicott's recommendation. His critique, especially of the handling of the particular case on which Winnicott's views are based, is well reasoned. Nonetheless, I believe that while the particular clinical example used by Winnicott might not have been the best for the purpose, the idea he was proposing does have merit.

18. In Sophocles' tale, Philoctetes, the Greek warrior, is persuaded to forgive his betrayers by Neoptolemus. However, he remains unconvinced till the image of Heracles appears before the two of them and commands Philoctetes to renounce suffering, forgive his enemies and proceed to the conquest of Troy.

19. The fact that Fordham University School of Law in New York City in 2002 held a conference on "The Role of Forgiveness in The Law" is encouraging in this regard.

CHAPTER 6: SACRIFICE

1. Freud acknowledged that his ideas were partly derived from William Robertson-Smith's (1889) *Lectures on the Religion of the Semites*. Levitt (2010) has, however, argued that Ludwig Fuerbach (1862) might have been the true progenitor of Freud's notions.
2. For prototypes of such altruism in animals, see Hrdy (1999).

REFERENCES

Abraham, K. (1917). "The spending of money in anxiety states." In Selected Papers of Karl Abraham, MD, pp. 299–302. London, UK: Hogarth Press, 1927.

———. (1924). The influence of oral erotism on character formation. In Selected Papers of Karl Abraham, MD, pp. 393–406. London, UK: Hogarth Press, 1927.

———. (1925). Psychoanalytical notes on Coue's system of self mastery. In Clinical Papers and Essays on Psycho–Analysis, pp. 306–327. London, UK: Hogarth Press, 1955.

Abram, J. (2007). *The Language of Winnicott, 2nd Edition.* London, UK: Karnac Books.

Abrams, S. (1978). The teaching and learning of psychoanalytic developmental psychology. *Journal of the American Psychoanalytic Association 26*: 387–406.

Akhtar, S. (1991). Three fantasies related to unresolved separation–individuation: a less recognized aspect of severe character pathology. *In Beyond the Symbiotic Orbit: Advances in Separation—Individuation Theory—Essays in Honor of Selma Kramer, M.D.* eds. S. Akhtar and H. Parens, pp. 261–284. Hillsdale, NJ: Analytic Press.

———. (1992a). Tethers, orbits, and invisible fences: clinical, developmental, sociocultural, and technical aspects of optimal distance. In *When the Body Speaks: Psychological Meanings in Kinetic Clues.* eds. S. Kramer and S. Akhtar, pp. 21–57. Northvale, NJ: Jason Aronson.

———. (1992b). *Broken Structures: Severe Personality Disorders and Their Treatment.* Northvale, NJ: Jason Aronson.

———. (1994) Object constancy and adult psychopathology. *International Journal of Psycho–Analysis 75*: 441–455.

———. (1996) "Someday . . ." and "if only" fantasies: pathological optimism and inordinate nostalgia as related forms of idealization. *Journal of the American Psychoanalytic Association* 44: 723–753.

———. (1997). *The psychodynamic dimension of terrorism. Psychiatric Annals 29*: 350–355.

———. (1999a). *Immigration and Identity: Turmoil, Treatment, and Transformation.* Northvale, NJ: Jason Aronson.

———. (1999b) The distinction between needs and wishes: implications for psychoanalytic theory and technique. *Journal of the American Psychoanalytic Association 47:* 113–151.

———. (1999c). *Inner Torment: Living Between Conflict and Fragmentation.* Northvale, NJ: Jason Aronson.

———. (2002). Forgiveness: origins, dynamics, psychopathology, and technical relevance. *Psychoanalytic Quarterly 71*: 175–212.

———. (2003). *New Clinical Realms: Pushing the Envelope of Theory and Technique.* Northvale, NJ: Jason Aronson.

———. (2009a). ed. *Good Feelings: Psychoanalytic Reflections on Positive Emotions and Attitudes.* London, UK: Karnac Books.

———. (2009b). *Comprehensive Dictionary of Psychoanalysis.* London, UK: Karnac Books.

———. (2009c). *Turning Points in Dynamic Psychotherapy: Initial Assessment, Boundaries, Money, Disruptions and Suicidal Crises.* London, UK: Karnac Books.

———. (2010). Happiness: origins, forms, and technical relevance. *American Journal of Psychoanalysis 70*: 219–244.

———. (2011a). ed. *Unusual Interventions: Alterations of the Frame, Method, and Relationship in Psychotherapy and Psychoanalysis.* London, UK: Karnac Books.

———. (2011b). *Matters of Life and Death: Psychoanalytic Perspectives.* London, UK: Karnac Books

———. (2011c). *Immigration and Acculturation: Mourning, Adaptation, and the Next Generation.* Lanham, MD: Jason Aronson.

———. (2012). *Psychoanalytic Listening: Methods, Limits, and Innovations.* London, UK: Karnac Books.

Akhtar, S., and Blue, S. (2012). Command and legacy: Martin Luther King, Jr. In *The African American Experience: Psychoanalytic Perspectives.* ed. S. Akhtar, pp. 87–116. Lanham, MD: Jason Aronson.

Alford, F. (1990). Psychoanalysis and social theory: sacrificing psychoanalysis to Utopia? *Psychoanalysis and Contemporary Thought 13*: 483–507.

Altman, L.L. (1977). Some viscissitudes of love. *Journal of the American Psychoanalytic Association 23*: 35–52.

Amati-Mehler, J., and Argentieri, S. (1989). Hope and hopelessness: a technical problem? *International Journal of Psychoanalysis 70*: 295–304.

Anderson, R.W. (2000). Response to Richard Kradin's 'Generosity: a psychological and interpersonal motivational factor of therapeutic relevance.' *Journal of Analytical Psychology 45*: 123–130.

Andreson, J. (1984). The motif of sacrifice and the sacrifice complex. *Contemporary Psychoanalysis 20*: 526–559.

Anthony, E. J. (1987). Risk, vulnerability, and resilience: an overview. In *The Invulnerable Child.* eds. E. J. Anthony and B. J. Cohler, pp. 3–47. New York, NY: Guilford Press.

Anthony, E. J., and Cohler, B. J. (1987).eds. *The Invulnerable Child.* New York, NY: Guilford Press.

Ashton, P. W. (2007). *From the Brink: Experiences of the Void from a Depth Psychology Perspective.* London, UK: Karnac.

Bach, S. (1977). On narcissistic state of consciousness. *International Journal of Psychoanalysis 58*: 209–233.

Badcock, C. R. (1986). *The Problem of Altruism.* New York, NY: Blackwell.

Balint, M. (1957).*The Doctor, His Patient, and the Illness.* New York, NY: International Universities Press.

———. (1968). *The Basic Fault: Therapeutic Aspects of Regression.* London, UK: Tavistock.

Barnland, D. C, and Yoshioko, M. (1990). Apologies: Japanese and American styles. *International Journal of Intercultural Relations 14*: 193–206.

Benedek, T. (1938). Adaptation to reality in early infancy. *Psychoanalytic Quarterly* 7: 200–214.

———. (1977). Ambivalence, passion, and love. *Journal of the American Psychoanalytic Association 25*: 53–79.

Bergler, E. (1935). Some special varieties of ejaculatory disturbance not hitherto described. *International Journal of Psychoanalysis 16*: 84–95.

———. (1945). Psychopathology of ingratitude. In *The World of Emotions,* ed. C. Socarides, pp. 135–142. New York, NY: International Universities Press, 1977.

———. (1961). *Problems of Curable and Incurable Neurosis: Neurotic Versus Malignant Masochism.* New York, NY: Liveright.

Bergman, M. S. (1971). Psychoanalytic observations on the capacity to love. In *Separation–Individuation,* eds. J.B. McDevitt and C.F. Settlage, pp. 15–41. New York, NY: International Universities Press.

———. (1992). *In the Shadow of Moloch: The Sacrifice of Children and Its Impact on Western Religions.* New York. NY: Columbia University Press.

Berliner, B. (1958). The role of object relations in moral masochism. *Psychoanlaytic Quarterly 27*: 38–56.

Bick, E. (1968). The experience of the skin in early object relations. *International Journal of Psychoanalysis 49*: 484–486.

Bion, W. (1957) Differentiation of the psychotic from the non–psychotic personalities. *International Journal of Psycho-Analysis 38*: 266–275.

Biswas-Diener, R. (2012) *The Courage Quotient: How Science Can Make You Braver.* San Francisco, CA: Jossey-Bass.

Blos, P. (1967). The second individuation process of adolescence. *Psychoanalytic Study of the Child 22*: 162–186.

Blum, H. P. (1997). Clinical and developmental dimensions of hate. *Journal of the American Psychoanalytic Association 45*: 359–375.

———. (2008). Resilience and its correlates. In *The Unbroken Soul: Tragedy, Trauma, and Resilience.* eds. H. Parens, H. Blum, and S. Akhtar, pp. 171–191. Lanham, MD: Jason Aronson.

Borneman, E. (1976). ed. *The Psychoanalysis of Money.* New York, NY: Urizen Books.

Bowlby, J. (1988). *A Secure Base: Parent–Child Attachment and Healthy Human Development.* New York, NY: Basic Books.

Brenner, C. (1976). *Psychoanalytic Technique and Psychic Conflict.* New York, NY: International Universities Press.

Brenner, I. (2004). *Psychic Trauma: Dynamics, Symptoms, and Treatments.* Lanham, MD: Jason Aronson.

———. (2008). On genocidal persecution and resilience. In *The Unbroken Soul: Tragedy, Trauma, and Resilience.* eds. H. Parens, H. Blum, and S. Akhtar, pp. 65–83. Lanham, MD: Jason Aronson.

Brinkley, J. (2012). "Yitzhak Shamir, Former Israeli Prime Minister and Militia Leader, Dies at 96." The New York Times, July 1, 2012, p. 18.

Brodsky, J. (1973). Elegy for Robert Powell. In *A Part of Speech.* New York, NY: Farrar, Strauss, and Giroux.

Bruner, J. (1990). *Acts of Meaning.* Cambridge, MA: Harvard University Press.

Buechler, S. (2012). *Still Practicing: The Heartaches and Joys of a Clinical Career.* New York, NY: Routledge.

Bunker, H. A. (1933). Review of 'The Meaning of Sacrifice' by R. Money–Kryle. *Psychoanalytic Quarterly 2*: 154–157.

Cairns, D. L. (1999) Representations of remorse and reparation in classical Greece. In *Remorse and Reparation*, ed. M. Cox, pp. 171–178. London: Jessica Kingsley Publishers.

Campbell, J., and Pile, S. (2011). Space travels of the Wolfman: phobia and its worlds. *Psychoanalysis and History 13*: 69–88.

Carcamo, C. E. (1943). The plumed serpent: psychoanalysis of the Maya–Aztec religion and of human sacrifice. *Review Psicoanál 1*: 5–38.

Carveth, D.(1992). Dead end kids: projective identification and sacrifice in 'Orphans.' *International Review of Psychoanalysis 19*: 217–227.

Casement, A. (1999). Response to Richard Kradin's 'Generosity: a psychological and interpersonal motivational factor of therapeutic relevance.' *Journal of Analytical Psychology 44*: 237–243.

Casement, P. (1991). *Learning from the Patient.* New York, NY: Guilford Press.

Celenza, A. (2007). *Sexual Boundary Violations: Therapeutic, Supervisory, and Academic Contexts.* Lanham, MD: Jason Aronson.

Chase, D. (2000). *Restorative justice: use of apologies in criminal law.* Virginia Lawyers Weekly February 21, 2000.

Chasseguet-Smirgel, J. (1985). *The Ego-Ideal: A Psychoanalytical Essay on the Malady of the Ideal.* New York, NY: W.W. Norton.

———. (1988). The triumph of humor. In *Fantasy, Myth, and Reality: Essays in Honor of Jacob Arlow.* eds. H.P. Blum, Y. Kramer, A. K. Richards, and A. D. Richards, pp. 197–213. Madison, CT: International Universities Press.

Chekov, A. (1927). Death of a government clerk. *Anton Chekov: Early Short Stories 1883–1883,* ed. S. Foote, transl. C. Garnet. New York, NY: The Modern Library.

Cheney, D. L., Seyfarth, R. M., and Silk, B. M. (1995). The role of grunts in reconciling opponents and facilitating interactions among adult female baboons. *Animal Behavior 50*: 249–257.

Chess, S., and Thomas, A. (1986). *Temperament in Clinical Practice.* New York, NY: Guilford.

Chiesa, M. (2001). Envy and gratitude. In *Kleinian Theory: A Contemporary Perspective.* ed. C. Bronstein, pp. 93–107. London, UK: Whurr Publishers.

Clinton, B. (2007). *Giving: How Each of Us Can Change the World.* New York, NY: Alfred A. Knopf.

Coen, S. (2002). *Affect and Tolerance in the Patient and the Analyst.* Northvale, NJ: Jason Aronson.

Coles, R. (1965). On courage. *Contemporary Psychoanalysis 1*: 85–98.

Colton, C. C. (1822). *Lacon, or Many Things in Few Words, Addressed to Those Who Think.* Whitefish, MT: Kessinger Publishing, 2004.

Cooper, A. M. (1988). The narcissistic–masochistic character. In *Masochism: Current Psychoanalytic Perspectives.* eds. R. A. Glick, and D. I. Meyers, pp. 117–138. Hillsdale, NJ: The Analytic Press.

Cords, M. (1992). Post-conflict reunions and reconciliation in long–tailed Macaques. *Animal Behaviour 44*: 57–61.

Crawford, S. (in press). Generosity. In *Being and Relating in Psychotherapy: Clinical and Theoretical Perspectives.* eds. C. Driver, S. Crawford and J. Stewart. Basingstoke, UK: Palgrave Macmillan.

Cyrulnik, B. (2004). *Parlerd'Amour au bord du Gouffre.* Paris, France: Odile Jacob.

———. (2005). *The Whispering of Ghosts.* trans. S. Fairfield. New York, NY: Other Press.

———. (2008). Children in war and their resiliences. In *The Unbroken Soul: Tragedy, Trauma, and Resilience.* eds. H. Parens, H. Blum, and S. Akhtar, pp. 21–36. Lanham, MD: Jason Aronson.

Darby, B. W., and Schlenker, B. R. (1982). Children's reactions to apologies. *Journal of Personality and Social Psychology 43*: 742–753.

———. (1989). Children's reactions to transgressions: effects on the actor's apology, reputation, and remorse. *British Journal of Social Psychology 28*: 353–364.

Das, L. S. (1997). *Awakening the Buddha Within.* New York, NY: Bantam Books.

Deutsch, H. (1942). Some forms of emotional disturbance and their relationship to schizophrenia. *Psychoanalytic Quarterly 11*: 301–321.

De Waal, F. B. (1989). *Peacemaking among Primates.* Cambridge, MA: Harvard University Press.

De Waal, F. B. and Aureli, F. (1996). Consolation, reconciliation, and a possible cognitive difference between Macaques and Chimpanzees. In *Reaching into Thought*, eds. A. E. Russon, K. A. Bard, and S.T. Parker, pp. 80–110. Cambridge, UK: Cambridge University Press.

De Waal, F. B., and van Roosmalen, A. (1979) Reconciliation and consolation among chimpanzees. *Behavioral Ecology and Sociobiology 5*: 55–66.

Diagnostic and Statistical Manual of Mental Disorders (4th ed.). (2000). Washington, DC: American Psychiatric Publishing Inc.

Durham, M. S. (1990). The therapist and the concept of revenge: the law of talion. *The Journal of Pastoral Care 44*: 131–137.

———. (2000). *The Therapist's Encounters with Revenge and Forgiveness.* London, UK: Jessica Kingsley Publishers

Edgcumbe, R., and Burgner, M. (1972). Some problems in the conceptualization of early object relationships. *Psychoanalytic Study of the Child 27*: 283–314.

Ehrenfels, C. (1908). *Die sadistischen Liebesopfer des Abend-und Morgenlandes.* [The sadistic love sacrifices of the West and the East]. *Sexual probleme* 4: 299–320.

Eidelberg, L. (1968). *The Encyclopedia of Psychoanalysis.* New York, NY: Free Press.

Emde, R. (1991). Positive emotions for psychoanalytic theory: surprises from infancy research and new directions. *Journal of the American Psychoanalytic Association 39 (S)*: 5–44.

Emde, R., Graensbauer, T., and Harmon, R. (1976). *Emotional Expression in Infancy.* New York, NY: International Universities Press.

Erikson, E. (1950). *Childhood and Society.* New York, NY: W. W. Norton.

———. (1969). *Gandhi's Truth: On the Origins of Militant Non–Violence.* New York, NY: W. W. Norton.

———. (1982). *The Life Cycle Completed: A Review.* New York, NY: W. W. Norton.

Erlich, H. S. (2008). Envy and gratitude: some current reflections. In *Envy and Gratitude Revisited.* eds. P. Roth and A. Lemma, pp. 50–62. London, UK: Karnac Books.

Esman, A. (1983). Stimulus barrier: a review and reconsideration. *Psychoanalytic Study of the Child 38:* 193–207.

Fadman, J., and Frager, R. (1979). *Theories of Personality.* São Paulo, Brasil: do Brasil Ltda.

Fairbairn, W. R. D. (1940). Schizoid factors in the personality. In *An Object Relations Theory of Personality, pp. 3–27.* New York, NY: Basic Books, 1952.

———. (1952). *An Object Relations Theory of Psychoanalysis.* New York, NY: Basic Books.

Feiner, A. (1977). Countertransference and the anxiety of influence. *Contemporary Psychoanalysis 13*: 1–15.

Feiner, A. H., and Levenson, E. A. (1968). The compassionate sacrifice: an explanation of a metaphor. *Psychoanalytic Review 55*: 552–573.

Fenichel, O. (1938). The drive to amass wealth. *Psychoanalytic Quarterly* 7: 69–95.

———. (1945*). The Psychoanalytic Theory of Neurosis.* New York, NY: W. W. Norton.

Ferenczi, S. (1914). The ontogenesis of the interest in money. In *First Contributions to Psychoanalysis, pp. 319–331.* New York, NY: Brunner/Mazel, 1980.

———. (1930). Thoughts on 'pleasure in passivity.' In *Final Contributions to the Problems and Methods of Psychoanalysis, pp. 224–227.* New York, NY: Brunner/Mazel, 1980.

Fleiss, R. (1942). The metapsychology of the analyst. *Psychoanalytic Quarterly 11*: 211–227.

Fodor, A. (1946). The origin of the Mosaic prohibition against cooking the suckling in the mother's milk. *International Journal of Psychoanalysis 27*: 140–144.

Fonagy, P. (2009). Commentary on 'Forgiveness.' In *Good Feelings: Psychoanalytic Reflections on Positive Emotions and Attitudes.* ed. S. Akhtar, pp. 441–452. London, UK: Karnac Books.

Fonagy, P. and Target, M. (1997). Attachment and reflective function: their role in self–organization. *Development and Psychopathology 9*: 679–700.

Ford, D. (2012). *Courage: Overcoming Fear and Igniting Self–Confidence.* New York, NY: HarperCollins Publishers.

Fox, M.J. (2002). *Lucky Man.* New York, NY: Hyperion Books.

Frady, M. (2006). *Martin Luther King Jr.: A Life.* New York, NY: Penguin Books.

Frank, A.W. (2004). *The Renewal of Generosity: Illness, Medicine, and How to Live.* Chicago, IL: University of Chicago Press.

Freud, A. (1936). *The Ego and Mechanisms of Defence*. New York, NY: International Universities Press, 1966.
———. (1956). Comments on 'A Mother's Observations.' *Psychoanalytic Study of the Child 11*: 427–433.
———. (1965). Normality and pathology in childhood. In *The Writings of Anna Freud, Vol 6*, pp. 3–273. New York, NY: International Universities Press.
Freud, S. (1895). Project for a scientific psychology. *Standard Edition 1*: 173–280.
———. (1901). The psychopathology of everyday life. *Standard Edition 6*: 1–279.
———. (1905a) On psychotherapy. *Standard Edition* 7: 257–268.
———. (1905b). Three essays on the theory of sexuality. *Standard Edition* 7: 135–243.
———. (1908). Character and anal erotism. *Standard Edition 9*: 167–176.
———. (1908). On the sexual theories of children. *Standard Edition 9*: 209–226.
———. (1909). Five lectures on psychoanalysis. *Standard Edition 11*: 9–55.
———. (1910a). 'Wild' psychoanalysis. *Standard Edition 11*: 219–228.
———. (1910b). A special type of object choice made by men. *Standard Edition 11*: 163–175.
———. (1910). Contribution to a discussion on suicide. *Standard Edition 11*: 231–232.
———. (1912). On the universal tendency to debasement in the sphere of love. Standard *Edition 11*: 178–190.
———. (1912). Recommendations to physicians practicing psychoanalysis. *Standard Edition 12*: 111–120.
———. (1913). Totem and taboo. *Standard Edition 13*: 1–161.
———. (1914). On narcissism. *Standard Edition 14*: 67–103.
———. (1915). Observations on transference love. *Standard Edition 12*: 157–171.
———. (1915). Instincts and their vicissitudes. *Standard Edition 14*: 117–140.
———. (1916). Some character types met with in psychoanalytic work. *Standard Edition 14*: 310–333.
———. (1917). A childhood recollection from 'Dichtung und Wahrheit.' *Standard Edition 17*: 145–156.
———. (1918). From the history of an infantile neurosis. *Standard Edition 17*: 1–122.
———. (1920). Beyond the pleasure principle. *Standard Edition 18*: 7–64.
———. (1926). Inhibitions, symptoms and anxiety. *Standard Edition 20*: 75–175.
———. (1927). The future of an illusion. *Standard Edition 21*: 5–56.
———. (1930). Civilization and its discontents. *Standard Edition 21*: 59–145.
———. (1933). New introductory lectures on psychoanalysis. *Standard Edition 22*: 7–182.

———. (n.d.). General index. *Standard Edition 23*: 313–326.

Fromm-Reichman, F. (1966). Psychoanalysis and psychotherapy. In *Selected Papers of Frieda Fromme-Reichman.* ed. D. Bullard. Chicago, IL: University of Chicago Press.

Fuerbach, L. (1862). Das Geheimnis des Opfersoder Der Mensch ist. In *Gesammelte Werke II, pp. 26–52.* Berlin, Germany: AkademieVerlag, 1990.

Gabbard, G. (2000). On gratitude and gratification. *Journal of the American Psychoanalytic Association 48*: 697–716.

Galdston, R. (1987). The longest pleasure: a psychoanalytic study of hatred. *International Journal of Psycho-Analysis 68*: 371–378.

Gallagher, M. (2000). Prayer asks forgiveness for anti–Semitism. *The Philadelphia Inquirer,* March 5, 2000, p. J–7.

Gandhi, M. K. (1929). *The Story of My Experiments with Truth: An Autobiography.* trans. M. Desai. Boston, MA: Beacon Press, 1957.

———. (1940). *An Autobiography: The Story of My Experiments with Truth.* transl. M. Desai. Boston, MA: Beacon Press, 1957.

Garmezy, N. (1985). Stress-resistant children: the search for protective factors. In *Recent Research in Developmental Psychopathology.* ed. J.E. Stevens, pp. 213–233. Oxford, UK: Pergamon Press.

Gartner, J. (1992). The capacity to forgive: an object relations perspective. In *Object Relations Theory and Religion: Clinical Applications.* eds. M. Finn and J. Gartner, pp. 21–31. Westport, CT: Praeger Publishers.

Garza-Guerrero, C. (2009). Commentary on 'Enthusiasm.' In *Good Feelings: Psychoanalytic Reflections on Positive Emotions and Attitudes.* ed. S. Akhtar, pp. 93–102. London, UK: Karnac Books.

Gay, P. (1988). *Freud: A Life for Our Time.* New York, NY: W.W. Norton.

Gediman, H. (1971). The concept of stimulus barrier: its review and reformulation as an adaptive ego function. *International Journal of Psychoanalysis 52*: 243–257.

Gedo, J., and Goldberg, A. (1973). *Models of the Mind.* Chicago, IL: University of Chicago Press.

Gill, M. (1982). *Analysis of Transference, Volume I: Theory and Technique.* New York, NY: International Universities Press.

Gilligan, C. (1982). *In a Different Voice.* Cambridge, MA: Harvard University Press.

Girard, R. (1977). *Violence and the Sacred.* Baltimore, MD: Johns Hopkins University Press.

Glenn, J. (1991). Transformation in normal and pathological latency. In *Beyond the Symbiotic Orbit: Advances in Separation–Individuation Theory,* eds. S. Akhtar and H. Parens, pp. 171–187. Hillsdale, NJ: Analytic Press.

Glover, E. (1940). *The Psychology of Fear and Courage.* London, UK: Penguin Books.

———. (1941). *On Fear and Courage*. London, UK: Penguin Books.

Goldberg, A. (1987). The place of apology in psychoanalysis and psychotherapy. *International Review of Psychoanalysis* 14: 409-422.

Gottlieb, R. M. (2004). Refusing the cure: Sophocles's Philoctetes and the clinical problems of the self-injurious spite, shame, and forgiveness. *International Journal of Psychoanalysis 85*: 669–689.

Green, A. (1986). Réponses à des questions inconcévables. *Topique 37*: 11–30.

Greenacre, P. (1971). *Emotional Growth: Volumes 1 and 2*. New York, NY: International Universities Press.

Greenson, R. (1960). Empathy and its vicissitudes. *International Journal of Psychoanalysis 41*: 418–424.

———. (1962). On enthusiasm. *Journal of the American Psychoanalytic Association 10*: 3–21.

———. (1967). *The Technique and Practice of Psycho-Analysis*. New York, NY: International Universities Press.

Greenspan, S. I. (1989). The development of the ego: biological and environmental specificity in the psychopathological developmental process and the selection and construction of ego defenses. *Journal of the American Psychoanalytic Association 37*: 605–638.

Griffith, J. L. (2010). *Religion That Heals, Religion That Harms: A Guide for Clinical Practice*. New York, NY: Guilford Press.

Grotstein, J. S. (1997a). Why Oedipus and not Christ?: a psychoanalytic inquiry into innocence, human sacrifice, and the sacred—part I: innocence, spirituality, and human sacrifice. *American Journal of Psychoanalysis 57*: 193–218.

———. (1997b). Why Oedipus and not Christ?: a psychoanalytic inquiry into innocence, human sacrifice, and the sacred—part II: the numinous and spiritual dimension as a metapsychological perspective. *American Journal of Psychoanalysis 57*: 317–355.

Grunberger, B. (1975). *Narcissism: Psychoanalytic Essays*. New York, NY: International Universities Press.

Grunert, U. (1979). The negative therapeutic reaction as a reactivation of a disturbed process of separation in the transference. *Bulletin of the European Psychoanlaytic Federation 65*: 5–19.

Gusdorf, G. (1948). *L'expériencehumaine du sacrifice*. Paris, France: Presses Universitaires de France.

Guttman, S. A., Jones R.L., and Parrish, S. M. (1980). eds. *The Concordance to the Standard edition of the Complete Psychological Works of Sigmund Freud*. Boston, MA: G.K. Hall.

Harding, J. (1999). Remorse and rehabilitation. *In Remorse and Reparation*, ed. M. Cox, pp. 107–115. London, UK: Jessica Kingsley Publishers.

Hartmann, H. (1939). *Ego Psychology and the Problem of Adaptation*. Trans. D. Rapaport. New York, NY: International Universities Press, 1958.

———. (1952). Mutual influences in the development of the ego and the id: earliest stages. *Psychoanalytic Study of the Child* 7: 9–30.

———. (1960). *Psychoanalysis and Moral Values*. New York, NY: International Universities Press.

Harvey, M. R., and Tummala–Narrra, P. (2007). *Sources and Expression Resiliency in Trauma Survivors: Ecological Theory, Multicultural Practice*. Binghamton, NY: Haworth Press.

Hauser, S. T., Allen, J.P., Golden, E. (2006) *Out of the Woods: Tales of Resilient Teens*. Cambridge, MA: Harvard University Press.

Hawking, S. (1998). *A Brief History of Time*. New York, NY: Bantam Books.

———. (2001). *The Universe in a Nutshell*. New York, NY: Bantam Books.

Heilbrunn, G. (1972). 'Thank you.' *Journal of the American Psychoanalytic Association 20*: 512–516.

Herman, J. (1992). *Trauma and Recovery*. New York, NY: Basic Books.

Hinshelwood, R. D. (1991). *A Dictionary of Kleinian Thought*, pp. 412–415. Northvale, NJ: Jason Aronson.

Hoffman, M. L. (1977). Sex differences in empathy and related behaviors. *Psychological Bulletin 84*: 712–722.

Hooberman, R.E. (2010). *Forgiving, Forgetting, and Moving On*. Lanham, MD: Jason Aronson.

Hrdy, S. B. (1999). *Mother Nature: A History of Mothers, Infants, and Natural Selection*. New York, NY: Pantheon Books.

Hunter, R. (1978). Forgiveness, retaliation, and paranoid reactions. *Journal of the Canadian Psychiatric Association 23*: 267–273.

Jacobs, T. (2008). On courage. *Psychoanalytic Psychology 25*: 550–555.

Jeste, D. V. and Vahia, I. V. (2008). Comparison of the conceptualization of wisdom in ancient Indian literature with modern views: focus on the Bhagavad Gita. *Psychiatry 71*: 197–209.

Jones, E. (1913). The God complex. In *Essays in Applied Psychoanalysis*, pp. 244–265. New York, NY: International Universities Press, 1964.

———. (1918). Anal erotic character traits. In *Papers on Psychoanalysis*, pp. 413–437. Baltimore, MD: Williams and Wilkens, 1950.

———. (1928). *Fear, guilt, and hate. In Papers on Psychoanalysis*. Baltimore, MD: Williams and Wilkins, 1950.

Kafka, J. S. (1992). *Multiple Realities*. New York, NY: International Universities Press.

Kagan, J. (1984). *The Nature of the Child*. New York, NY: Basic Books.

Kaufman, W. (1976). Some emotional uses of money. In *The Psychoanalysis of Money*. ed. E. Borneman, pp. 227–252. New York, NY: Urizen Books.

Kay, M. W. (1976). ed. *Webster's Collegiate Thesaurus*. Springfield, MA: G and C Merriam.

Kelley, K. (2010). *Oprah: A Biography*. New York, NY: Crown Publishers.

Kernberg, O. F. (1975). *Borderline Conditions and Pathological Narcissism*. New York, NY: Jason Aronson Press.

———. (1976). *Object Relations Theory and Clinical Psychoanalysis*. New York, NY: International Universities Press.

———. (1980). *Internal World and External Reality: Object Relations Theory Applied*. New York, NY: Jason Aronson.

———. (1984). *Severe Personality Disorders: Psychotherapeutic Strategies*. New Haven, CT: Yale University Press.

———. (1988). Clinical dimensions of masochism. In *Masochism: Current Psychoanalytic Perspectives*. eds. R.A. Glick, and D.I. Meyers, pp. 61–79. Hillsdale, NJ: The Analytic Press.

———. (1989). The narcissistic personality disorder and the differential diagnosis of antisocial behavior. *Psychiatric Clinics of North America 12*: 533–570.

———. (1992). *Aggression in Personality Disorders and Perversions*. New Haven, CT: Yale University Press.

———. (1995a). *Love Relations: Normality and Pathology*. New Haven, CT: Yale University Press.

———. (1995b). Hatred as a core affect of aggression. In *The Birth of Hatred: Developmental, Clinical, and Technical Aspects of Intense Aggression*, eds. S. Akhtar, S. Kramer, and H. Parens, pp. 53–82. Northvale, NJ: Jason Aronson.

———. (2012). *The Inseparable Nature of Love and Aggression: Clinical and Theoretical Perspectives*. Washington, DC: American Psychiatric Publishing Inc.

Kestenberg, J. S. (1972). Psychoanalytic contributions to the problem of survivors from Nazi persecution. *Israel Annals of Psychiatry and Related Disciplines 10*: 311–325.

Kestenberg, J. S., and Brenner, I. (1996). *The Last Witness: the Child Survivor of the Holocaust*. Washington, DC: American Psychiatric Press.

Khan, M. (1963). The concept of cumulative trauma. *Psychoanalytic Study of the Child 18*: 286–306.

Kidder, R. M. (2006). *Moral Courage*. New York, NY: Harper Collins.

Kimball, S.A. (2007). Refusing the infanticidal: interpretative closure in teleological readings of Abraham's sacrifice. In *The Infanticidal Logic of Evolution and Culture*, pp. 125–143. Newark, DE: University of Delaware Press.

Klauber, J. (1968). The psychoanalyst as a person. In *Difficulties in the Analytic Encounter*, pp. 123–139. New York, NY: Jason Aronson, 1981.

Klein, G. (1976). *Psychoanalytic Theory*. New York, NY: International Universities Press.

Klein, M. (1932). The significance of early anxiety–situations in the development of the ego. In *The Psycho-Analysis of Children*, pp. 176–193. New York, NY: Free Press, 1975.

———. (1937). Love, guilt, and reparation. In *Love, Guilt, and Reparation and Other Works*, pp. 306–343. New York, NY: Free Press, 1975.

———. (1940). Mourning and its relation to manic depressive states. In *Love, Guilt and Reparation and Other Works*—1921–1945, pp. 344–369. New York, NY: Free Press, 1975.

———. (1946). Notes on some schizoid mechanisms. In *The Selected Melanie Klein*, ed. J. Mitchell, pp. 175–200. New York, NY: Free Press, 1986.

———. (1948). *Contributions to Psychoanalysis (1921–1945)*. London, UK: Hogarth.

———. (1957). Envy and gratitude. In *Envy and Gratitude & Other Works 1946–1963*, pp. 176–235. New York, NY: Free Press.

———. (1959). Our adult world and its roots in infancy. In *Envy and Gratitude & Other Works 1946–1963*, pp. 247–263. New York, NY: Free Press.

Kogan, I. (1995). *The Cry of Mute Children: A Psychoanalytic Perspective of the Second Generation of the Holocaust*. London, UK: Free Association Books.

———. (2007). *The Struggle Against Mourning*. Lanham, MD: Jason Aronson.

Kohut, H. (1971). *The Analysis of the Self*. New York, NY: International Universities Press.

———. (1972). Thoughts on narcissism and narcissistic rage. *Psychoanalytic Study of the Child* 7: 360–400. New Haven, CT: Yale University Press.

———. (1977). *Restoration of the Self*. New York, NY: International Universities Press.

———. (1985). On courage. In *Self Psychology and the Humanities*. ed. C.B. Strozier, pp. 5–50. New York, NY: W. W. Norton.

Kradin, R. (1999). Generosity: a psychological and interpersonal motivational factor of therapeutic relevance. *Journal of Analytical Psychology 44*: 221–236.

Krohn, A. (1974). Borderline "empathy" and differentiation of object representations: a contribution to the psychology of object relations. *International Journal of Psychoanalysis 3*: 142–165.

Krueger, D. W. (1986). ed. *The Last Taboo: Money as a Symbol and Reality in Psychotherapy and Psychoanalysis*. New York, NY: Brunner/Mazel.

Krystal, H. (1973). Psychic reality. Paper presented to the Michigan Psychoanalytic Institute, Farmington Hills, MI.

———. (1981). The aging survivor of the Holocaust. *The Journal of Geriatric Psychiatry 14*: 165–1989.

———. (1985). Trauma and the stimulus barrier. *Psychoanalytic Inquiry 5*: 131–161.

Kulish, N. (1996). A phobia of the couch: a clinical study of psychoanalytic process. *Psychoanalytic Quarterly 65*: 465–494.

Lacan, J. (1955). *The Seminar Book—II: The Ego in Freud's Theory and in the Technique of Psychoanalysis*. trans. S. Tomaselli. Cambridge, UK: Cambridge University Press.

LaFarge, L. (2009). The workings of forgiveness: Charles Dickens and David Copperfield. *Psychoanalytic Inquiry 29*: 362–373.

LaForgue, R. (1929). 'Active' psychoanalytical technique and the will to recovery. *International Journal of Psychoanalysis 10*: 411–422.

Lansky, M. (2001). Hidden shame, working through, and the problem of forgiveness in 'The Tempest.' *Journal of the American Psychoanalytic Association 49*: 1005–1033.

———. (2003). Modification of the ego ideal, forgiveness, and the resolution of hate in Sophocles' 'Philoctetes.' *Psychoanalysis and Contemporary Thought 26*: 463–491.

———. (2005). The impossibility of forgiveness: shame fantasies as instigators of vengefulness in Euripides' 'Medea.' *Journal of the American Psychoanalytic Association 53*: 437–464.

———. (2007). Unbearable shame, splitting, and forgiveness in the resolution of vengefulness. *Journal of the American Psychoanalytic Association 55*: 571–593.

———. (2009). Forgiveness as the working through of splitting. *Psychoanalytic Inquiry 29*: 374–385.

Laplanche, J., and Pontalis, J. B. (1973).*The Language of Psychoanalysis*. trans. D. Nicholson-Smith. New York, NY: W. W. Norton.

Levine, S. (2006). Catching the wrong leopard: courage and masochism in the psychoanalytic situation. *Psychoanalytic Quarterly 75*: 533–556.

Levitt, C. (2010). Freud, Smith, and Feuerbach on sacrifice. *Canadian Journal of Psychoanalysis 18*: 20–42.

Lewinsky, H. (1951). Pathological generosity. *International Journal of Psychoanalysis 32*: 185–189.

Lewis, C. S. (1942). *The Screwtape Letters*. Belfast, Ireland: Geoffrey Bles.

Lichtenberg, J. D. (1989). *Psychoanalysis and Motivation*. Hillsdale, NJ: Analytic Press.

Lowenstein, R. M. (1958). Remarks on some variations in psychoanalytic technique. *International Journal of Psychoanalysis 39*: 202–210.

Mackinnon, R., and Michels, R. (1971). *The Psychiatric Interview in Clinical Practice*. Philadelphia, PA: Saunders and Company.

Madanes, C. (1990). *Sex, Love, and Violence: Strategies for Transformation*. New York, NY: W.W. Norton.

Mahler, M. S. (1942). Pseudo-imbecility: a magic cap of invisibility. *Psychoanalytic Quarterly 11*: 149–164.

———. (1958). On two crucial phases of integration of the sense of identity: separation-individuation and bisexual identity. *Journal of the American Psychoanalytic Association 6*: 136–149.

———. (1968). *On Human Symbiosis and the Vicissitudes of Individuation.* New York, NY: International Universities Press.

———. (1975). On the current status of the infantile neurosis. In *The Selected Papers of Margaret S. Mahler, Vol. 2*, pp. 189–194. New York, NY: Jason Aronson, 1979.

Mahler, M. S., Pine, F., and Bergman, A. (1975). *The Psychological Birth of the Human Infant.* New York, NY: Basic Books.

Maimonides, M. (1200). *Mishne Torah.* trans. E. Touger. New York, NY: Moznaim, 1989.

Mairs, N. (1966). *Waist–High in the World: A Life among the Non–Disabled.* Boston, MA: Beacon Press.

Maleson, F. (1984). Multiple meanings of masochism in psychoanalytic discourse. *Journal of the American Psychoanalytic Association 41*: 91–1020.

Mandela, N.R. (1994). *The Long Walk to Freedom.* Boston, MA: Back Bay Books, 1995.

Marshall, G. (1998). Sapir-Whorf hypothesis. In *A Dictionary of Sociology, 2nd Edition*, pp. 576–577. Oxford, UK: Oxford University Press.

Masten, A. S. (2001). Ordinary magic: resilience processes in development. *American Psychologist 56*: 227–238.

McCullough, M. E., Worthington, E. L., and Rachal, K.C. (1997). Interpersonal forgiving in close relationships. *Journal of Personality and Social Psychology 73*: 321–336.

McMillen, D. L. and Helmreich, R. L. (1969).The effectiveness of several types of ingratiation tecniques following argument. *Psychonomic Science 15*: 207–208.

McWilliams, N., Lependorf, S. (1990). Narcissistic pathology of everyday life: the denial of remorse and gratitude. *Contemporary Psychoanalysis 26*: 430–451.

Meeks, T. W. and Jeste, D. V. (2009). Neurobiology of wisdom: a literature overview. *Archives of General Psychiatry 66*: 355–365.

Meissner, W. W. (1996). Review of '*In the Shadow of Moloch: The Sacrifice of Children and Its Impact on Western Religions*' by M. S. Bergmann. *Journal of the American Psychoanalytic Association 44*: 293–297.

Meltzer, D. (1973). *Sexual States of Mind.* London, UK: Karnac Books, 2008.

———. (1975). Compulsive generosity. *Contemporary Psychoanalysis 11*: 135–145.

Melville, H. (1851) *Moby Dick; Or, the Whale.* Berkeley, CA: University of California Press, 1979.

Menaker, E. (1979). Masochism and the emergent ego. In *Selected Papers of Esther Menaker*, ed. L. Lerner, pp. 72–101. New York, NY: Human Sciences Press.

Menninger, K., and Holzman, P. (1973). *Theory of Psychoanalytic Technique*. New York, NY: Basic Books.

Mesch, D. (2009). *Women and philanthropy: a literature review*. Accessed at www.philanthropy.iupui.edu on 05/22/12.

Mish, F. C. (1987). ed. *Webster's Ninth New Collegiate Dictionary*. Springfield, MA: G and C Merriam.

Money-Kyrle, R. (1930). *The Meaning of Sacrifice*. London, UK: Hogarth Press.

Moore, B., and Fine, B. (1968). *A Glossary of Psychoanalytic Terms and Concepts*. New York, NY: American Psychoanalytic Association.

———. (1990). *Psychoanalytic Terms and Concepts*. New Haven, CT: Yale University Press.

Moore, B. and Fine, B. (1995). *Psychoanalysis: The Major Concepts*. New Haven, CT: Yale University Press.

Moses, R. (1999). *Apology and reparation*. Presented at the 1st Izmir Conference on Psychotherapy and Psychoanalysis, Izmir, Turkey, October 21–24th, 1999.

Mosher, P. (1991) *Title, Key Word, and Author Index to Psychoanalytic Journals—1920–1990*. New York, NY: American Psychoanalytic Association.

Nersessian, E. and Kopf, R. (1996). *Textbook of Psychoanalysis*. Washington, DC: The American Psychiatric Press.

Niederland, W. (1968). Clinical observations on the 'survivor syndrome.' *International Journal of Psychoanalysis 49*: 313–315.

Nietzsche, F. (1905).*Thus Spake Zarthustra*. New York, NY: Modern Library Series.

Nooteboom, C. (1980). *Rituals*. New York, NY: Penguin.

Nunberg, H. (1926). The will to recovery. *International Journal of Psychoanalysis* 7: 64–78.

———. (1947). Circumcision and problems of bisexuality. *International Journal of Psychoanalysis 28*: 145–179.

Ohbuchi, K., Kameda, M., and Agarie, N. (1989). Apology as aggression control: its role in mediating appraisal and response to harm. *Journal of Personality and Social Psychology 56*: 219–227.

Olinick, S., Poland, W., Grigg, K., and Granatir, W. (1973). The psychoanalytic work ego: process and interpretation. *International Journal of Psychoanalysis 54*: 143–151.

Olsson, P. (1994). A psychoanalytic study of integrity, inner courage, and 'good character.' *Mind and Human Interaction 5*: 34–41.

O'Malley, M. N. and Greenberg, J. (1993). Sex differences in restoring justice: the down payment effect. *Journal of Research in Personality 17*: 174–185.

O'Neil, M. K. (2009). Commentary on 'Courage.' In *Good Feelings: Psychoanalytic Reflections on Positive Emotions and Attitudes*. ed. S. Akhtar, pp. 55–62. London, UK: Karnac Books.

Orange, D. (2009). Toward the art of the living dialogue: between constructivism and hermeneutics in psychoanalytic thinking. In *Beyond Postmodernism: New Dimensions in Clinical Theory and Practice*. eds. R. Frie and D. Orange, pp. 117–142. London, UK: Routledge.

O'Shaughnessy, E. (2008). On gratitude. In *Envy and Gratitude Revisited*. eds. P. Roth and A. Lemma, pp. 79–91. London, UK: Karnac Books.

Pacella, B. (1980). The primal matrix configuration. In *Rapprochement: The Critical Subphase of Separation-Individuation*. eds. R.F. Lax, S. Bach, and J.A. Burland, pp. 117–131. New York, NY: Jason Aronson.

Parens, H. (1970). *The Development of Aggression in Early Childhood*. New York, NY: Jason Aronson.

———. (2004). *Renewal of Life: Healing from the Holocaust*. Rockwell, MD: Schreiber.

———. (2009). Resilience. In *Good Feelings: Psychoanalytic Reflections on Positive Emotions and Attitudes*. ed. S. Akhtar, pp. 329–361. London, UK: Karnac Books.

Parens, H., Blum, H., and Akhtar, S. (2008). eds. *The Unbroken Soul: Tragedy, Trauma, and Human Resilience*. Lanham, MD: Jason Aronson.

Person, E. (2007). Forgiveness and its limits: a psychological and psychoanalytic perspective. *Psychoanalytic Review 94*: 389–408.

Person, E., Cooper, A., and Gabbard, G. (2005). *Textbook of Psychoanalysis*. Washington, DC: American Psychiatric Press.

Pine, F. (1997). *Diversity and Direction in Psychoanalytic Technique*. New Haven, CT: Yale University Press.

Poland, W. (1975). Tact as a psychoanalytic function. *International Journal of Psycho-Analysis 56*: 155–161.

———. (2007). Courage and morals. *American Imago 64*: 253–259.

Potamianou, A. (1992). *Un Bouclierdans L'Economie des Etats Limites L'Espoir*. Paris, France: Presses Universitaires de France.

Prince, R. (1984). Courage and masochism in psychotherapy. *Psychoanalytic Review 71*: 47–62.

Procci, W. (1987). Mockery through caricature: a variation of introjection utilized by a masochistic woman. *Journal of the American Academy of Psychoanalysis 15*: 51–66.

Pruett, K. (1988). *The Nurturing Father*. New York, NY: Grand Central.

Rangell, L. (1952). The analysis of a doll phobia. *International Journal of Psychoanalysis 33*: 43–

———. (1963). On friendship. *Journal of the American Psychoanalytic Association 11*: 3–54.

Rappaport, D. (1998). Destruction and gratitude: some thoughts on 'The use of an object.' *Contemporary Psychoanalysis 34*: 369–378.

Reeve, C. (1998). *Still Me*. New York, NY: Ballantine.

———. (2009). *Nothing Is Impossible*. New York, NY: Random House.

Reik, T. (1941). *Masochism in Modern Man*. trans. M. H. Beigel and G. M. Kurth. New York, NY: Ferrar and Rinehart.

Ren, R., Yan, K., Su, Y., et al. (1991) The reconciliation behavior of Golden Monkeys (Rhinopiethecusroxellanaeroxellanae) in small breeding groups. *Primates 32*: 321–327.

Robertson-Smith, W. (1889). *Lectures on the Religion of the Semites*. London, UK: Black, 1927.

Rosen, I. (2009). Atonement. In *Good Feelings: Psychoanalytic Reflections on Positive Emotions and Attitudes*. ed. S. Akhtar, pp. 371–390. London, UK: Karnac Books.

———. (2009). The atonement-forgiveness dyad: identification with the aggressed. *Psychoanalytic Inquiry 29*: 411–425.

Rosenfeld, H. (1971). Theory of life and death instincts: aggressive aspects of narcissism. *International Journal of Psychoanalysis 45*: 332–337.

Rothstein, A. (1986). The seduction of money: expression of transference love. *Psychoanalytic Quarterly 55*: 296–300.

Rycroft, C. (1968). *A Critical Dictionary of Psychoanalysis*. London, UK: Penguin.

Sanders, K. (1995). *A behavioral study on forgiveness*. Senior Thesis. Claremont McKenna College.

Sandler, A. M. (1989). Comments on phobic mechanisms in childhood. *Psychoanalytic Study of the Child 44*: 101–114.

Sandler, J. (1976). Countertransference and role-responsiveness. *International Review of Psychoanalysis 3*: 43–47.

Sandler, J., and Freud, A. (1985). *The Analysis of Defense: The Ego and the Mechanisms of Defense Revisited*. New York, NY: International Universities Press.

Sandler, J., and Joffe, W. J. (1966).On skill and sublimation. Journal of the American *Psychoanalytic Association 14*: 335–355.

Sarnoff, C. (1976). *Latency*. New York, NY: Jason Aronson.

Schafer, R. (2002). Defences against goodness. *Psychoanalytic Quarterly* 71: 5–19.

———. (2005). Cordelia, Lear, and forgiveness. *Journal of the American Psychoanalytic Association 53*: 389–409.

Scheper-Hughes, N. (1999). Undoing: social suffering and the politics of remorse. In *Remorse and Reparation*, ed. M. Cox, pp. 145–170. London, UK: Jessica Kingsley Publishers.

Scher, S. J., and Darley, J.M. (1997). How effective are the things people say to apologize? Effects of the realization of the Apology Speech Act. *Journal of Psycholinguistic Research 26*: 127–140.

Schlesinger, H. (2003). *The Texture of Treatment: On the Matter of Psychoanalytic Technique*. Hillsdale, NJ: Analytic Press.

Schneider, K. (1950). *Psychopathic Personalities*. trans. M. W. Hamilton. Springfield, IL: Charles C. Thomas, 1958.

Schreber, D. P. (1903). *DenkwürdigkeiteneinesNervenkrankennebstNacträge und einemAnhangüber die Frage: 'UnterwelchenVoraussetzungendarfeinefürgeisteskrankerachtete Person gegenihrenerklärtenWillen in eineHeilenstaltfestgehalten warden?'* Leipzig, Germany: Mutze.

Searles, H. F. (1956). The psychodynamics of vengefulness. *Psychiatry 19*: 31–39.

———. (1958). Positive feelings in the relationship between the schizophrenic and his mother. In *Collected Papers on Schizophrenia and Related Subjects,* pp. 216–253. New York, NY: International Universities Press, 1965.

Seelig, B., and Rosof, L. (2009). Altruism. In *Good Feelings: Psychoanalytic Reflections on Positive Emotions and Attitudes*. ed. S. Akhtar, pp. 63–91. London, UK: Karnac Books.

Settlage, C. F. (1992). Psychoanalytic observations on adult development in life and in the therapeutic relationship. *Psychoanalysis and Contemporary Thought 15*: 349–375.

———. (1994). On the contribution of separation-individuation theory to psychoanalysis: developmental process, pathogenesis, therapeutic process and technique. In *Mahler and Kohut: Perspectives on Development, Psychopathology, and Technique*. eds. S. Kramer and S. Akhtar, pp.17–52. Northvale, NJ: Jason Aronson.

Settlage, C. F., Bemesderfer, S. Rosenthal, J., Afterman, J., and Spielman, P. (1991) The appeal cycle in early mother-child interactions: The nature and implications of a finding from developmental research. *Journal of the American Psychoanalytic Association 39*: 987–1014.

Shapiro, B. (2008). Resilience, sublimation and healing: reactions to a personal narrative. In: *The Unbroken Soul: Tragedy, Trauma, and Resilience*. eds. H. Parens, H.P. Blum, and S. Akhtar, pp. 117-157. Lanham, MD: Jason Aronson.

Shengold, L. (1989). *Soul Murder: The Effects of Childhood Abuse and Deprivation*. New Haven, CT: Yale University Press.

Siassi, S. (2004). Transcending bitterness and early parental loss through mourning and forgiveness. *Psychoanalytic Quarterly 73*: 915–937.

———. (2007). Forgiveness, acceptance, and the matter of expectation. *International Journal of Psychoanalysis 88*: 1423–1440.

———. (2009). On 'Leaps of faith: is forgiveness a useful concept'? by Henry Smith. *International Journal of Psychoanalysis 90*: 642–645.

———. (2013). *Forgiveness in Intimate Relationships: Psychoanalytic Reflections.* London, UK: Karnac Books.

Silberer, H. (1909). Report on method of eliciting and observing certain symbolic hallucination–phenomena. In *Organization and Pathology of Thought.* ed. D. Rapaport, pp. 208–233. New York, NY: Columbia University Press, 1951.

———. (1914). *Problem der Mystik und ihrer Symbolik.* Leipzig: Hugo Heller.

Silk, J. B. (1998). Making amends: adaptive perspectives on conflict remediation in monkeys, apes, and humans. *Human Nature 9*: 341–368.

Silk, J. B. Cheney, D. L., and Seyfarth, R. M. (1996).The form and function of post–conflict interactions between female baboons. *Animal Behaviour 52*: 259–268.

Skeat, W. (1993).*The Concise Dictionary of English Etymology.* New York, NY: Wordsworth Editions Ltd.

Skinner, J. (1961). Ritual matricide: a study of the origins of sacrifice. *American Imago 18*: 71–102.

Smith, H. F. (2002). A footnote on forgiveness. *Psychoanalytic Quarterly 71*: 327–329.

———. (2008). Leaps of faith: is forgiveness a useful concept? *International Journal of Psychoanalysis 89*: 919–936.

Socarides, C. (1966). On vengeance: the desire to "get even." *Journal of the American Psychoanalytic Association 14*: 356–375.

Sohn, L. (1999). A defective capacity to feel sorrow. In *Remorse and Reparation,* ed. M. Cox, pp. 69–104. London, UK: Jessica Kingsley Publishers.

Sorce, J. F., Emde, R. N., Campos, J., and Klinnert, M. (1985). Maternal emotional signaling: its effect on the visual cliff behavior of 1-year-olds. *Developmental Psychology 21*: 195–200.

Southwick, S. M., Vythialingan, M., and Charney, D. S. (2005). The psychobiology of depression and resilience to stress: implications for prevention and treatment. *Annual Review of Clinical Psychology 1*: 255–291.

Sperling, O. (1963). Exaggeration as a defense. *Psychoanalytic Quarterly 32*: 533–548.

Spitz, R. (1946). The smiling response: a contribution to the ontogenesis of social relations. *Genetic Psychology 34*: 57–125.

Stern, D. (1985). *The Interpersonal World of the Infant.* New York, NY: Basic Books.

Stern, D. B. (2010). *Partners in Thought: Working with Unformulated Experience, Dissociation, and Enactment.* New York, NY: Routledge.

Stolorow, R. D. (1971). On forgiveness. *American Journal of Psychoanalysis 31*: 102–103.

Stone, L. (1961). *The Psychoanalytic Situation*. New York, NY: International Universities Press.

———. (1981). Notes on the non-interpretative elements in the psychoanalytic situation and process. In *Transference and Its Context: Selected Papers on Psychoanalysis*, pp. 153–175. New York, NY: Jason Aronson.

Stone, M. (1980). *The Borderline Syndrome*. New York, NY: McGraw Hill.

Steiner, J. (1993). *Psychic Retreats: Pathological Organizations in Psychotic, Neurotic and Borderline Patients*. London, UK: Routledge.

Strenger, C. (1989). The classic and romantic visions in psychoanalysis. *International Journal of Psychoanalysis 70*: 595–610.

Surya Das, L. (1997). Awakening the Buddha within. In *Tibetan Wisdom for the Western World*. New York, NY: Bantam Books.

Tahka, V. (1993). *Mind and Its Treatment: A Psychoanalytic Approach*. New York, NY: International Universities Press.

Tavuchis, N. (1991). *Mia Culpa: A Sociology of Apology*. Palo Alto, CA: Stanford University Press.

The Dalai Lama. (2008). *Worlds in Harmony*. Berkeley, CA: Parallax Press.

Thoma, H. and Kachele, H. (1994). *Psychoanalytic Practice, Volume 2: Clinical Studies*. Northvale, NJ: Jason Aronson.

Tillich, P. (1952). *The Courage to Be*. New Haven, CT: Yale University Press.

Treurniet, N. (1997). On an ethic of psychoanalytic technique. *Psychoanalytic Quarterly 66*: 596–627.

Tutu, D. (1999). *No Future Without Forgiveness*. New York, NY: Doubleday.

Tutu, D., and Tutu, M. (1989). *Made for Goodness*. New York, NY: Harper Collins.

Tylim, I. (2005). The power of apologies in transforming resentment into forgiveness. *International Journal of Applied Psychoanalytic Studies 2*: 260–270.

Tyson, R. L. (1978). Notes on the analysis of a prelatency boy with a dog phobia. *Psychoanalytic Study of the Child 33*: 427–458.

Vaillant, G. (1977). *Adaptation to Life*. Boston, MA: Little, Brown.

Varvin, S. (2009). Commentary on 'Resilience.' In *Good Feelings: Psychoanalytic Reflections on Positive Emotions and Attitudes*. ed. S. Akhtar, pp. 363–369. London, UK: Karnac Books.

Volkan, V. D. (1997). *Blood Lines: From Ethnic Price to Ethnic Terrorism*. New York, NY: Farrar, Strauss and Giroux.

Von Bergen, J. M. (2012). A Penn class in Giving 101: officials from China being schooled here in the ways of charities. *The Philadelphia Inquirer*, p. A-3, May 4, 2012.

Waddington, C. (1947). *Organizers and Genes*. Cambridge, UK: Cambridge University Press.

Waelder, R. (1936). The principle of multiple function. *Psychoanalytic Quarterly 5*: 45–62.

Wagenheim, H. (1985). Aspects of analysis of an adult son of deaf–mute parents. *Journal of the American Psychoanalytic Association 33*: 413–447.

Wangh, M. (1959). Structural determinants of phobia. *Journal of the American Psychoanalytic Association* 7: 675–695

Wangh, S. (2005). Revenge and forgiveness in Laramie, Wyoming. *Psychoanalytic Dialogue 15*: 1–16.

Webster's Ninth New Collegiate Dictionary. (1998). New York, NY: Merriam Webster.

Weiner, E. S., and Simpson, J. A. (1989). eds. *Oxford English Dictionary*. London, UK: Oxford University Press.

Weiss, D. (1965). The Red Badge of Courage—Part 2. *Psychoanalytic Review 52*: 130–154.

Werman, D. S. (1979). Chance, ambiguity, and psychological mindedness. *Psychoanalytic Quarterly 48*: 107–115.

White, M., and Gribbin, J. (2002). *Stephen Hawking: A Life in Science*. Washington, DC: Joseph Henry Press.

Whorf, B. (1956) *Language, Thought, and Reality*. Cambridge, MA: Massachusetts Institute of Technology Press.

Winnicott, D. W. (1947). Hate in the countertransference. In *Collected Papers: Through Paediatrics to Psychoanlaysis*, pp. 194–203. London, UK: Hogarth, 1958.

———. (1955). Metapsychological and clinical aspects of regression within the psychoanalytical setup. *International Journal of Psychoanalysis 36*: 16–26.

———. (1957). The mother's contribution to society. In *Home Is Where We Start From*. ed. C. Winnicott, R. Shepherd, and M. Davis, pp. 123–127. London, UK: Penguin Books.

———. (1958). The capacity to be alone. *International Journal of Psychoanalysis 39*: 416–420.

———. (1960). Parent infant relationship. In *The Maturational Processes and the Facilitating Environment*, pp. 37–55. New York, NY: International Universities Press, 1965.

———. (1960). Ego distortion in the terms of true and false self. In *Maturational Processes and the Facilitating Environment*, pp. 140–152. New York, NY: International Universities Press.

———. (1962). Ego integration in child development. In *Maturational Processes and the Facilitating Environment*, pp. 45–53. New York, NY: International Universities Press.

———. (1963). The development of the capacity for concern. *Bulletin of the Menninger Clinic 27*: 167–176.

———. (1968). Children learning. In *Home Is Where We Start From*, pp. 142–149. London, UK: Penguin Books.

———. (1969). The use of an object. *International Journal of Psychoanalysis 50*: 711–716.

———. (1970). Cure. In *Home Is Where We Start From*, pp. 112–120. London, UK: Penguin Books.

———. (1971). *Playing and Reality*. New York, NY: Basic Books.

———. (1971). On 'The use of an object.' In *Psychoanalytic Explorations*. eds. C. Winnicott, R. Shepherd, and M. Davis, pp. 217–246. Cambridge, MA: Harvard University Press.

Winterich, Karen Page, Vikas Mittal, and William T. Ross, Jr. (2009). Donation behavior toward in-groups and out-groups: the role of gender and moral identity. *Journal of Consumer Research 36*: 199–214.

Wolf, E. (1994). Self object experiences: development, psychopathology, treatment. In *Mahler and Kohut: Perspectives on Development, Psychopathology and Technique*. eds. S. Kramer and S. Akhtar, pp. 65–96. Northvale, NJ: Jason Aronson.

Wolfe, T. (1979). *The Right Stuff*. New York, NY: Penguin Books.

Valent, P. (1988). Resilience in child survivors of the Holocaust. *Psychoanalytic Review 85*: 517–535.

Yeats, W. B. (1933). *The Winding Stair and Other Poems*. London, UK: MacMillan and Company.

Young-Eisendrath, P. (1996). *The Resilient Spirit: Transforming Suffering into Insight and Renewal*. New York, NY: Addison-Wesley Publishing Company Inc.

INDEX

ABOUT THE AUTHOR

Salman Akhtar, MD, is a professor of psychiatry at Jefferson Medical College, and Training and Supervising Analyst at the Psychoanalytic Center of Philadelphia. He has served on the Editorial Boards of the *International Journal of Psychoanalysis* and *Journal of the American Psychoanalytic Association,* and is currently the Book Review Editor of the *International Journal of Applied Psychoanalytic Studies.* His sixty-two books include *Broken Structures* (1992), *Quest for Answers* (1995), *Inner Torment* (1999), *Immigration and Identity* (1999), *New Clinical Realms* (2003), *Objects of Our Desire* (2005), *Regarding Others* (2007), *The Damaged Core* (2009), *Turning Points in Dynamic Psychotherapy* (2009), *The Comprehensive Dictionary of Psychoanalysis* (2009), *Immigration and Acculturation* (2011), *Matters of Life and Death* (2011), *Psychoanalytic Listening* (2012) and *Good Stuff* (2013), as well as thirty-seven edited volumes in the realm of culture and psychoanalysis, including *Freud along the Ganges* (2005), *The Crescent and the Couch* (2008), *Freud and the Far East* (2009), and *The African American Experience* (2012), which deal with India, the Islamic world, the Far Eastern culture, and the African American population of the United States, respectively. Dr. Akhtar is the recipient of the Best Paper of the Year Award from the *Journal of American Psychoanalytic Association* (1995), the Edith Sabshin Award (2000) from the American Psychoanalytic Association, the Kun Po Soo Award (2004), the Irma Bland Award (2005) and the Nancy Roeske Award (2012) from the American Psychiatric Association, the Sigmund Freud Award for Distinguished Contribution to Psychoanalysis from the American Society of Psychoanalytic Physicians (2000), and the Robert Liebert Award (2003) for Distinguished Contributions to Applied Psychoanalysis from the Columbia University

Center for Psychoanalytic Training and Research. More recently, he recieved the Sigourney Award (2013), which is the most prestigious honor in the field of psychoanalysis. Dr. Akhtar has delivered invited lectures at academic institutions in countries around the world including Australia, Belgium, Brazil, Canada, Chile, China, England, France, Germany, India, Italy, Japan, Mexico, Peru, Serbia, and Turkey. His books have been translated into many languages including German, Rumanian, Spanish, and Turkish. He has also published seven volumes of poetry and is a Scholar-in-Residence at the Inter-Act Theatre Company in Philadelphia.